Paul Ricoeur and Narrative

Paul Ricoeur and Narrative

Context and Contestation

edited by Morny Joy

University of Calgary Press

University of Calgary Press
2500 University Drive N.W.
Calgary, Alberta, Canada T2N 1N4

Canadian Cataloguing in Publication Data

Main entry under title:

Paul Ricoeur and narrative

Includes some text in French.
ISBN 1-895176-90-5

1. Ricoeur, Paul. 2. Narration (Rhetoric) I. Joy, Morny.
B2430.R553P38 1997   194   C97-910015-1

COMMITTED TO THE DEVELOPMENT OF CULTURE AND THE ARTS

Financial support provided in part by the Alberta Foundation for the Arts.

Printed and bound in Canada by Kromar Printing.

♾ This book is printed on acid-free paper.

Contents

Preface

The aim of this book is to make Paul Ricoeur's work on narrative accessible to a wider audience. Students and scholars in many of the humanities and social sciences will find much of interest here. In March, 1994, a network of interdisciplinary researchers were invited to gather at The University of Calgary under the auspices of the Calgary Institute for the Humanities. This book took shape as a result of that meeting. The essays presented here illustrate varied responses to and analyses of Ricoeur's long-standing and multifaceted fascination with aspects of narrative. The book does not attempt a comprehensive coverage of all of Ricoeur's theories, nor even an intensive study of the philosophical developments involved in his investigations. This has been undertaken elsewhere. Instead, the book provides a survey of many of the key concepts that Ricoeur uses concerning narrative. It offers valuable applications of his ideas, not just in the contexts of philosophical and theological discussions, but also in such areas as architecture, medieval and contemporary literature, psychology, psychoanalysis, sociology, and feminist theory.

This book would not exist without the support provided by many people at different stages of its development. I thank the Calgary Institute for the Humanities and especially its director, Jane Kelley for sponsoring the conference. Funding for the conference was provided by The University of Calgary and the Social Sciences and Humanities Research Council of Canada. Dr. O.H.D. Blomfield, David Carr, Shadia Drury, Esther Enns, Art Frank, John McCarthy, and Haijo Westra participated in the conference and provided valuable discussion, which has shaped the contents of this book.

A roundtable discussion concerning narrative within First Nations traditions also formed an important part of the conference. Because of the primarily oral nature of that culture, the proceedings of that session were videotaped and made available to the participant communities. The participants were Clara Schenkul and Julia Cruikshank (Whitehorse, YT), Allice Legat, Rita Blackduck, Sally Zoe, Joan Ryan, and Marta Johnson (Northwest Territories).

Rose Ferronato helped with the typing; John King offered editorial advice; Joan Eadie prepared the index.

This book has been published with the help of a grant from the Humanities and Social Sciences Federation of Canada, using funds provided by the Social Sciences and Humanities Research Council of Canada.

                                                                    M.J.

Foreword:
Recounting Narrative

DAVID PELLAUER

What Paul Ricoeur has to say about narrative in his fascinating three-volume work *Time and Narrative* and the essays most closely associated with it is important in many ways, and not just for philosophers, as the essays in this volume nicely demonstrate.[1] However, it may still be useful for readers to review briefly what he has to say about narrative there, as well as to indicate its place in his philosophy. In this way, we shall see that this topic has a place within a much larger philosophical enterprise, yet it can also be considered independently of that undertaking because of its immediate implications for an even wider range of issues.

In fact, Ricoeur's discussion of narrative can be shown to arise out of concerns internal to his philosophical reflections that go all the way back to the beginning of his work. What he first presented himself as undertaking was the project of working out a philosophy of the will that we may summarize as an attempt to elaborate a philosophy of freedom, but of a finite freedom, a freedom that can be used for evil as well as for good. This freedom always runs up against the limits of what Ricoeur called the absolute involuntary and the transcendence that we experience and attempt to articulate as going beyond even this apparent final limit. Already in this earliest work, given its focus on freedom, we find a tie to human action as voluntary action, as this occurs within the setting of such limits, as it encounters and responds to them, along with the ways in which we attempt to make sense of such action. This concern for action, its possibility, and its intelligibility – for meaningful action – is a central strand that runs throughout all Ricoeur's subsequent work. Indeed, we can now see, given that subsequent work, and the benefit of hindsight, that his initial concern for human freedom and meaningful action already pointed to the possibility, if not the necessity, of taking up narrative as one of the ways in which human beings talk about such things and thereby seek to make sense of them. That is, because we tell stories or histories about what people have done, do, and may or will do, as well as of the world within which all this takes place, reflection on narrative is already implicated in any attempt at a comprehensive philosophy of human freedom.

Narrative as a likely topic for Ricoeur's investigations becomes even more obvious midway through this never-completed project of a philosophy of the will when he takes up the problem of evil. He had set this aside at first in order to consider what philosophy, apart from any consideration of evil, and using the methods of descriptive phenomenology, could say about the essential structures underlying human freedom. To discover these essential structures, however, is not yet to have considered their concrete application in actual existence. This is why we need also to take into account the fact that human beings in practice not only misuse their freedom but that such misuse seems, and indeed is experienced as, inevitable (which for Ricoeur does not mean necessary). This misuse of freedom seems impossible to account for on strictly philosophical grounds, at least if philosophy too quickly defines itself as purely rational reflection. In contrast, evil is something contrary to reason, if not wholly irrational, and hence apparently beyond the competence of such reflection. This is why in *The Symbolism of Evil* Ricoeur makes a hermeneutical turn, a shift in method, from a phenomenological description aimed at essential structures to an interpretation of what people have in fact said about their experience of evil.[2] This turn, which denies the possibility of a method of direct intuition or of a purely deductive reasoning based on self-evident premises as a way to make adequate sense of the human experience of evil, has shaped all his subsequent work. His proposed alternative solution to the question of how then to proceed was to seek a way for philosophy to take up, by re-enacting in a reflective manner, people's experience of evil in a way that could make sense of the ways they have spoken about it, particularly about its origin. This is a kind of discourse, he suggests, that also points to the ways in which human beings have understood the possible overcoming of the fault, his preferred term for this complex of phenomena. Because it is a kind of second-order discourse on an already second-order discourse that seeks understanding, we can see why he characterizes this approach as belonging within the realm of interpretation, of hermeneutics.

Starting from these methodological assumptions, what he shows is that people talk about the origin and end of evil in a language best characterized as confession or testimony, a kind of discourse that overlaps both the religious and the legal spheres, and that intimately involves the one who speaks. This is a language, especially in its religious dimensions, shaped by symbols and their elaboration and interpretation through myth and ritual. It is this focus on myth, which is already a kind of narrative, that directly anticipates *Time and Narrative*, although there, owing to further development of his hermeneutical theory, Ricoeur chooses to begin beyond the symbolically laden discourse of originary religious discourse with Aristotle's reflections on the nature of Greek tragedy in his *Poetics*.[3] This new shift in starting point, if not in method, can be read in terms of a more or less standard interpretation of the origins of Greek philosophy as having broken in some significant way with the earlier religious and mythic traditions, such as found in Homer and Hesiod. Ricoeur does not make this point, but I think it is important in that it is already indicative of a number of directions in which his narrative theory can be developed further. For example, we may ask whether it is possible to expand his narrative theory to include reflection on symbolically laden religious discourse, including religious narratives, discourse that does not presuppose such a break in its originary uses. Or, if we wish to stay close to a perspective like that found in the *Symbolism of Evil*, that is, one that takes people's use of symbolic discourse seriously, albeit critically and reflectively, how can we learn to think starting from such uses of narrative?[4]

His hermeneutical turn led Ricoeur, at the end of the *Symbolism of Evil*, to the conclusion that philosophy has to learn to think starting from the symbol. In a well-known phrase from that work, philosophy needs to make sense of and to be able to make use of the fact that a symbol can give rise to thought. There was a second important aspect to this development in his thinking. Because symbols are taken up into language in myth, philosophers have to learn to be attentive to what he characterizes as "the fullness of language," a fullness that will include such symbolically laden forms of language. This is an important assertion, one that I do not think has been fully appreciated as yet by the philosophical community, much less the wider realm of scholarly discourse, even when one recognizes something like a "linguistic turn" as having characterized much of recent philosophy. This is so for two reasons.

Much of twentieth-century philosophy, especially in English-speaking countries, has been driven by significant developments in the theory of logic that began in the mid-nineteenth century, associated with names like Boole, Frege, Russell and Whitehead, which gave rise to new techniques of philosophical analysis. In many ways, this history is well-known, at least to philosophers; in others, it is beginning to be rewritten as contemporary work has run up against some of the limits implicit in such a paradigm shift. In an effort to make sense of these limits, if not get beyond them, philosophers and historians of philosophy are beginning to reconsider in detail, and critically, how this turn in philosophical method came about.[5] Suffice it to say here that a central portion of this development lay in the discovery of new forms of logical systems, ones that could be applied to arguments in ways far beyond the capacities of the traditional logic of the syllogism, whose basic form runs all the way back to Aristotle. Originally these new developments were intended to respond to issues that had arisen in mathematics and the philosophy of mathematics, beginning with the discovery of non-Euclidean forms of geometry, which seemed to call into question the assumption that mathematics provides the most obvious case of rigorous knowledge, knowledge necessarily characterized by certainty. Subsequently, they were applied to the quest for an ideal language, one that could say all that there was to be meaningfully and truthfully said, and hence that would define the limits of knowledge. But in both cases the central goal of applications of this newer logic, as an attempt to capture the necessary structure of valid arguments and to systematize such arguments, remains the same. Given a valid argument form or mathematical proof and true premises, the conclusion, properly drawn, cannot be false. It must be true. Hence logical analysis is a way of testing whether a conclusion said to be true does in fact "follow" from its premises, on the presupposition that we also have a workable model of "implication." Going the other direction, such analysis ought also to provide a technique for generating new truths from existing ones by working out their implications, which can serve in turn as the premises of further arguments. Here many philosophers believed, and still believe, even when they acknowledge the limitations of models of so-called ideal languages, was a set of techniques that could be applied across the board to the problems of philosophy in all its forms, not simply to mathematics or the philosophy of mathematics but to all questions of epistemology and to ethics as well.

Such techniques have proved immensely insightful. However, given Ricoeur's commitment to the fullness of language, such an approach can also be seen to have its limits in that it still must aim at working exclusively with univocal propositional forms equivalent to "*S* is *P*" or reducible to such forms, even when they are considered in terms of a theory of "functions." It is exactly symbolic language, in whatever form it may take, on Ricoeur's interpretation that resists reduction to such propositional form, for symbolic language says more than one thing at once. For a philosophical approach determined to deal only with univocal propositions, such apparently equivocal language must be shown to in fact contain or be reducible to such univocal assertions or to misuse them, or, some have suggested, it must simply be ruled out of court as irrational, where "irrational" this time means nonsensical, and hence incapable of any real meaning or truth value. Yet the implication of Ricoeur's attempts to be respectful of and to learn from the symbols of evil and what in fact people have said about them is that this is a misleading because truncated set of alternatives. If symbols are double-meaning expressions, as he maintains,[6] that is, if they always mean more than what they literally say, then the techniques of logical analysis are ill-suited to deal with this aspect of language.

This implication becomes clearer, I believe, with his subsequent more general hermeneutical reflections. These develop his initial work on the symbols of evil from a more or less *ad hoc* application of interpretation to a particular realm of symbols and symbolic discourse toward a more general theory. Such a theory can apply to other forms of complex uses of language, such as poetic metaphor and extended discourse that is more than one sentence long, and whose truth may not be equivalent to the sum or conjunction of the truth values of its individual sentences, even when they are translated into propositional form.

Narrative, for Ricoeur, is one such form of complex, extended discourse that any philosophy committed to the fullness of language must investigate. Note that he does not claim that it is the only such form. In fact, when we begin to enumerate other such forms, say political discourse or lyrical poetry, not to mention, perhaps, "philosophical" discourse, and then to think of how they may intersect and be interwoven with one another, we can see that there are still many other consequences of his larger theory of language to be developed and investigated.

Time and Narrative can be read as addressing a number of the concerns arising out of these developments in Ricoeur's thinking. In the first place, it is meant to complement his work on metaphor, which itself is one more development of his hermeneutical theory and his commitment to the fullness of language. Metaphor, according to Ricoeur, is a form of discourse that like a symbol somehow says more than one thing at the same time. As he puts it in *The Rule of Metaphor*, a live metaphor says both "is" and "is not" at the same time, and as such may be seen as the locus or even as the process of semantic innovation in language, a place and an occurrence where new meaning arises through a redescription of reality.[7] Narrative, too, shares in this capacity for semantic innovation, albeit on a more extended level of discourse than a single metaphor, which according to Ricoeur's theory operates at the level of the sentence rather than at that of the single word, which was the dominant interpretation of a rhetoric of tropes that died out under the weight of its ever burgeoning taxonomic schemes. However, as he notes, following Monroe Beardsley, a metaphor is already a poem in miniature. Hence it is already on its way to becoming extended discourse. As we know, many poems in fact are such extended metaphors, which run over many sentences, if not over the whole poem. This is why he can say that his work on metaphor and that on narrative go hand in hand.

When he turns to narrative, however, Ricoeur shifts his terminology from description and redescription to figuration, configuration, and refiguration. What is at stake here is in part indicated by the title of these volumes: *time* and narrative. For it is Ricoeur's major thesis in this work that narrative is the way we finally make sense of the temporality of our experience, a fact that has eluded, and Ricoeur believes and argues must elude, all philosophical attempts to account for it. As he says, in *Time and Narrative:*

> one presupposition commands all the others, that what is ultimately at stake in the case of the structural identity of the narrative function as well as in that of the truth claim of every narrative work, is the temporal character of human experience. The world unfolded by every narrative work is always a temporal world. Or, as will be repeated in the course of this study: time becomes human time to the extent that it is organized after the manner of a narrative; narrative, in turn, is meaningful to the extent that it portrays the features of temporal experience.[8]

Narrative, to put it another way, does not give us the missing philosophy of time. It instead resolves the problem by making use of it in order to refigure our temporal experience, which for reflection includes both a lived and a cosmic aspect, in such a way that it makes sense to us.

Narrative makes sense of time by drawing upon the inherent relation, however indirect, of all narrative to human action, which we have seen is a long-term concern of Ricoeur's. To state this in another more technical way, this time using the vocabulary of *Time and Narrative*, narrative allows us to refigure time by configuring it on the basis of the mimesis of an already figured human action, starting from everyday, already acquired language about such action. This move is central, even if such narrative may subsequently distort our language and our experience in an innovative, quasi-metaphorical, but semantically significant, way. Ricoeur's argument for this point is complex. It draws centrally upon what he calls the threefold structure of mimesis at work in narrative. The first aspect of such mimesis is that human action is, as just said, already symbolically mediated or "figured" in the ordinary language we use to identify and speak of it in everyday life. It is this aspect of an already existing mimesis of action that gets taken up into the second dimension of mimesis in narrative, so for Ricoeur there is both continuity and discontinuity in the move from life to narrative.[9] It is this second form of mimesis, the one internal to narrative, that is constituted by the fact that narrative has a plot. We might even say that there is a kind of dialectical relation at work here: narrative has a plot because it is mimetic, and it is mimetic because it has a plot, where in both cases the mimesis is directly or indirectly about human action. Here Ricoeur, it must be recognized, is following Aristotle in holding that the characteristic mark of narrative is that it has a plot, or better, in order to capture the dynamic sense of what is at issue here, that narrative *emplots* what it says. In a non-trivial sense, what is at issue here is that narratives, at least well-formed ones, have a beginning, middle, and end. As such, they are extended forms of discourse marked by at least quasi-causal connections. But beyond this, there is more at stake. Narratives, thanks to their emplotment, have a specific temporality that weaves their episodes into a comprehensible whole that cannot be reduced to an atemporal idea. Hence, while it may be true to say, "this is a story about the struggle between good and evil," such a judgment overlooks what is at issue in the fact that the story in question is a story or narrative. The plots of narratives, be they stories or histories, are marked, Ricoeur says, by a concordant discordance that reflects the tension in our lived experience of time (and, I would argue, human action). It is recognition of this tension that allows us to agree with Augustine when he says, "What then is time? I know well enough what it is, provided that nobody asks me; but if I am asked what it is and try to explain, I am baffled."[10] A similar point could be made, I am suggesting about action, and with it, freedom. We know well enough what it is as long as no one asks; we can even perform it, but when asked, we do not know how to answer. Or, at least, our answers quickly seem less than adequate and to point down blind alleys like freedom versus determinism.

It is worth noting in passing that this distinction of different dimensions of mimesis allows Ricoeur to separate in his analyses of narrative those structures that are part of any narrative as a narrative and those that belong to hearing or reading it. This is an important methodological point for those interested in the study of narrative in that it gives us a way of keeping distinct what a narrative says and what an audience makes of what it says, and not confuse the one with the other. Here Ricoeur is influenced by his critical attentiveness to structuralism with its emphasis on formal modes of explanation, but it is a point that has implications far beyond any commitment to such a technique for approaching language and our uses of language. This is because it allows us to incorporate explanatory techniques into our hermeneutic quest for understanding. As he suggests, sometimes we need to explain more in order better to understand, and there is no understanding, finally, without such a critical explanatory moment.

What he calls "mimesis$_3$," finally, refers to our recognition of the configuration of the action in a narrative that we appropriate through hearing or reading and the application of our imagination to what we hear or read. This brings us back once again to action in that it is on the basis of what we make of the world of the text, as Ricoeur calls it, where this action takes place, even more so than the characters of their actions, that we discover through our understanding of narrative new possibilities for our own action in that this world is one that potentially we might inhabit. It is this possibility that shapes our own possible activity. This world of the text found in narrative is, of course, as a world, one marked by temporality. Insofar as we can make sense of such a world, Ricoeur's point is that we also learn to make sense of time and our own temporal experience, and vice versa. In fact, because there is, in the best of cases, a creative or semantically innovative aspect at work in narrative, as in metaphor, we may gain new insight into making sense of time – and, again, of action, and with it, of our freedom.

A further important dimension of this process of appropriation in relation to narrative also needs to be briefly noted. That is that through the stories we tell and retell, that we read and reread, we also discover and convey what he calls a "narrative identity," an identity that may refer to communities as well as to individual subjects. This theme is further developed in his Gifford Lectures, published as *Oneself as Another*, but already the implication is that our narrative identity is not only related to who we are and what we do. Like narrative, it has a complex temporality; like narrative, it may be best characterized as a kind of concordant discordance.[11]

All the details of Ricoeur's argument in *Time and Narrative* are not at issue here. Let it suffice to say that he begins by setting out the problem of both time and narrative through an examination of Augustine's reflections on time in the *Confessions* and Aristotle's contribution to reflection on the nature of plot in his *Poetics*. From here, he moves on to a statement of his own theory of threefold mimesis, as the basis for what is to follow. That is a long discussion of both history and fiction as belonging to what he now calls the "narrative field" that encompasses them. The discussion of history is important on its own grounds in light of contemporary controversy among historians as to the role of narrative in writing history, particularly under the impact of the social sciences and their efforts to reduce things to atemporal formulae and numbers. Ricoeur's position is that, however sophisticated the techniques of historical research may become, there is an unbreakable tie to narrative in the writing of history, and thereby to the meaning of history, even when historians make use of forms of discourse and even models of explanation from other disciplines, and even when they draw upon the techniques of literary fiction in order better to convey what they mean to say.

There is less controversy about whether literary fiction belongs to the narrative field, although, as is well known, there are many conflicts among authors and critics about whether the concept of plot is really required, whether characterization is not more important than plot, and even whether recent forms of the novel, for example, can be said to be about time in the sense Ricoeur intends. However, it must be said that too often such critics unthinkingly identify what is at issue for Ricoeur about temporality with simple chronology, which is not what he has in mind. In narrative, beginning, middle, and end need not come in that order. Indeed, modern writers often delight in confusing and even distorting their relationships as much as possible. Ricoeur's major points about literary fiction, rather, are that such forms of narrative cannot really be explained by attempts to reduce them to generative underlying atemporal logical deep structures, as in the work of structural narratologists, and that fiction is in fact a place where we learn to play with forms of making sense of time through the invention of various techniques. Examples of such techniques are indirect free discourse, stream of consciousness, and the possibilities of interplay within narrative between, for example, the temporality of the narrating, of what happens in the narration, and of the world in which this all takes place. To this list may be added his discussion in *Time and Narrative*, II, of the role of tradition in literary fiction, the often odd use of verb tenses in fiction ("tomorrow was Christmas"!), and the important notions of point of view and narrative voice as elements of narrative technique. Even the French *nouveau roman*, which in many ways has tried to be or at least has been alleged to be an anti-novel, or a non-narrative narrative, which Ricoeur does not discuss, could be shown, I believe, to reflect these points, indicating the insightfulness of his analyses.

History and fiction, therefore, for Ricoeur both belong to the wider category of narrative discourse. In fact, they learn from and even depend upon one another, even though a distinction can finally be drawn between them owing to history's commitment to a "real" past, a past that has left traces in the present, and to standards of evidence that do not apply in the case of fiction. To this model, which occupies the second half of *Time and Narrative*, I, and all of *Time and Narrative*, II, he adds at the beginning of *Time and Narrative*, III, a long analysis of attempts by philosophy to achieve a phenomenology of time. The details of this need not concern us here. The point is that there is an inherent aporetics of temporality that will always undermine attempts to make sense of time on strictly philosophical grounds, thereby strengthening our understanding of why a narrative solution to the question of time may be necessary. This discussion is followed by a turn to the hermeneutical considerations that arise at the level of mimesis$_3$, particularly as they apply to a theory of appropriating narratives through reading or hearing, and what this says about a hermeneutical consciousness as part of our human condition and of our identity, both as individuals and as members of larger communities. For example, at this level we need to add to the complex temporal interactions that occur within narrative, those that may occur between the narrative and its audience. For Ricoeur, these are mediated and appropriated through our imagination before they are taken up in explicit reflection or applied in subsequent action.

I hope it is obvious to the reader that *Time and Narrative* is a complex and incredibly rich work, one that is well worth the effort of following the different strands of its argumentation. Let me conclude, however, by turning to a brief discussion of what I see to be a few of its implications for a broader concern for narrative across the disciplines. In so doing, I would also like to indicate what I see to be several points that could be taken up by those interested in making use of Ricoeur's work for their own investigations. At the same time, such work may help us better to appreciate, and where necessary expand, or even correct, his account of narrative.

A first point has to do with what I shall call the empirical dimensions of narrative, particularly in the sense of actually telling and listening to or reading narratives. In his account of the intelligibility of narrative discourse, Ricoeur appeals to, without really developing, what he calls our narrative understanding. This has a Kantian ring to it, and I think this connection is plausible given the overall shape of his philosophical investigations. However, the idea of narrative understanding may also be taken in something more like what generative linguistics has taught us to think of as a "competence." This is a perhaps innate or evolved capacity of the human mind to develop abilities such as learning and using a language, which will always be instantiated in terms of some particular language, but that are based upon and constrained by underlying deep structures. Such a notion is not that far removed from the Kantian *Verstand*, in fact. However such a model does involve a temporal dimension and the complication that the underlying structure can be expressed in different forms. We might see a further reason for drawing this parallel in the fact that Ricoeur himself has sometimes characterized his overall stance as a kind of post-Hegelian Kantianism. I take it that he means by this that there are structures that organize human experience, but they are to be understood to change over time and hence themselves to be marked by the historicity that characterizes hermeneutic consciousness and self-understanding.

Linguistics, further, adds the claim that such underlying structures are in some sense built-in, so to speak, probably in a physiological man- ner amenable to empirical investigation. I am not a physiologist nor a linguist, so this is not the direction I want to pursue, although the possi- bility of cognitive science turning to narrative discourse is an intriguing one. What interests me are the possibilities of a more empirical inquiry than is found in Ricoeur's own work into how human beings learn to tell and listen to narrative from what broadly speaking we may call a developmental perspective. Narrative discourse, after all, is according to Ricoeur one kind of use of language, and hence may be related to such a capacity, its development, and its use. A number of essays in this volume take up this topic from the point of view of how adults use nar- rative in a variety of different situations. These accounts already are in- dicative of the way in which the broad topic of narrative discourse and narrative theory can be fruitful across a wide range of disciplines. What interests me more, however, is the possibility of investigation into how human beings as children come to learn to tell and to understand stories. At one point in *Time and Narrative*, II, Ricoeur suggests that he believes narrative is a universal aspect of the human condition, at least as it cur- rently exists.[12] Yet it is true that some people are better storytellers than others, just as it is true that some are better story interpreters than oth- ers. Might it not be possible to show that these are skills that we in some sense learn, even if they are based upon some underlying competence or possibility within us? Ought we to go further and hypothesize that research into such learning might turn out like so many other aspects of human development to fall into a series of identifiable stages or at least a theory of such stages, with the concomitant arguments to be sure whether there is only one such sequence or many. Such results, if obtain- able, would have a pedagogical value in that they could help us to help each other to make better sense of narrative, and in so doing one might hope that we could also learn to better appreciate the possibilities and the limits of such discourse.

A second area of possible empirical inquiry is how people actually use narrative in their day-to-day lives, in contrast to the well-formed narratives of the literary tradition, even in its more popular and generic forms. Much daily storytelling need not be, indeed is not, well-formed. It is often stereotypical, and this allows people to interrupt and to talk back and forth, all the while keeping the narrative line or lines going, or at least getting enough of the point that an abrupt change of subject is often justifiable. Investigation into concrete instances of such phenom- ena would take us in the direction of the pragmatics of discourse analysis, which is already a recognized area of linguistic investigation. What Ricoeur's narrative theory provides, I am suggesting, is a means of focusing on a certain portion of that discourse to see how it works or perhaps does not work, not just in itself, but also in relation to other forms of everyday discourse, which may not have such a theoretical basis behind them. Such investigation, of course, may feedback on narrative theory both critically and correctively in that it may show just what such a theory cannot account for and what it may leave out.

One area of investigation within such discourse analysis that would have immediate repercussions on narrative theory is what it might contribute to filling out our understanding of what Ricoeur calls "mimesis$_1$," the repertoire of our prefigured conceptual network or networks regarding human action that the mimesis at work in narrative emplotment draws upon. I have already indicated that the entry into narrative involves both continuity and discontinuity in Ricoeur's account. Knowing more about what we draw upon in making such a move, and even how we draw upon it, could have large implications, for example, for our account of the nature of fiction. Insofar as all narrative involves a break with mimesis$_1$, all narrative can be said, must be said, to have a fictive dimension. What we do not really understand on this account, however, is the significance of this assertion. Following Ricoeur, I want to maintain the distinction between history and fiction, not to reduce them to the latter alone. Yet, with him, I am also willing to admit that historiography does draw upon the techniques and forms constitutive of fictional narrative. Investigation into less than well-formed use of narrative discourse, I am suggesting, especially as it is found in everyday discourse, even allowing for the possible influence of all that we might place under the heading of ideological influences, social conformity, and tradition, may help us better to understand just what it is that constitutes the basis of fiction as fiction. In better understanding the range of ways in which people make use of narrative, as well as the range of situations where they do make use of it, we may have a better basis to understand the origins of our distinction between history and fiction because we have a greater insight into the commencement of forms of narrative discourse.

A third area where attempts to apply Ricoeur's account of narrative to a wide range of examples could be useful is that it may provide us with a better basis for the possible analogical extension of this theory to other forms of extended discourse, leading eventually to the difficult question or questions dealing with the intersection of narrative and other forms of discourse. At this point, I believe, we are at the limits of Ricoeur's philosophy of language, which asserts the existence of such a plurality of forms of discourse, each having its own specificity, but also being able to intersect and even interweave with other such forms. In the final study of *The Rule of Metaphor*, he discusses the relation of philosophical to metaphorical discourse, but the emphasis is mainly on establishing the autonomy, if not the independence, of philosophical in relation to metaphorical discourse. He has nowhere told us or even attempted to enumerate exhaustively just how many forms of discourse there are or may be, even though in his writings on the Bible he does list a number of them. Nor do we as yet really have what can be called a theoretical account of the intersecting or interweaving of different forms of discourse, beyond the claim that such interactions do take place.[13] Further insight into the nature and limits of narrative discourse would not by itself give us such an account, but it would add to it, especially when complemented by comparable accounts of different modes of discourse, including philosophical discourse. But that is a story for another time.

Notes

1 Paul Ricoeur, *Time and Narrative*, 3 vols., trans. Kathleen Blamey and David Pellauer (Chicago: University of Chicago Press, 1984–88); "That Fiction 'Remakes' Reality," *The Journal of the Blaisdell Institute* 12 (1978): 44–62; "The Human Experience of Time and Narrative," *Research in Phenomenology* 9 (1979): 17–34; "The Function of Fiction in Shaping Reality," *Man and World* 12 (1979): 123–41; "Narrative Time," *Critical Inquiry* 7 (1980): 169–90; "Mimesis and Representation," *Annals of Scholarship*, 2:3 (1981): 15–32; "Can Fictional Narratives Be True?" in A.-T. Tynieniecka, ed., *The Phenomenology of Man and the Human Condition* (Dordrecht: D. Reidel, 1983), 3–19; "Narrative and Hermeneutics," in J. Fisher, ed., *Essays on Aesthetics* (Philadelphia: Temple University Press, 1983), 149–60; *The Reality of the Historical Past* (Milwaukee: Marquette University Press, 1984); "The Text as Dynamic Identity," in M. J. Valdés and O. Milko, ed., *Identity of the Literary Text* (Toronto: University of Toronto Press, 1985), 175–76; "History as Narrative and Practice. Peter Kemp Talks to Paul Ricoeur in Copenhagen," *Philosophy Today* 29 (1985): 213–22; "Narrated Time," *Philosophy Today* 29 (1985): 259–72; "Life: A Story in Search of a Narrator," in *Facts and Values: Philosophical Reflections from Western and Non-Western Perspectives*, ed. M.C. Doeser and J.N. Kraay (Dordrecht: Martinus Nijhoff, 1986), 121-32; "Narrative Identity," *Philosophy Today* 35 (1991): 73–81. For discussion of this work, cf. P. Kemp and D. Rasmussen, ed., *The Narrative Path: The Later Works of Paul Ricoeur* (Cambridge: MIT Press, 1989); Ch. Bouchindhomme and R. Rochlitz, ed., *'Temps et Récit' de Paul Ricoeur en débat* (Paris: Cerf, 1990); David Wood, ed., *On Paul Ricoeur: Narrative and Interpretation* (New York: Routledge, 1991).

2 Paul Ricoeur, *The Symbolism of Evil*, trans. Emerson Buchanan (New York: Harper & Row, 1967). There was an intermediary step on the way to this hermeneutical turn, laid out in *Fallible Man*, rev. trans. Charles A. Kelbley (New York: Fordham University Press, 1986). There, from the perspective of a more Kantian transcendental reflection on the condition of possibility of evil, Ricoeur considers how evil, or as he calls it, the fault, might be possible for human beings. He conceptualizes

this possibility in what he calls the "fragility" that is one of the constitutive conditions of the human condition. Such fragility makes evil or the misuse of freedom possible but not necessary. As such, it neither predicts nor prevents the fault from occurring; hence, it cannot explain its occurrence when it does happen. This is why there is still a need for a further step, and a different, more applicable method, in order to take up the question of actual evil.

In fact, according to the Preface to *Fallible Man*, Ricoeur at one time projected a third volume that would seek to begin with thought that began from the symbol and that would take up such topics as the human sciences, psychoanalysis, criminology, and political thought. While his subsequent work may be read as reflecting many aspects of this project, it also reflects its complexity and might be seen as a series of steps – or as Ricoeur himself prefers to call them, detours – leading to such a volume.

3 He also uses Augustine's reflections on the nature of time in the *Confessions*, which in a way keeps the religious dimension on the horizon of his inquiry.

4 For Ricoeur's own attempts to apply his hermeneutical theory to the biblical tradition, see "Biblical Hermeneutics," *Semeia* 4 (1975): 29–148; *Essays on Biblical Interpretation*, ed. Lewis S. Mudge (Philadelphia: Fortress Press, 1980); *Figuring the Sacred: Religion, Narrative, and Imagination*, ed. Mark I. Wallace (Minneapolis: Fortress Press, 1995). Cf. my "*Time and Narrative* and Theological Reflection: Some Preliminary Reflections," *Philosophy Today* 31 (1987): 262–86.

5 See, for example, the "Opinionated Introduction" to William Aspray and Philip Kitcher, ed., *Minnesota Studies in the Philosophy of Science*, vol. XI: *History and Philosophy of Modern Mathematics* (Minneapolis: University of Minnesota Press, 1988).

6 Cf., for example, his essay "The Problem of Double Meaning as Hermeneutic Problem and as Semantic Problem," in Paul Ricoeur, *The Conflict of Interpretations: Essays in Hermeneutics* (Evanston: Northwestern University Press, 1974), 62–78. This whole collection is central to the working out of his hermeneutical reflections subsequent to the *Symbolism of Evil*.

7 Paul Ricoeur, *The Rule of Metaphor: Multi-Disciplinary Studies of the Creation of Meaning in Language*, trans. Robert Czerny *et al.* (Toronto: University of Toronto Press, 1977).

8 *Time and Narrative*, I, 3.

9 I have developed the importance of this claim elsewhere in discussing the similarities and differences between Ricoeur's narrative theory and that of David Carr's *Time, Narrative, and History* (Bloomington: Indiana University Press, 1986). "Limning the Liminal: Carr and Ricoeur on Time and Narrative," *Philosophy Today* 34 (1991): 51–62.

10 Augustine, *The Confessions*, trans. R. S. Pine-Coffin (New York: Penguin Books, 1961), Book 11, 14:17.

11 This question of identity, including what Ricoeur calls "narrative identity," is taken up at greater length in Ricoeur's Gifford Lectures, published as *Oneself as Another*, trans. Kathleen Blamey (Chicago: University of Chicago Press, 1992). The emphasis on agency and ethics in this volume once again makes clear the tie to freedom and action that runs throughout Ricoeur's philosophy.

12 In discussing Walter Benjamin's suggestion that we may be at the end of an era where narrating has a place, he says, "Perhaps, in spite of everything, it is necessary to have confidence in the call for concordance that today still structures the expectations of readers and to believe that new narrative forms, which we do not yet know how to name, are already being born, which will bear witness to the fact

that the narrative function can still be metamorphosed, but not so as to die. For we have no idea of what a culture would be where no one any longer knew what it meant to narrate things" (*Time and Narrative*, II, 28).

13   There is one discussion of how the parables of Jesus, which are themselves narratives, are embedded in the larger narrative of the gospels in "The Bible and the Imagination," in *Figuring the Sacred*, 144–66. This is a particular account, more like the account of symbols and myths in the *Symbolism of Evil* than a theoretical statement, however. Cf. also the essay "Naming God" in the same collection (217–35) for a discussion of how different genres in the Bible – narrative, prescriptive, hymnic, wisdom – interact polyphonically to name God as their common referent. It may be possible for someone to expand these investigations to similar texts of the secular literary tradition. It would be a useful exercise, I believe.

Introduction

The work of Paul Ricoeur reflects a profound and complex interrogation of contemporary philosophical resources so as to provide meaning in a world beset by personal, cultural, and international conflicts. Ricoeur is a mediator who strives to elicit constructive insights by placing disparate views in conversation. This dialectical interplay is not in the service of an ultimate solution (as with Hegel) but seeks a position that incorporates both the conservative and innovative forces he discerns at work in such exchanges. Ricoeur continues to surprise and challenge his readers with the vast amount of intellectual territory he covers, the extravagance of his conceptual experimentation, and the magnanimous respect he pays to his interlocutors.

From the beginning, Ricoeur has been fascinated by the power of words and symbols and by the creative capacity of human beings to make sense of their world. He affirms this response in the face of those forces that inhibit inventive variation. Rather than defer to a reproductive imagination (to use Kant's terminology), which simply replicates experience, Ricoeur has sought to express the dynamics of a productive imagination in a *poietic* (from Aristotle's *poiesis*) mode of depiction.[1] Such an appeal to literary forms of expression permits him to avoid the impasses that occur when strictly rational or logical procedures cannot do justice to the human predicament.

In his work both on metaphor and on narrative, Ricoeur seeks a poetic/*poietic* resolution that does not remain simply on the level of ideas, for it is intimately related to *praxis* (the practical application of theory). Again, he borrows the term from Aristotle, to imply that poetic delineations of narrative do not remain self-referential, but have definite practical implications. Whatever new appreciations occur from our interaction with literary figures and forms can be the basis for changes in our worldviews and our actions.

A central aspect of all Ricoeur's work has been his focus on *hermeneutics* or interpretation theory. This term is not used in the traditional Biblical manner of textual exegesis. Instead, Ricoeur's approach is hermeneutical in that it accepts that we are constantly part of a process of interpretation and reinterpretation. We are involved in a constant evolution whereby the past is being integrated into the present, and the present refining its perception of the past and of its own definitions. This hermeneutic perspective implies that there is no personal a-historical, objective identity to be constituted, any more than there is a supreme plot to be deciphered. Ricoeur sets out a hermeneutical circle that holds that we are influenced by the reading of narratives (with their own accompanying history of interpretations) as much as we influence their subsequent readings. "At the very heart of what we call experience [there is a tension] between the efficacy of the past we undergo and the reception of the past that we bring about."[2] Indeed, Ricoeur would acknowledge that basically our identity is a composite of all such readings to which we have been exposed.

At the core of hermeneutics, then, is an awareness that any interpretation takes place in a context where one must be open-minded and prepared to revise both our self-understandings and our sense of responsibility to the world:

> It is the task of hermeneutics, in return, to reconstruct the set of operations by which a work lifts itself above the opaque depths of living, acting, and suffering, to be given by an author to readers who receive it and thereby change their acting.[3]

At the same time, we cannot evade our responsibility to the past. As a result, one of the most poignant pleas in the whole of *Time and Narrative* occurs in Vol. I, where Ricoeur relates the need for narrative as a mode of self-understanding to a specific debt to the past. This issues from a growing awareness that our present identity can involve reclaiming lost heritages, whether personal or collective, that have not been allowed their impact on the stage of history. This reflects the movement towards what has been termed "history of the lost and forgotten," i.e., reading not official archives but diaries and other memorabilia of the underdogs of history: slaves, convicts, colonized men and women. For Ricoeur, the narrative of identity that can be construed from this evidence is not just an interesting hobby or a peripheral pursuit. It illuminates, within the categories of space and time, records whose rehabilitation adds to a more equitable heritage of knowledge. Narrative identity, on this reading, is not just a psychological construct, but a composite of detailed memory and present re-evaluation. Narrative is both a testament to the diversity of past human accomplishment and the possible basis for further self-determination. Narratives of whatever nature (of victory or of defeat) furnish the building blocks by which we construct a sense of identity. The debt is not just to the past, but to ourselves:

> We tell stories because in the last analysis human lives need and merit being narrated. This remark takes on its full force when we refer to the necessity to save the history of the defeated and the lost. The whole history of suffering cries out for vengeance and calls for narrative.[4]

Given such an exhortation, it appears that within the parameters of Ricoeur's model, the hermeneutical contact of reader and text is not just a continuous dialectic but also a productive one. Nevertheless, the outcome will never be certain nor the narrative all-encompassing. The mode of consciousness and identity that emerge (i.e., narrative identity) will never have the consolation of a total or final mediation, as in Hegel.[5]

The various essays in this collection represent diverse hermeneutical encounters with the work of Ricoeur. Each engages with an aspect of Ricoeur's work on the topic of narrative – some in ways that seek to elucidate Ricoeur's theories, others in ways that contest his thought or his position on certain issues. As such, they attest to the wide range of disciplines and approaches that Ricoeur's work has influenced. Yet, in both their constructive and critical modes, all the contributions seek to amplify aspects of Ricoeur's work that have not yet had the benefit of such interdisciplinary perspectives.

In the opening essay, **Jocelyn Dunphy Blomfield** surveys the narrative elements that have suffused Ricoeur's work from *Freud and Philosophy* (1970)[6] until his more recent *Oneself as Another*.[7] Dunphy Blomfield portrays Ricoeur as concerned with the creative element (in spite of obstacles) that surfaces both in the "semantics of desire" of psychoanalysis and in the search for identity that features in more formal narratives.

It is worth noting that the term "hermeneutics of suspicion" was coined as a result of *Freud and Philosophy*.[8] Ricoeur used the term "suspicion" in relation to the work of Marx, Nietzsche, and Freud, who, in their respective ways, questioned the illusions of consciousness. Although Ricoeur acknowledges that we need a form of hermeneutics that demystifies false appearances in the retrieval of the past, he also wants to indicate the constant and vibrant impulse to affirm life – a hermeneutics of restoration, of renewal. Dunphy Blomfield shows this double form of hermeneutics at work in the narratives of psychoanalysis, where such paradigmatic tales as those of Oedipus and Job do not privilege the initial suffering and guilt, but surmount them to testify to a hard-won wisdom that only the nuances of narrative can convey.

Jamie Scott turns his attention to an actual work of testimony –
Bonhoeffer's Letters and Papers from Prison.[9] Ricoeur had focused on testimony in an early essay, "The Hermeneutics of Testimony,"[10] and he returns to it briefly in *Time and Narrative.*[11] Ricoeur understands testimony,
as a form of narrative, as being in the service of judgment. It provides
information that helps the hearer determine a position regarding a sequence of events or a person's character.[12] As a narrative form, it construes meanings and motives and ties them to action. Scott analyzes
Bonhoeffer's letters and papers as a testament to his own experience
and justification of his martyrdom. At the same time, he depicts a dialectic of literary and literal testimony – the former being Bonhoeffer's
actual writings; the latter, Bonhoeffer's actual sacrifice of his life. Both
testimonies can be understood as a form of transformation, of witness
to a greater truth embodied in the ideals of Christianity.

In looking at the relation of Ricoeur's ideas on narrative to architecture, **Graham Livesey** traces the trajectory of Ricoeur's development
from the figure of metaphor to the form of *muthos* (plot). In charting
Ricoeur's gradual expansion from an early interest in creative narrative
genres (including Biblical material)[13] to the creative element in narrative
(*muthos*), Livesey points to metaphor. Ricoeur's work, *The Rule of Metaphor*, was an exacting exercise that documented metaphor, not simply as
a linguistic trope, but as the exemplar of a creative moment that fosters
new insight.[14] The resultant "redescription of reality" was refined by
Ricoeur in his three volumes on *Time and Narrative*, where Ricoeur developed the position that the *muthos*/plot plays the same role in narrative that metaphor does in a semantic frame of reference. Metaphor, for
Ricoeur, is not simply an instance of semiotic substitution, but a vibrant
wordplay that encourages new insights into the way the world is perceived and recorded. *Muthos*, as plot, functions in a similar fashion in
narrative to metaphor with words, so that novel ways of appreciating
the world are portrayed. The narrative redescription of activity by
"emplotment" (the English translation of Ricoeur's term *mise-en-intrigue*)
is a *poietic* act of configuration that Livesey then compares to the work
of an architect. He sees this in the way that architecture gives form to a
disparate range of elements and requirements in the same way that a
plot brings a perspective to bear on a heterogeneous set of circumstances
or experiences.

The phrase, "redescription of reality," first used describing the effects
of metaphor, was also even more finely articulated in *Time and Narrative*
by the introduction of the term "mimesis." In the past, this term has
often been employed to refer to reproduction as simply a reduplication,

but Ricoeur introduces a more complex tripartite model of mimesis$_1$, mimesis$_2$ and mimesis$_3$. "Mimesis$_1$" refers to the way in which human action occurs in an unthematized or unreflective manner (prefiguration); "mimesis$_2$" refers to the organization of these activities in a comprehensible form by means of *muthos*/plot (configuration); "mimesis$_3$" refers to the effects of reading or reception, by which a person can change his or her ideas and behavior as a result of discovering new dimensions of life (refiguration). Livesey concedes that architects tend to concentrate on mimesis$_2$ (configuration), but observes that all the patterns we make in life are forms of figural intersection – whether a configural definition of space by an architect or the more broadly based mimetic involvements of human beings in shaping their world.

The construct of narrative identity is another dimension of Ricoeur's more recent work on narrative that has been particularly helpful. Ricoeur believes a narrative form of identity can rescue us from our contemporary dilemmas as defined by the postmodern impasse between repetition and indeterminacy. Speaking with specific reference to the problem of self and identity he says:

> Without the recourse to narration, the problem of personal identity would in fact be condemned to an antimony with no solution. Either we must posit a subject identical with itself through the diversity of its different states, or, following Hume and Nietzsche, we must hold that this identical subject is nothing more than a substantialist illusion whose elimination merely brings to light a pure manifold of cognitions, emotions and volitions.[15]

In place of the ontological understanding of identity as an abstract timeless entity, Ricoeur wishes to substitute an appreciation of narrative as a modality of awareness that allows for development and change while simultaneously providing a form of self-constancy. To incorporate these requirements, Ricoeur talks of a person's life as composed of many different narrative plots. Each plot (*muthos*) lends cohesion and coherence to the manifold influences that ceaselessly threaten to overwhelm us. So it is that a particular plot is constructed by a person in a specific context. This plot can help a person establish a bridgehead from which he or she can thematize (i.e., emplot) a set of events that may otherwise be either too chaotic or distressing. In this way, as Ricoeur relates in a recent article: "we learn to become the *narrator of our own story* [stories] without becoming the author of our life.[16]

To illustrate this understanding of identity, **Morny Joy** examines three narratives of women survivors of incest. The telling of their stories is indeed a form of therapy – it helped these women gain a perspective on their spattered lives. This does not imply the happy-ever-after ending of a linear plot, but rather the type of *poietic* resolution that does not appeal either to the arrogant certainties of modernism or the gratuitous fragmentation of a nihilistic mode of postmodernism.

Yet, in his recent work, *Oneself as Another*, Ricoeur admitted he was not satisfied with the model of narrative identity he had proposed earlier in *Time and Narrative*. In the later work he introduces the terms *"idem"* and *"ipse"* to refer to different aspects of identity. *"Idem"* refers to those aspects of identity that are defined by objective criteria that can be replicated. *"Ipse"* refers to responses of a more existential nature that have developmental connotations. Both terms, however, overlap with reference to notions of permanence in time. Ricoeur sees narrative as mediating these two different ascriptions of identity, allowing for the intricate interplay of the different needs for permanence without being caught in the extremes of immutability or constant change. The personal connotations of *ipse* will disrupt the tendencies of *idem* to rigidity. In the narratives of women who have suffered incest, their need is to establish an identity, not to dismantle one. Ricoeur's narrative model allows the exploration and building of what could be termed a "strategic identity," that supports but never controls this delicate process.

Pamela Anderson's paper is a critical reading of Sophocles' narrative text, *Antigone*, as it is presented in the context of *Oneself as Another*.[17] Her concern is to tease out the way in which she believes Ricoeur remains part of a modern male-centered tradition by reading this female figure of myth as disrupting the text. Although Ricoeur generally works to distance his philosophical thinking from Hegel, in his reading of Antigone, he follows closely Hegel's interpretation in reading women as being in dialectical opposition to men, particularly regarding the public/private distinction. It is thus interesting to note that, although Ricoeur strives to accommodate the diffuse influences of life in a narrative form that honors the manifold while organizing it, he does not recognize the rigid demarcations that all too often dictate to women stereotypical and artificial roles. Anderson looks particularly to French thinker Luce Irigaray to provide other readings of women in myth that question such standard categorization. Such a critical evaluation of the simplistic association of women with the domestic and private realms is a necessary task, as women today challenge these traditional confinements in both theory and practice. Women are questioning both the roles and the plots that have been assigned to them. Ricoeur's theories on narrative are evaluated and found wanting in that they tend to assume social and cultural formulas that are not appropriate for many present-day women.

Another area of dispute regarding Ricoeur's formulation of narrative is addressed by **Hank Stam** and **Lori Egger**. David Carr has written elsewhere querying whether Ricoeur has succumbed to the "standard view" of separating life from narrative in his threefold version of mimesis.[18] Stam and Egger expand on this observation to review the role of narrative in psychology, where they contend that a variant of this standard view is employed to impose narrative structures in the guise of normal standards. In contrast, Stam and Egger do not see Ricoeur as requiring such a definite exposition, particularly in his writings on psychoanalysis. Here Ricoeur refers to life as an "inchoate narrative" that in its configuration by narrative can be transformed. These configurations, though prefigured, never conform to a set pattern. In this way, Stam and Egger do not understand Ricoeur as dividing life and narrative according to manufactured criteria. But, nonetheless, he wishes to contain it. In this sense, for Stam and Egger, Ricoeur and Carr are not that different. Stam and Egger believe that what is required is an investigation of what "life" or "reality," as insisted on by Carr, actually entails. By looking at transcripts of therapy sessions, Stam and Egger would claim that "reality" is configured by a process of negotiation between the therapist and client. Configuration (or mimesis$_2$), then, need not always simply be the disclosure of latent patterns. As in therapy, it should allow for helpful interventions that may bring to light unanticipated possibilities. It is thus a dynamic and shared process, in the course of which a mutually acceptable narrative account of past events (an interpretation, not an exact replication) is reached.

Helen Buss wants to make the reader nervous by conflating two narrative genres, history and fiction, that Ricoeur prefers to keep in separate, though interactive spheres. Invoking the term "archive," which she feels, particularly in women's memories, trangresses the boundaries between history and fiction, Buss wants to introduce her own language game. While Ricoeur posits the imagination as "the depository of oral and written traditions,"[19] Buss reliteralizes the concept of imagination as another form of archive and depicts the building that houses this imaginative archive as the body. Buss believes that, until there is a concept of imagination as embodied, it is not possible to read fully the literary narration of imagination acts. Buss extends Ricoeur's claim: "We *belong-to* history before telling stories or writing stories,"[20] by maintaining that we *belong-to* our bodies, and we belong to our bodies' histories before and while we tell stories. Such a move reflects contemporary women's concerns that experience must not be confined to conceptual definitions but must reflect all aspects of life. Though Ricoeur wants to ground narrative in the everyday world, Buss makes it clear that Ricoeur has yet to incorporate the more visceral and emotional aspects of a lived reality into his work on narrative.

It is something of a jump from present-day interests of women to late medieval religious song manuscripts belonging to women's communities, particularly as it appears these songs were of a secular nature, though featuring in collections of sacred texts. The secularity involved, however, while it did pertain to the body, was more devoted to stories of misgotten or unfulfilled love. **Hermine Joldersma** wonders what such narratives meant, given that the women who read or recited them probably never "lived" such stories themselves. Joldersma finds Ricoeur's notion of narrative as a "thought experiment" helpful. That is, as Ricoeur postulates, the narrative mode "sets before the imagination and meditation situations ... by means of which we learn to join the ethical aspect of human behavior to happiness and unhappiness, to fortune and misfortune."[21] Thus, such imaginative variations seemed to function for these women in a particular way. Although apparently secular on first hearing, they can indicate figurative depictions of the longing of the soul for God. Such narratives, however, need not be reduced to allegories, for they were also indicators of how the Christian struggle took place in the lives of actual human beings. Thus, Ricoeur's understanding of narratives as presenting us with a world we might inhabit, that through the refiguration or reception implicit in mimesis$_3$ we can make it our own, is relevant. The late medieval song experiments give us a graphic insight into the particular flavor of the Christian values of the women of that time, whose ultimate vision was not of this world.

David Brown is also concerned with a particular community, but more with its collective identity. Brown is interested in how Ricoeur's notion of narrative identity can be expanded from a personal to a communal setting that is not confined to a demographic definition. The "belonging" to such a group is problematic in that it relies on the sharing of subjective experiences. Brown illustrates how such an identity is achieved by mapping out the processes of social interaction through narrative-based discourse, whereby identity is accomplished, negotiated, contested, repaired. His ethnographic study of a support group of Latin-American seniors in a Canadian town details how Ricoeur's concept of narrative identity can be used fruitfully to incorporate the experience of social change in family and work, with particular reference to effects of aging and immigration among women.

Communal identity is also the focus of **Dominique Perron's** paper, but she wonders if Ricoeur's ideas can be applied to a specific form of identity – what, in French, is called *"l'identitaire."* Such a construct refers to a horizon of cultural identity, whose boundaries are difficult to define, as it is composed of individual, social, and national components.

Yet Perron states that an appreciation of *l'identitaire* is necessary for anyone who wants to comprehend the link between fiction and society of Québec's contemporary narrative. Whereas individual identity can be attributed to transformations that are the result of refiguration/reception (mimesis$_3$) of narratives that embody cultural codes, *l'identitaire* can be characterized as the culmination of all such individual processes. Perron looks to the work of writer Jacques Poulin to document the sense of *l'identitaire* with which the Québécois of today resonate. This is a world of fluidity, of uncertainty, of difference, of contrary impulses that find actual location in the present difficult. Yet this seeming non-identity is still a form of identity, forged by interaction with Poulin's ambivalent texts that explore the paradoxes of existence. Perron allows that while Ricoeur's definition of narrative identity may not be sufficiently comprehensive to encompass such a composite and uncertain identity, his description of refiguration (mimesis$_3$) as an integral part of identity formation does have certain affinities for Québec's self-appropriation of Poulin's texts.

Bernard Dauenhauer also amplifies Ricoeur's account of the elements inherent in the establishment of personal/narrative identity but, in this instance, it is in the direction of political identity. Firstly, Dauenhauer distinguishes between personal and political identity and finds that this differentiation leads to problems regarding the establishment of conditions for a normative identity. Thus, his second task is an investigation of the conditions that separate defensible from indefensible narratives of identity. Dauenhauer draws on Ricoeur's distinction between *idem* and *ipse* regarding the nature of identity to clarify his findings. One condition that a defensible narrative must satisfy is that the demands of *idem*, which, in this context, have connotations of fixed political allegiances, should never become determinate in a way that dominates the singularity of *ipse*. That is, political identity should always preserve the difference between *idem* (regulative) and *ipse* (existentially responsive) as discrete forms of identity. Consequently, change or reform is possible. The second condition is that the thoroughgoing historicality of the constitution of a society must be admitted. That is, the recognition that no society is ever free from the multiple influences of the past that continue to influence it, no matter how rigid or dogmatic its present declarations. Such a society ideally would respect the diversity of possible political positions, i.e., no one position is decisive. Again, in this context, the collective and regulative *idem* does not dictate terms to the particularity of *ipse*, and a demarcation is maintained. This innovative expansion of Ricoeur's model of narrative identity in the service of defining the adequacy of political narratives helps to guard against tyranny that would impose its notion of identity on a populace. Such a dialectical exercise is very much in keeping with the spirit of Ricoeur's work.

The contribution of **Catherine Bryn Pinchin** is politically engaged from another point of view. Pinchin is worried that the apparent suspension of literal reference that is at the core of Ricoeur's theory of metaphor and fiction allows for a non-critical acceptance of the ideologies that are embedded in the political fabric. Even if it is conceded that in Ricoeur's theory of metaphor the bracketing of the actual referent is in the service of emergent meaning brought about by the clash between literal and figurative perceptions instigated by metaphor, Pinchin fears this is an evasion of reality. She wonders whether a theory of metaphor so deeply implanted in an unexamined power position, and so committed to preserving values that "are the common treasure of mankind"[22] can be respected as a critical tool. The test cases for Pinchin are the contemporary postmodern texts written by women or people of color whose purpose is to disrupt the conventions that Ricoeur appears to leave unchallenged. Such a critique is powerful and relevant, unless it can be demonstrated that the hermeneutics of suspicion can function in both evaluative and recuperative modes, and that metaphor, while creative in intent, is not simply a substitution for outdated prototypes of newer versions, but has the potential to revise and reconstitute oppressive practices.

The status of *muthos* and *mimesis* and the extent of their connection with Greek culture and values is **Jim Fodor's** concern. Although Ricoeur fully appreciates the concrete specificity of narratives in the formation of an adequate hermeneutic, he nonetheless does not discuss in detail the varieties of cultures that contribute to distinct community-forming narratives. That is, Ricoeur attempts to promote a more or less general narrative theory which neither favors nor precludes any one specific narrative tradition, even though he himself has been shaped by (and in turn shapes) the Jewish-Christian heritage. However, Fodor wonders about the extent to which Aristotle's and Ricoeur's respective understanding of narrative presuppose the presence of dissimilar living, concrete myths which inform the habits, skills, judgments, and practices of a specific community. In particular, Fodor questions whether *muthos/* plot can be divorced from its Greek location within Aristotle's theory of tragedy. This is a matter of concern to Fodor because the values promoted by a Greek tragic worldview are incompatible with those of Christianity. Thus, in contrast to other contributors to this volume (e.g., Brown, Perron, who do not see any problem in applying Ricoeur's theories in other contexts), Fodor would hold that Ricoeur's project is too formal and abstract to take into account the variations of narrative traditions and their accompanying culturally specific values and judgments – in particular a Christian conception of tragedy and redemption.

While Fodor worries about the relevance of Ricoeur for the Christian narrative, **Terence Tilley** finds that Ricoeur's work can be of assistance in formulating a type of narrative theology that is effective in a postmodern, post-death-of-God age. Tilley finds that Ricoeur's work concerning mimesis$_3$ and reception does need clarification, even modification to further emphasize implementation, but these changes do not undermine the basis of his work on narrative. Tilley refines Ricoeur's statement: "The effects of fiction, effects of revelation and transformation are essentially effects of reading,"[23] to include a theory of performative action. One cannot remain simply at the textual level, but must put the new insights gleaned into a *praxis* that changes both personal character and the world we inhabit. Ricoeur has always had an implicit theory of effects contained in his narrative theory, although Tilley's elaboration highlights the practical element that must be implemented by a narrative theology, if it is to avoid the abstract dislocations of purely postmodern wordplay.

It is interesting to speculate just what sort of actions a postmodern narrative theology might support. Usually, when such guidance is sought, an appeal is made to ethics – and when one turns to Ricoeur for insight on this matter, at first glance, his work does not seem promising. However, **Robert Sweeney** discloses a discontinuous current of thought from Ricoeur's earliest work until today that demonstrates the presence of ethics, in different guises, as a strong underlying element. From Ricoeur's early association with the French personalist school and the work of Emmanuel Mounier, by way of notions of value he derived from German phenomenology, to the ethics presented in *Oneself as Another*, there are indications that he has been well aware of the issues involved and the need for an ethical stance. Sweeney focuses on Ricoeur's discussion of the two central ethical traditions: teleological (Aristotle) and deontological (Kant) and their implications for a theory of narrative. There are both positive connections (*liaisons*) and negative connections (*déliaisons*). On Sweeney's reading, Ricoeur insists that we first underscore the gap between the imaginary component of narrative and moral judgment – that is, there is an initial refraining from all moral censure of inventive plots and characters. Here the imaginative variants are entertained as thought experiments regarding new ways of thinking and acting that could or could not be adopted. But this non-committal step must never stand in isolation. For the wager behind such exploration in narrative form is to test out original combinations between love and hate, life and death, pleasure and suffering, good and evil. These probings are, in Ricoeur's words, in the service of discovering a world that could be inhabited. The first step of distanced consideration is to be followed by critical appraisal. What Ricoeur leaves unsaid is that these explorations are not of frivolous or harmful ways of life – and this is where he is often misunderstood. Sweeney's paper supports an appreciation that ethics and morality are always intended in these imaginary experimentations. For Ricoeur, literary fictions can be considered as interrogations regarding the theme of the good life – which constitutes the first "ethico-moral cornerstone." Thus, narrativity and ethics are more intertwined than might appear at first approximation.

Finally, in completing this survey of Ricoeur's work on narrative, it seems appropriate to acknowledge the crucial role of the hermeneutic circle, which is an integral part of all Ricoeur's work. As **Linda Fisher** indicates, the hermeneutic circle describes the interpretive principle whereby the objects of understanding are comprehended in relation to a whole which, in turn, is grasped in relation to the various parts that comprise the whole. Another formulation, influenced by Heidegger's analysis of this circle, stresses the structure of anticipatory pre-understanding which relates all subsequent explanations back to this understanding, which precedes it. The delineation of the three parts of mimesis in the treatment of narrative is a subtle reformulation of the flow of the hermeneutic circle. Part/whole, understanding/explanation are components that figure prominently, although they are never thematically developed in Ricoeur's work on narrative as they are in his philosophical essays. When Ricoeur states that "narrative identity is the poetic resolution of the hermeneutic circle,"[24] he brings together many implicit ideas that have informed his work on narrative. Fisher describes how in relating time and narrative, Ricoeur is aware that there are paradoxes or aporias that cannot be solved by conceptual formulas. Narration, particularly in its three stages of mimesis, defines ways in which the complex interrelationships of life can be made accessible, in a *poietic* way, even if they ultimately escape rational categories. We constantly progress through the stages of mimesis in an unending cycle, but each turn brings greater insight, further appreciation of our finite existence. In narrative, the hermeneutic circle occurs as we live through the stories we create from our immersion in other stories. Our lives are thus enriched. "An examined life is a life recounted." Narrative, as conceived by Ricoeur, provides the contemporary variant of Socrates' admonition regarding the practice of a wise and fulfilled life.

Morny Joy

Notes

1 Morny Joy, "Hermeneutics and *Mimesis*," *Studies in Religion/Sciences Religieuses* 19/ 1 (1990): 78-9.

2 Paul Ricoeur, *Time and Narrative*, III, trans. K. Blamey and D. Pellauer (Chicago: University of Chicago Press, 1988), 220.

3 Paul Ricoeur, *Time and Narrative*, I, trans. K. McLaughlin and D. Pellauer (Chicago: University of Chicago Press, 1984), 53.

4 Ricoeur, *Time and Narrative*, I, 75.

5 Ricoeur, *Time and Narrative*, III, 206.

6 Paul Ricoeur, *Freud and Philosophy: An Essay on Interpretation*, trans. D. Savage (New Haven: Yale University Press, 1970).

7 Paul Ricoeur, *Oneself as Another*, trans. K. Blamey (Chicago: University of Chicago Press, 1992).

8 Ricoeur, *Freud and Philosophy*, 32-6.

9 Dietrich Bonhoeffer, *Letters and Papers from Prison*, ed. E. Bethge (London: SCM Press, 1953).

10 Paul Ricoeur, "The Hermeneutics of Testimony," *Essays on Biblical Interpretation*, ed. L.S. Mudge (Philadelphia: Fortress Press, 1980), 119-54. Originally published in 1972.

11 Ricoeur, *Time and Narrative*, III, 114, 117-8.

12 Ricoeur, "The Hermeneutics of Testimony," 123.

13 Paul Ricoeur, "The Bible and the Imagination," *The Bible as a Document of the University*, ed. H.D. Betz (Chicago: University of Chicago Press, 1981), 49-76.

14 Paul Ricoeur, *The Rule of Metaphor: Multidisciplinary Studies of the Creation of Meaning in Language*, trans. R. Czerny *et al.* (Toronto: University of Toronto Press, 1977), 303.

15 Ricoeur, *Time and Narrative*, III, 246.

16 Paul Ricoeur, "Life: A Story in Search of a Narrator," *Facts and Values: Philosophical Reflections from Western and Non-Western Perspectives*, ed. M.C. Doeser and J.N. Kraay, (Dordrecht: Martinus Nijhoff, 1986), 131.

17 Ricoeur, *Oneself as Another*, 241-9.

18 David Carr, "Discussion: Ricoeur on Narrative," *Paul Ricoeur: Narrative and Interpretation*, ed. David Wood (London: Routledge, 1990), 160.

19 Paul Ricoeur, "Can Fictional Narratives be True?", *Analecta Husserliana* 14 (1983): 5.

20 Ricoeur, "Fictional Narratives," 14.

21 Ricoeur, "Life: A Story," 123-4.

22 Ricoeur, "Fictional Narratives," 16.

23 Ricoeur, *Time and Narrative*, III, 101.

24 Ricoeur, *Time and Narrative*, III, 248.

A Response by Paul Ricoeur

I want to express my gratitude to Morny Joy and all those who have contributed to this volume based on the Colloquy held at the University of Calgary.

The subtitle "Context and Contestation" indicates quite precisely the outcome that was reached, namely, on the one hand, a reconstruction of the conceptual framework within which my narrative theory constitutes one segment, and, on the other hand, a testing of this theory with regard to multiple fields of inquiry where it sometimes finds an expansion, sometimes a contestation. I am pleased to be able to write this preface not just in acknowledgment of this work, but also to add to its critical aspect what assistance I see stemming from recent developments within my own thinking. In this way, I hope to contribute to the expansion of thinking about narrative intended by Morny Joy.

I would like first of all to underscore my emphasis, since *Oneself as Another*, on the importance of the idea of *homo capax* as integrating a wide conceptual field. With this theme I have tried to bring together those diverse capacities and incapacities that make human beings acting and suffering beings. If the notions of *poiesis* and *praxis* were given ample development in my earlier work, those of being acted upon and of suffering were less so. This disequilibrium is apparent in my treatment of the four modes of what I call our power to act that together make up the underlying structure of *Oneself as Another*.

For example, at a first level, that of language, I think I do a good job of showing the necessity to return from the logical structure of the proposition or statement, dealt with by semantics, to the act of utterance, which is taken up by pragmatics, and from there to the utterer's ability to speak. However, I did not emphasize enough our difficulty, even our incapacity to bring to language the emotional, often traumatic experience that psychoanalysis attempts to liberate. Similarly, on the second level, that of ordinary action and its intervention in the course of events, I had no difficulty in returning from the objective structures of action (whose "readability" I had earlier pointed to by assimilating them to something like a text) to the ability to act of which the agent is certain and concerning which s/he is confident. In this sense, the capacity to designate myself as the author of my acts gets added to the general level of our ability to speak. But I left unclear the face of impotence that goes with this ability, owing not only to those infirmities of every sort that may affect the human body as the organ of action, but also to the interference of outside powers capable of diminishing, hindering, or preventing our use of our abilities. In this regard, the sufferings that humans inflict on one another weigh heavily in the scale of our abilities and inabilities within the sphere of ordinary action. I would say the same thing about my analysis of the relations between our affirmation of personal or collective identity and what I have called the narrative function. The distinction I proposed between *idem*-identity and *ipse*-identity only reinforces our capacity to tell about things and to tell about ourselves, and thereby to answer the question: who am I? But the employment of this capacity does not always just happen smoothly, as is indicated by the inability of many survivors of extermination camps to bring their wounded memories to verbal expression in narrative. Finally, the fourth category, that of imputability, which governs the transition from the first descriptive studies to the three chapters devoted to my "little ethics," also calls for a significant complement concerning the difficulty of many of our contemporaries to recognize themselves not just as the authors of their acts, but as accountable for the consequences of these acts, especially when they do harm to others – that is, finally, when they add to the world's suffering. We can speak in this regard of an incapacity to enter a symbolic order, including beyond motivating impulses, structuring prohibitions. This incapacity has as its effect an inability to discern or derive the morally significant aspect of action in relation to some norm. These incapacities, which affect the imputability of human action, today pose serious problems for educators, judges, and political leaders inasmuch as they diminish what we can call our aptitude for citizenship.

Why have I begun with this exordium on the dialectic of acting and being acted upon? For the following reason. It seemed to me in reading the essays brought together in this volume by Morny Joy that several of the critiques that are here developed with lucidity as well as generosity may find the beginnings of a response in the direction I have just indicated.

As regards my recourse to psychoanalysis, I would be less concerned today to argue on the plane of the Freudian "metapsychology" (even though I would have nothing to add or to withdraw from what I have said about the dialectic between a hermeneutic of suspicion and one of renewal). Instead I would pursue the sense of the analytic experience itself, insofar as a significant part of psychic suffering there finds itself caught up in a quest for expression in language and aided by the mediation of a third person who in a way "authorizes" speaking.

But this displacement is motivated by a more important shift that affects my narrative theory overall. In *Time and Narrative*, I proceeded thanks to a kind of short-circuit that placed into direct relation the structured forms of narrative and our experience of time. In so doing, I passed over in silence the mediation of memory and forgetting, where the dialectic of acting and being acted upon or suffering finds a privileged site of manifestation. What is more, to memory and suffering are attached those modes of narrative at the pre-literary level that I sacrificed to the benefit of dealing with sophisticated forms of narrative literary fiction and historiography. The place and role of what I would today call the narrative of conversion were only sketchily indicated in my discussion of what I called mimesis$_1$. But it is at this level of the pre-literary narrative that we find expressed the wounds, abuses, and failures of individual and collective memory. Yet it is not just the stage of the "prefiguration" of narrative that can be enriched by taking memory into account, but also that of "refiguration" (mimesis$_3$). In this respect, the effects of "redescribing reality" have to be extended from time to space and to the embodied lived experience. In this way, the architectural act of construction has be taken into account in an expanded phenomenology of the act of dwelling (where we also take into account the misfortune of those who are homeless). Then, once handed over to the contingencies of space and time, the notion of identity, so closely linked to the narrative function, loses its abstract and atemporal appearance.

Does the rootedness of narrative in memory, combined with the dialectic of acting and suffering, allow me to do justice to narratives composed by women? By giving a place today to the theme of the wounded memory along with that of the therapeutic function of narrative, I hope to have made some progress in this direction. In any case, I would like to note that, confronted on the ethnological plane with the dominant tendency across space and time of the subordination of women to male power, following Françoise Hértier, in *Masculin-Féminin*, I would like to link the defense of the rights of women to the moral, juridical, and political affirmation of the common humanity of the two sexes. It is to this humanity that I apply my analysis of acting and suffering. That today there is not only a female way of suffering as well as of acting, and that my analysis of common humanity suffers the limits of a male way of thinking and writing is something that I in no way would deny. The complements and corrections that women writers bring to my analysis nonetheless do not seem to me to require a basic revision of my sexually neutral theses. In particular, I would persist in saying that even the eminently female figure of Antigone bears witness to a conflict that bears on our common humanity, that of the relation between unwritten laws and political power that claims to rule by decree. The figure of Antigone not only interrupts a text but also the structure of power. It breaks away from the stereotypes of political power, and first of all those relative to the female condition as interpreted by the male figure of power. The question why it should be a male who incarnates power and a women who calls this into question is a good one; but it only arises against the background of a humanity at stake that surpasses both sexual roles. In this regard, George Steiner's book *Antigones* can help in articulating the many dialectics this plot sets in motion: human/divine, moral absolutes/historical power, youth/age, life/death, male/female. And there is still the question of unraveling, among the different female roles, that of the sister over against brothers who are enemies.

To the rootedness of narrative in memory I would like to add its rootedness in the imagination. The dialectic between memory and imagination unfolds at a deeper level than that of the pair literary fiction and historiography. One consequence is that the dialectic of acting and suffering, along with the visceral and emotional aspects of the latter, may be more easily discerned at the point of articulation that links memory and imagination, the former intending a passed past, the latter a possible non-reality. It is also at this primordial level that the junction between the narrative function and corporeality takes place, as well as the multiple fashions of the act of corporeally inhabiting or dwelling within the world. Yet it is also true that only language can articulate these modes, these moods, so as finally to turn them into "imaginative variations." We might apply to this discursive plane Hölderlin's line celebrating our "poetically" dwelling within the world.

I do not want to end these considerations, where personal and communal identity are still considered on a pre-political level, without having said a few words about the notion of testimony. Today, I would prefer to speak of attestation in order to speak of the kind of certitude and confidence that I apply to our capacity to act (by speaking, doing, telling, assuring my responsibility). The contrary of attestation is precisely suspicion, the driving force behind the hermeneutics of suspicion already referred to above. I reserve the term testimony for the recognition rendered to another who incarnates and exemplifies in my eyes the ideal of a good life. It is within the framework of testimony so understood that narrativity and morality and their interaction are to be articulated.

Next, as concerns collective identity, I would like to say that the consideration of memory brings an important insight. Ought we not to take the phenomenon of commemoration, which is by nature both collective and public, as strictly correlative with the individual bringing to mind [*remémoration*] of the past? It is only within the philosophical tradition that Charles Taylor in his *The Sources of the Self* places under the heading of inwardness that memory is treated as a fundamentally personal phenomenon. But it is together that we remember; and it is within the social medium of language that we articulate our most individual memories in the mode of narrative. On the basis of this notion of collective memory we can do justice to the idea of the narrative identity of the communities to which we belong. We can also see that this collective identity can suffer the same abuses and failures as do the wounded memories of individuals. Here is where today I would take up the question of the identity crises of so many contemporary historical communities.

It is on the basis of this analysis of collective narrative identity that the problem of identity at the political level arises. What I said above about the category of imputability, thanks to which agents have the capacity to hold themselves accountable for the consequences of their acts, allows us to articulate the normative and narrative dimensions of collective identity on the plane of politics. In this regard, the commemorations just referred to are the site where the intersection of the normative and the narrative gets articulated, within the framework of narratives that we can call political narratives, such as the founding narratives of a political community. What is more, the dialectic between memory and imagination, which gets underway on the individual level, continues its course on the collective and political plane in the form of ideology and utopia, which I have dealt with elsewhere in terms of what I called the social imaginary. Utopia, in particular, constitutes a form of discourse that challenges positions of power. In this sense, the analyses I have devoted to the power of redescription of metaphor and that of the refiguration of narrative receive a noteworthy extension thanks to which the structuring and contestatory functions of this social imaginary find their unstable equilibrium.

But I willingly grant that we ought not to demand too much of a theory of metaphor or a theory of narrative, even when extended to the public sphere. It is within an ethics that we have to seek the reference to norms. Yes, imagination can be taken to be a means of initiation to the critical function, insofar as it teaches us to dream of a different way just as narrative teaches us to recount things in a different way. A critical force is held in reserve within this double "a different way." In this regard, even the retrospective gaze of the historian applied to the past of our culture and to its founding texts is not opposed to the exploring gaze directed toward what might be possible of the social imaginary. History is not limited to describing and explaining past facts – or let us say, what actually happened – it can also take the risk of resuscitating and reanimating the unkept promises of the past. In this way, it rejoins what people who have disappeared may have imagined and frees it from the contingency of unachieved realizations so as to hand it over to the imagination of the future. However, I repeat, we must not ask of a theory of the imagination, even one completed by a narrative theory, both elevated to the collective plane, what can only be demanded of an ethics. Analyses of the redescription of reality of metaphor or of the refiguration brought about through narrative are not stamped with a normative signficance, such as required by a political theory, unless they are coupled on the ethical plane with analyses of the modes of practical reason, inherited from the *phronesis* of the Greeks and the *prudentia* of medieval thinkers. It is the passage from the norm to a concrete decision, taken within situations of uncertainty at the very heart of the tragic dimension of all action, that constitutes the critical moment par excellence of a morally intelligible action. Imagination and memory – metaphor and narrative – only provide handholds, at best incitement, for our making sense of this. But neither function includes as such within itself the dimension of evaluation. From politics, they only expect an absence of censorship. Whereas the distinction between good and evil, the permitted and the forbidden, requires the whole panoply of an ethics, which itself traverses the successive levels from the desire of a good life, with and for others in just institutions, to that of the norm under the double figure of obligation and interdiction, then finally to that of practical wisdom, of the prudential judgment. Only then can imagination and narrative be asked to nourish the dream, to exemplify concretely and in a way embody, the prudential judgment in which the whole of ethics joins together in the everydayness of our daily life and work.

Paul Ricoeur

Translated by David Pellauer

Une réponse de Paul Ricoeur

Je veux exprimer ici ma gratitude à Morny Joy et à tous ceux qui ont contribué à l'ouvrage collectif issu du Colloque de Calgary. Le sous-titre choisi « Context and Contestation » désigne avec exactitude le résultat atteint, à savoir, d'une part, la reconstruction de l'enchaînement conceptuel dont ma théorie narrative constitue un segment, d'autre part, la mise à l'épreuve de cette théorie dans de multiples champs du savoir où elle trouve, tantôt une expansion, tantôt une contestation. Le propos de la préface que j'ai le plaisir d'écrire en signe de reconnaissance est d'accompagner cette lecture critique à l'aide de développements récents de ma réflexion. Ainsi j'espère contribuer à l'effet d'amplification recherché par Morny Joy.

J'aimerais porter au premier plan mon insistance, depuis *Soi-même comme un Autre*, sur la fonction de rassemblement conceptuel que j'attache à l'idée de l'*homo capax*. Sous ce thème j'essaie de regrouper les capacités et incapacités diverses qui font des humains des êtres agissants et souffrants. Si les notions de *poiesis* et de *praxis* sont amplement développées dans mon oeuvre, la contrepartie du subir, du pâtir et du souffrir l'est moins. Ce déséquilibre est très sensible dans le traitement des quatre modalités de ce que j'appelle *puissance d'agir*, et qui constituent ensemble la structure de base de *Soi-même comme un Autre*.

Ainsi, au premier niveau, celui du *langage*, je montre bien la nécessité de remonter de la structure logique de la proposition (*statement*), prise en charge par la sémantique, à l'acte d'énonciation (*utterance*), relevant de la pragmatique, et de là au *pouvoir-dire* de l'énonciateur (*utterer*). Mais j'omets de souligner la difficulté, voire l'incapacité à porter au langage l'expérience émotionnelle souvent traumatique que la psychanalyse s'emploie à libérer. De même, au second niveau, celui de l'*action ordinaire* et de son intervention dans le cours des choses, je n'ai pas de peine non plus à remonter des structures objectives de l'action (dont j'avais autrefois

xlv

souligné les caractères de lisibilité qui l'assimilent à un texte) aux *pouvoirs-faire* dont l'agent de l'action a la certitude et la confiance qu'ils sont les siens; au pouvoir-dire s'ajoute ainsi la capacité de se désigner soi-même comme l'*auteur* de ses propres actes. Mais je laisse dans l'ombre la face d'impuissance, liée non seulement aux infirmités de toutes sortes affectant le corps humain comme organe d'action, mais aussi à l'interférence de pouvoirs étrangers capables de diminuer, d'empêcher, de ruiner les pouvoirs propres; à cet égard, les souffrances que les humains s'infligent les uns aux autres pèsent lourd dans la balance des pouvoirs et non-pouvoirs dans la sphère de l'action ordinaire. Je dirai la même chose de mon analyse des rapports entre l'affirmation d'identité personnelle ou collective et la fonction *narrative*. La distinction que je propose entre identité-*idem* et identité-*ipse* ne renforce que la capacité de raconter et de se raconter et ainsi de répondre à la question : qui suis-je ? Or cette capacité ne va pas de soi, comme en témoigne l'impuissance de rescapés des camps d'extermination à élever leur mémoire blessée au plan de l'expression verbale par le récit. Enfin, la quatrième catégorie, celle de l'*imputabilité*, qui commande la transition des premières études descriptives aux trois études consacrées à ma « petite éthique », appelle elle aussi un complément significatif concernant la difficulté de nos contemporains à se reconnaître non seulement comme auteurs de leurs actes, mais comme comptables des conséquences de ces actes, en particulier lorsqu'ils ont fait tort à autrui, c'est-à-dire finalement ajouté à la souffrance du monde; on peut parler à cet égard d'une incapacité à entrer dans un ordre symbolique, comportant outre des incitations motivantes des interdits structurants; or cette incapacité a pour effet l'impuissance à dériver du rapport à la norme le caractère *moralement* signifiant de l'action. Ces incapacités, qui affectent l'imputabilité de l'agir humain, posent aujourd'hui les plus graves problèmes aux éducateurs, aux juges, aux responsables politiques, dans la mesure où elles diminuent ce qu'on peut appeler l'aptitude à la citoyenneté.

Pourquoi cet exorde sur la dialectique de l'agir et du pâtir ? Pour la raison suivante. Il m'est apparu, à la lecture des essais rassemblés par Morny Joy, que plusieurs des critiques qui y sont développées avec autant de lucidité que de générosité pouvaient trouver un début de réponse dans la direction que je viens d'esquisser.

Concernant mon recours à la psychanalyse, je serais aujourd'hui moins soucieux d'argumenter au plan de la « métapsychologie » freudienne (quoique je n'aurais rien à ajouter ou à retrancher à la dialectique entre herméneutique du soupçon et herméneutique du renouveau). Je m'interrogerais plutôt sur le sens de l'expérience analytique elle-même, dans la mesure où une part significative de la souffrance psychique s'y révèle confrontée à la quête d'expression langagière et trouve un secours dans la médiation d'un tiers qui en quelque sorte « autorise » la parole.

Mais ce déplacement est motivé par un changement plus important qui affecte la théorie narrative dans son ensemble. Dans *Temps et récit* j'avais procédé à une sorte de court-circuit qui mettait dans un rapport direct les formes structurées du récit avec l'expérience du temps; je passais ainsi sous silence la médiation de la *mémoire* et de l'*oubli*, où la dialectique de l'agir et du souffrir trouve un lieu privilégié de manifestation. De plus, à la mémoire et à l'oubli sont attachées les modalités du récit de niveau pré-littéraire que j'avais sacrifiées au bénéfice de la fiction sophistiquée et du récit historiographique; la place et le rôle de ce que j'appellerai récit de conversation sont à peine esquissés au titre de *mimesis* I. Or c'est au niveau du récit pré-littéraire que s'expriment les blessures, les abus, les défaillances de la mémoire individuelle et collective. Mais ce n'est pas seulement le stade de « préfiguration » du récit qui peut être enrichi par la prise en compte de la mémoire, mais aussi le stade de la « refiguration » (*mimesis* III). A cet égard les effets de « redescription de la réalité » doivent être étendus du temps à l'espace et au vécu corporel. Ainsi l'acte architectural de construire devrait être pris en considération dans une phénoménologie élargie de l'acte d'habiter (compte tenu du malheur des sans-abri). Par là même la notion d'identité, si étroite liée à la fonction narrative, perdrait toute apparence abstraite et intemporelle, une fois livrée aux aléas de l'espace et du temps.

Est-ce que l'enracinement du récit dans la mémoire, combiné à la dialectique de l'agir et du souffrir, me permettrait de rendre justice aux récits composés par des femmes ? En donnant aujourd'hui une place au thème de la mémoire blessée et à celui de la fonction thérapeutique de récit, j'espère aller aux devants de cette requête. Toutefois, j'aimerais dire que, confronté au plan ethnologique à la tendance dominante à travers l'espace et le temps à la subordination des femmes au pouvoir masculin, je serais enclin à rattacher, à la suite de Françoise Héritier, dans *Masculin-Féminin*, la défense des droits des femmes à l'affirmation morale, juridique et politique de l'humanité commune aux deux sexes. C'est à cette humanité commune que j'applique mon analyse de l'agir et du souffrir. Maintenant, qu'il y ait une manière féminine non seulement de souffrir, mais d'agir, et que mon analyse visant l'humanité commune souffre des limites propres à une réflexion et à une écriture masculines, je ne le contesterai aucunement. Les compléments et les rectifications que des écrivains du sexe féminin apportent à mes analyses ne me paraissent pas néanmoins requérir un remaniement fondamental de mes thèses sexuellement neutres. En particulier, je persisterai à dire que même la figure éminemment féminine d'Antigone témoigne d'un conflit intéressant l'humanité commune, celui des rapports entre les lois non écrites et celles que le pouvoir politique édicte. Ce n'est pas seulement dans le texte que la figure d'Antigone fait irruption, mais dans la structure du pouvoir. Du même coup, elle rompt avec les stéréotypes du pouvoir politique et d'abord avec ceux relatifs à la condition féminine interprétée par la figure masculine du pouvoir. Maintenant, la question de savoir pourquoi il fallait que ce soit un homme qui incarne le pouvoir et une femme qui le mette en question, cela reste une bonne question; mais elle ne se pose pas sur le fond d'un enjeu d'humanité qui dépasse les rôles sexués. A cet égard, la lecture des *Antigones* de G. Steiner serait d'un grand secours pour articuler entre elles les multiples dialectiques que l'intrigue mobilise : humain-divin, morale absolue-pouvoir historique, jeunesse-vieillesse, vie-mort, homme-femme. Resterait encore à démêler, parmi les multiples rôles féminins, celui de la *soeur* face aux *frères* ennemis.

A l'enracinement du récit dans la mémoire, j'aimerais ajouter son enracinement dans l'imagination. Or la dialectique entre mémoire et imagination se joue à un niveau plus fondamental que la paire littéraire fiction-historiographie. Il en résulte que la dialectique de l'agir et du souffrir, avec les aspects viscéraux et émotionnels de ce dernier, se laisse plus directement discerner au point d'articulation entre mémoire et imagination, la première visant un passé révolu, la seconde un possible irréel. C'est aussi à ce niveau primordial que la jonction entre fonction narrative et corporéité s'opère, ainsi que les modalités multiples de l'acte d'habiter corporellement le monde. Il reste que seule le langage peut articuler ces modalités, ces *moods*, pour en faire des « variations imaginatives »; c'est à ce plan discursif que peut être entendue la parole d'Hölderlin célébrant la manière « poétique » d'habiter le monde.

Je ne voudrais pas quitter ces considérations, où l'identité personnelle et communautaire sont encore considérées à un niveau pré-politique, sans avoir dit quelques mots sur la notion de *témoignage*. Je privilégie aujourd'hui le terme *attestation* pour dire la sorte de certitude et de confiance que j'applique à *ma* capacité d'agir (en parlant, faisant, racontant, assumant ma responsabilité). Le contraire de l'attestation est précisément le soupçon, moteur de l'herméneutique du soupçon évoquée plus haut. Je réserve le terme *témoignage* pour la reconnaissance rendue à un *autre* qui incarne et exemplifie à mes yeux l'idéal d'une vie bonne. C'est alors dans le cadre du témoignage ainsi compris que s'articulent la narrativité et la moralité.

En ce qui concerne maintenant l'identité *collective*, j'aimerais dire que la considération de la mémoire apporte un éclairage important. Ne doit-on pas tenir le phénomène de *commémoration*, par nature collectif et public, pour strictement corrélatif de la *remémoration* individuelle du passé ?

Ce n'est que dans la tradition philosophique que Charles Taylor, dans *The Sources of the Self*, place sous le titre de l'*Inwardness*, que la mémoire est traitée comme un phénomène fondamentalement personnel. Mais c'est *ensemble* que nous nous souvenons; et c'est dans le médium social du langage que nous articulons nos souvenirs les plus propres sur le mode narratif. Sur la base de la notion de mémoire collective il pourrait être rendu justice à l'idée d'identité narrative des communautés auxquelles nous appartenons. On comprend en outre que cette identité collective puisse souffrir des mêmes abus et des mêmes défaillances que la mémoire blessée des individus. C'est par là que j'aborderais aujourd'hui la question de la crise « identitaire » de maintes communautés historiques contemporaines.

C'est à partir de cette analyse de l'identité narrative collective que se pose le problème de l'identité prise au niveau *politique*. Ce que j'ai dit plus haut sur la catégorie d'imputabilité, en vertu de laquelle un agent a la capacité de se tenir comptable des conséquences de ses actes, permettrait d'articuler la dimension *normative* et la dimension *narrative* de l'identité collective au plan politique. A cet égard les commémorations évoquées plus haut sont le lieu d'articulation entre le normatif et le narratif, dans le cadre de récits qu'on peut dire politiques, tels les récits fondateurs de la communauté politique. En outre la dialectique entre la mémoire et l'imagination, amorcée au plan individuel, continue sa course au plan collectif et politique, sous la forme de l'idéologie et de l'utopie, dont j'ai traité par ailleurs au titre de l'imaginaire social. L'utopie, en particulier, constitue le discours contestataire à l'égard des positions de pouvoir. Ainsi les analyses consacrées au pouvoir de « redescription » de la métaphore et de « refiguration » du récit reçoivent une extension remarquable à la faveur de laquelle la fonction structurante et la fonction contestatrice de l'imaginaire social trouvent leur équilibre instable.

Mais j'accorde volontiers qu'il ne faut pas trop demander à une théorie de la métaphore et à une théorie narrative, même élargies à la sphère publique. C'est dans une *éthique* qu'il faut puiser la référence aux normes. Certes, l'imagination peut être tenue pour une initiation à la fonction critique, dans la mesure où elle enseigne à rêver autrement, de la même façon que le récit enseigne à raconter autrement. Une force critique est tenue en réserve dans ce double « autrement ». A cet égard, même le regard rétrospectif de l'historien appliqué au passé de notre culture et à ses textes fondateurs n'est pas opposé au regard explorateur du possible de l'imaginaire social. L'histoire ne se borne pas en effet à décrire et à expliquer les *faits* passés – disons : ce qui a lieu effectivement; elle peut aussi se risquer à ressusciter et à réanimer les promesses non tenues du passé; elle rejoint ainsi l'imaginaire des humains disparus et le libère de la contingence des réalisations inachevées, pour le reverser au compte de l'imaginaire du futur. Mais, je le répète, il ne faut pas demander à une théorie de l'imaginaire complétée par une théorie narrative, élevées l'une et l'autre au plan collectif, ce qui doit être demandé à une éthique. Les analyses de la « redescription de la réalité » et de la « refiguration » par le récit ne revêtent une signification normative, requise par la théorie politique, que si elles sont couplées au plan éthique avec les analyses des modalités de la sagesse pratique, héritière de la *phronesis* des Grecs et de la *prudentia* des Médiévaux. C'est alors le passage de la norme à la décision concrète, prise dans des situations d'incertitude au coeur du tragique de l'action, qui constitue le moment critique par excellence d'une action *moralement* sensée. L'imagination et la mémoire – la métaphore et le récit – n'offrent là que des points d'appui, au mieux des incitations; mais ni l'une ni l'autre fonction ne comporte en tant que telle la dimension de l'*évaluation*; elles n'attendent du politique que l'abstention de toute censure. Mais la distinction du bien et du mal, du permis et du défendu, requiert l'appareil entier d'une éthique, qui elle-même traverse les niveaux successifs du désir de la vie bonne, avec et pour les autres dans des institutions justes, puis celui de la norme sous la double figure de l'obligation et de l'interdiction, enfin celui de la sagesse pratique, du *jugement prudentiel*. Alors seulement il peut être demandé à l'imagination et au récit de nourrir le rêve, d'exemplifier concrètement et en quelque sorte charnellement, le jugement prudentiel dans lequel se rassemble toute l'éthique dans la quotidienneté de nos jours.

Paul Ricoeur

From a Poetics of the Will to Narratives of the Self: Paul Ricoeur's *Freud and Philosophy*

JOCELYN DUNPHY BLOMFIELD

To introduce discussion of Paul Ricoeur's work on narrative through his *Freud and Philosophy* is to throw light on two special aspects of his work, time and experience, relating them to each other via his life-project, indicated in Ricoeur's own books and interviews.

Freud and Philosophy: an Essay on Interpretation is now thirty years old.[1] Five hundred and fifty-one pages in its English version, translated into German, Spanish, Portuguese, Italian and Japanese, this monumental work is only now making its mark. Its context is the changing paradigms of thought and the cultural and ideological conflict of the 1960s in France.[2] Still sparsely cited in the professional literature, and misread even by some scholarly critics,[3] it combines massiveness and density of argument with great coherence and architectural clarity. Ricoeur thematizes his investigation of Freud through the notion of a "semantics of desire," maintained as a conceptual constant. Other themes underlie, accompany, and emerge from this notion. One enriches the current debate on epistemology. It emphasizes the "post-critical" problem of knowledge that Ricoeur raises in *The Symbolism of Evil*,[4] and which is raised by Polanyi[5] at the same time in terms to scientific theory, and by Gadamer[6] in his development of a Heideggerian hermeneutics. For Ricoeur, this theme takes the direction of semantics. Allied to it is the philosophical quest of creativity, which Ricoeur later describes as that of his whole life. "Since I began to reflect my unique problem has been creativity."[7]

The title I have chosen for this study, "From a Poetics of the Will to Narratives of the Self," enlists Ricoeur's inquiry into creativity to chart the wider context of *Freud and Philosophy*. It relates his study of Freud to the major works written before and after it. *Philosophy of the Will*, projected as a three-volume work, was to conclude with a "poetics," or theory of creative action, in the sense of Aristotle's use of the Greek *poiesis* as purposeful making, the idea of "making something." The work remains in two volumes, the second in two parts, without the projected *Poetics*. *Freud and Philosophy* grew out of a dilemma revealed by examining that well-known aspect of willing: the doing of evil. In describing the non-creative aspect of willing in *The Symbolism of Evil*, Ricoeur recognized that there is no directly experiential language of evil-doing. The only language of wrong-doing is the language of "confession" or avowal. Found in epic, poetry, and myth, the language of the religions of the world, none of this language can be called philosophical. It is always symbolic. Moving from the notion of symbol in the broad anthropological field, Ricoeur looked to the work of Freud, which was already investigated by philosophers, including his former teacher Roland Dalbiez and phenomenologists such as Merleau-Ponty and de Waelhens, and by psychoanalysts in France, including Lacan, Vergote and the many theorists and commentators quoted in *Freud and Philosophy*.

Ricoeur warns against restricting *Freud and Philosophy* (and by this token the works that followed it) to the "resolution of this antinomy" raised in *The Symbolism of Evil*.[8] The "turn" to language he begins there leads him to structuralism[9] and analytic philosophy,[10] and to the analyses of linguistic trope and genre found in *The Rule of Metaphor* [11] and *Time and Narrative*.[12]

Without trying to extract a disguised completion of *Poetics of the Will* from Ricoeur's later books, one can legitimately trace the exploration of creative action throughout his work. The second part of my title, "Narratives of the Self," refers to Ricoeur's research in the 1980s and 1990s and his investigation of ways of expressing the self as an acting self or agent. Ricoeur emphasizes human action and suffering.[13] He develops the Kantian study of the "free and good will." One finds the theme of creativity in his study of testimony in *Oneself as Another*,[14] in the re-editions of early articles on politics and religion,[15] and in the "Intellectual Autobiography," where he does not flinch from crossing "the line of separation" between intellect and self to confront the shattering of life.[16]

Placed in the context of this search for creativity within "the profound temporal dimension" of human experience, what light does *Freud and Philosophy* cast on Ricoeur's studies of narrative? Ricoeur places his major study of Freud's work at a crossroads where many disciplines meet, all having in common a preoccupation with language and how it works.[17] Its French title, *De l'Interprétation, essai sur Freud*, suggests, and the first chapter states, that the study of Freud begins with a conceptual investigation, but not directly into narrative as such. Interpretation is set out first of all in linguistic terms. Later, in his 1978 paper, "The Question of Proof in Freud's Psychoanalytic Writings," when he is working on *Time and Narrative*, Ricoeur assesses the question of a psychoanalytic "fact," and emphasizes "what is capable of entering into a story or narrative" as the final criterion.[18] But the importance of the dimensions of narrative emerge and are stressed in *Freud and Philosophy* in the following way:

Firstly, there is the book's own history. It grew from the final paper, read by Ricoeur at the 1960 Colloquy on *The Unconscious*, organized by the dynamic psychiatrist Henri Ey at his Centre at Bonneval outside Paris. This meeting grouped an interdisciplinary body including André Green, Jean Hyppolite, Jacques Lacan, Jean Laplanche, Serge Leibovici, Serge Leclaire, Henri Lefebvre, Maurice Merleau-Ponty, Paul Ricoeur, Antoine de Waelhens and others. The Colloquy concluded with a paper by Ricoeur that shows us the conceptual germ of the book that appeared five years later.[19] *Freud and Philosophy* grew from the 1961 Yale University Terry Lectures and was also developed from lectures at the University of Louvain in Belgium. It was followed in France by the polemics already noted, succeeded a few years later by the violence of May 1968, which began at Nanterre, the campus where Ricoeur was Doyen.[20] With the passing of time, this narrative of the book's history continues to take new shapes and meanings. In the 1990s we can appreciate its mediating and transcendental quality, not as easily grasped at the time of publication.

Secondly, *Freud and Philosophy* has an inner progression, which is the pattern of its own exploration. One could title this the progression of Freud's research, from his *Project for a Scientific Psychology* of 1895[21] to the conflicting themes that Ricoeur shows as governing *Civilization and its Discontents* of 1939.[22] Ricoeur points out at the start that *Freud and Philosophy* differs from work by psychoanalysts since its author is not analyzed;[23] it is a book of philosophy, not of analytic theory and differs too from work of psychoanalytic dissidents since it stops with the work of Freud. Above all, it differs from previous philosophic work because it does not confine Freud to the study of the pathological, but sees his work as an "interpretation of culture." Hence the book's title. Ricoeur perceives that: "Today we are in search of a comprehensive philosophy of language to account for the multiple functions of the human act of signifying and for their inter-relationships."[24]

If what Freud brings out is that in the area of meaning "psychical productions" raise a particular question: "How do desires achieve speech?",[25] then "the function of psychoanalytic theory is to place the work of interpretation within the region of desire ... it grounds and limits all the particular concepts appearing in the field."[26] *Freud and Philosophy* is about desires and their language, characterized from the start as a "semantics of desire,"[27] which brings together Freud's dynamic concepts – discharge, repression, cathexis, etc. – its conceptual progression leads to its being qualified as unique because of its method:

> [T]he analyst's work, which we described at first as a struggle against the resistances, is now seen as a struggle against substitute satisfactions – precisely in the transference where the patient is particularly looking for such satisfaction.... That which makes the analytic relationship possible as an intersubjective relation is indeed ... the fact that the analytic dialogue ... brings to light the demand in which desire ultimately consists; but only the technique of transference, as a technique of frustration, could reveal the fact that desire is at bottom an unanswered demand.[28]

The book's central section, the *Analytic*, examines Freud's building and rearranging of theory. This scholarly exploration includes investigation of his concepts by analytic philosophers and English-language philosophers of science. It forms an early chapter in the narrative of the opening of French philosophy to English-speaking culture which took off in the late 1960s. The book's final section, *Dialectic*, brings together Ricoeur's exploration of the conceptual horizon of psychoanalysis, his analysis of Freud's concepts and their import, and the fulfillment or close of the book's thematic sweep. The achievement of an argument sustained over such length, and with such breadth and consistency of scholarly inquiry, forms a narrative of the kind which Ricoeur later describes in *Time and Narrative* as a "quasi-plot."

This being so, in the third place, it is appropriate to consider compositional strategies of *emplotment*. Ricoeur notes again and again the careful planning of his readings. The book is a "debate with Freud," presented as a contribution to "a comprehensive philosophy of language to account for the multiple functions of the human act of signifying and their inter-relationships."[29] It proposes, not "an interpretation on a single level, but ... a series of readings each of which is both completed and corrected by the following one."[30] Given that not "desires as such" are to be at the centre of inquiry, but "their language,"[31] between the specific topic, psychoanalysis, and the wide extent of language lies the horizon, "the hermeneutic field,"[32] and that two hermeneutic activities are possible. Freud, like Marx and Nietzsche, is a "master of suspicion," master of a "reductive" hermeneutics that performs the necessary work of demystifying. But the task is also to seek what Ricoeur in the 1960s calls a hermeneutic of "restoration." Other words used in this sense include "recollection," "reminiscence," "retrieval," "restitution." What Ricoeur seeks is a rediscovery through psychoanalysis of "the fullness of language," lost sense, creative power and possibility. Interpretation is an activity involving both reduction of illusion and restoration of meaning.[33]

As Freud began his work he had presented his first theories in the "energetics" model derived from physics. Patients' experiences required interpretation of actions and symptoms. Ricoeur asks: "What is the status of representation or ideas in relation to instinct, aim of instinct and affect?"[34]

Ricoeur's sustained reading of Freud explores the "hermeneutic field" of language through Freud's reworkings of his models and ideas, and the great theoretical positions of his time – of Dilthey, Husserl, and Weber, for example – as well as Freud's own colleagues in psychiatry and psychoanalysis. Ricoeur also analyses the increasing role of Greek mythology in shaping Freud's conception of the world and the human psyche, especially in his later years.

The debate between Ricoeur's two hermeneutics, the reductive and the restorative, is delicately balanced. It is not possible for an attentive reader to accuse Ricoeur (as Adolf Grunbaum[35] and some others do) of denying energetics in favour of hermeneutics. Ricoeur makes clear that: "It is completely misleading to raise the question [of theory in psychoanalysis] in the context of a factual or observational science."[36]

Rather, what is important is to see how particular experiences can be conceptualized: "The concepts of analysis are to be judged according to their status as conditions of the possibility of analytic experience, insofar as the latter operates in the field of speech."[37]

Gadamer points out that hermeneutics is not an alternative method.[38] It is an approach to experience that has a different starting-point, perhaps comparable to that of post-Einsteinian physics – a comparison which Ricoeur himself does not make. In comparing psychic activity and the things of external reality he remains Kantian in his schematization:

> Instincts are like the Kantian thing – the transcendental = X; they too are never attained except in that which stands for and represents them. In this way we will be led from the problematic of instincts to the problematic of the representatives of instincts.[39]

Dialectic, the third section of *Freud and Philosophy*, first of all defines the unique quality of psychoanalytic activity by language:

> [A]nalytic experience unfolds in the field of speech and ... what comes to light is another language, dissociated from common language, ... which presents itself to be deciphered through its meaningful effects – symptoms, dreams, various formations.... Not to recognize this specific feature leads one to eliminate as an anomaly the interrelationship of hermeneutics and energetics in analytic theory.[40]

Secondly, this unique experience is defined by the relationship of transference: "[T]he correlation between energetics and hermeneutics which we have focused on ... reappears in a decisive manner on the level of praxis."[41]

Then the empirical and interpretive are linked by the practical, unique aspect of psychoanalytic work and theory:

[A] greater familiarity with critical thought would have obviated many scholastic discussions about the realism of the unconscious and of the topography – as though one were forced to choose between a realism of agencies (*Ucs., Pcs., Cs*) and an idealism of meaning and non-meaning. In the area of physics, Kant has taught us to combine an empirical realism with a transcendental idealism – I say a transcendental idealism, and not a subjective or psychological one, as would be the case with a too well-intentioned theory which would not be long in annulling the result and gain of the topography.[42]

Ricoeur's inspiration for his careful and coherent reading of Freud thus is Kant. To note this fact dissolves polemics that originate in empiricist or in dogmatist presuppositions. Yet what are the implications of this theoretical awareness for the appreciation of narrative?

The most famous narrative of all in psychoanalytic literature is Freud's retelling of the myth of Oedipus. How does Ricoeur understand this myth, and how does it develop his own research into human experience?

It is interesting that both "Consciousness and the Unconscious" – the "germ" article – and the last section of *Freud and Philosophy* offer a double reading of *Oedipus*. Freud, writes Ricoeur, presents *Oedipus* as a "tragedy of destiny."[43] But it is also "possible to apply to Sophocles' drama ... an antithetic of reflection ... the 'force of truth' proceeds from the seer," making *Oedipus,* via the combination of tragedy with comedy comparable to Elizabethan theatre and, via the double view thus presented, a "tragedy of truth." "The core is not the problem of sex, but the problem of light."[44] This parallel reading comes at the end of a corollary that Ricoeur develops to Freud's theoretical structure. His long investigation of Freud's work concludes by characterizing the achievement of psychoanalysis as an "archaeology of the subject."[45] This is then balanced by the hypothesis of a logically entailed "teleology"[46]: the "figures of spirit" that successively create meaning and fulfillment – liberation in Hegel's language – for the human subject. This challenging last section recasts desire as the quest for identity and sublimation. Desire's curative praxis will be wisdom, and this is where the role of Ricoeur's second *King Oedipus* belongs. The question that remains is what vision, wisdom, healing can we hope for in psychoanalysis?

The reading of *Oedipus* shows that another narrative underlies those of desire, knowledge, and wisdom. It is the experience of suffering. This is how Martha Nussbaum opens a recent study, *The Therapy of Desire:*

The idea of a practical and compassionate philosophy – a philosophy that exists for the sake of human beings, in order to address their deepest needs, confront their most urgent perplexities, and bring them from misery to some greater measure of flourishing – this idea makes the study of Hellenistic ethics riveting for a philosopher who wonders what philosophy has to do with the world.[47]

Does Nussbaum's endorsement of philosophy's task as the healing and strengthening of human suffering correspond with what Ricoeur finds in the work of Freud? In one way, yes. Ricoeur notes in *Freud and Philosophy*: "Suffering accompanies the task of culture like fate. The fate illustrated by the Oedipus tragedy."[48]

The reading of *Oedipus* as a tragedy of truth does not deny its sense as a tragedy of destiny and of sex. Ricoeur brings out the fact that Freud sees the reality of suffering as the reality of necessity. Later on, he talks about it mythologically as "*Ananke.*" What is the place of suffering for Freud in the last analysis? Ricoeur writes:

> Strangely enough, Freud has a more finely developed conception of the evils that are the burden of existence than he has of pleasure. The empire of suffering is more extensive than that of mere unpleasure. It extends to everything that makes up the harshness of life. What is the meaning in Freud's works of this disparity between the diversity of suffering and the monotony of enjoyment? In the face of manifold suffering, does man's only recourse lie in unvaried enjoyment and in bearing the excessive suffering with resignation? I am inclined to think that the whole of Freud's work tends towards the second hypothesis. This hypothesis brings us back to the reality principle.[49]

In a sense, suffering is at the heart of Ricoeur's discussion for Freud's work is about coming to grips with "*Ananke*" as the reality principle, as the principle of hard necessity. *Freud and Philosophy* takes this harsh necessity as one pole of his thinking. The other pole is Ricoeur's effort to take that notion further. Ricoeur's method sometimes includes a tactic of moving on from an intractable problem or aporia. One of his translators, Charles Kelbly, refers to this as "widening the argument." But this moment of a shift in argument may be similar to that which held him up in *Philosophy of the Will* – the need to go beyond recognizing the principle of harsh necessity or nature and to recognize and deal with the principle of creation. Was this the discarded notion of a *Poetics* as the final volume?

Looking at the principle of reality, the notion of necessity and the difficulties of conceptualizing experience, Ricoeur notes Freud's speculation. Freud moves from considering resignation in terms of a principle of reality to speculating in mythological language about the meaning of "*Ananke.*" "*Ananke*" is a mythological term for necessity. Ricoeur redevelops the argument in Freud's own terms. It is a struggle between the mythological figures of *Eros* (love, desire) and *Thanatos* (death). This is not Ricoeur's own conclusion. He follows Freud's late reworkings with regard to infantile guilt, and looks at the theme of narcissism to examine guilt in its "non-infantile" sources. He notes:

Guilt remains ambiguous and suspect. In order to break its false prestige, we must always focus on it the double illumination of a demystifying interpretation that denounces its archaism and a restorative interpretation that places the birth of evil in the mind or spirit itself.[51]

If Ricoeur's method in *Freud and Philosophy* is spelled out at the beginning as "a semantics of desire,"[52] the use of the double hermeneutic to defeat the prestige of guilt gives the argument a new dimension. Suffering may not be diminished, but neither is it merely to be endured: "Job receives no explanation of his suffering; he is merely shown something of the grandeur and order of the whole."[53]

The last pages of *Freud and Philosophy* include a rethinking of the human dimension of religion through this "critique of narcissism," which Ricoeur notes he has "constantly called the false Cogito."[54] The false Cogito is the narcissism of rationality: the certainty of knowledge and of consciousness.[55] The critique is described metaphorically as a "cleavage" that strikes both religion and "mere resignation." The response to this liberation is not an infantile or reactionary return to old myths, but "the love of Creation,"[56] the final phrase of Ricoeur's book.

This final word of *Freud and Philosophy* is the end of an exploration that has included Freud's complete opus and the cultural context it challenged. A justified rhetorical conclusion, it is neither a leap of faith out of philosophy, nor a sophist's evasion of "harsh reality." Rather, it is a carefully developed praxis, justified at both levels of investigative thought.

If Freud's solution to suffering is harsher than that of the Hellenist philosophers that Nussbaum describes, the possibility of using Freud's thought to get beyond mere resignation offers hope of a different kind. Each psychotherapy contains a world of cultural meanings. Ricoeur did not repeat his conclusion in other works. His "Intellectual Autobiography" leaves us to think he may have had some dissatisfaction with it.[57] In articles written some years after *Freud and Philosophy*, he took the question of language further, but tackled issues of concrete epistemology, rather than central existential questions or the appearance of a completed narrative.[58]

One can note, on the one hand, that the conclusion of Ricoeur's version of Freud's narrative of psychoanalysis and suffering humanity does not evade the harshness of human experience or the task of psychic realism: "[T]he reading of Freud is what helped me place the 'giving up of the father' at the heart of the problematic of faith."[59] On the other hand, Ricoeur's solution is not metaphysical or "onto-theological," nor does it propose false hope. It attests to a capacity to transcend guilt and the infantile need for consolation, and demonstrates the expression of love as praxis.

What of the interface between *Freud and Philosophy* and *Time and Narrative*? If we think of the double hermeneutic as the challenge and centre of interest of *Freud and Philosophy*, how to explain the preference that some readers still show for demystification, and for the work of the "masters of suspicion," rather than for the constructive approach of recollecting meaning or bringing back what has been lost? This question is well handled by David Carr,[60] Charles Taylor,[61] and Hayden White[62] in current discussion of Ricoeur's narrative theory. With regard to the questions raised by Ricoeur's work on narrative, Charles Taylor has written that he finds Ricoeur's originality in his privileging of fiction over referentiality in narrative. I would agree only in part with this view. Ricoeur privileges epistemology as the "long way" to ontology. He also privileges natural science. He is interested in recent philosophers of science like Prigogine. He does not reduce philosophy to these fields, and his strength is to insist on holding the two together – on relating the fictional to the referential.

One can say that *Freud and Philosophy* stands between Ricoeur's major early work and his later studies of narrative as a double analysis: of the entire work of Freud, and the lack of freedom which Freud has revealed in human existence, against the possibility of free creative action. If *Philosophy of the Will* turns us towards an examination of language so as to speak more competently of the ambiguities of existence, *Freud and Philosophy* shows polarities not only in human action but polarities of thought in our descriptions and evaluations. It is a book of great value to philosophers and to psychoanalysts. It offers writers of narrative new ways of thinking about pattern and action.

Notes

1 Paul Ricoeur, *Freud and Philosophy : an Essay on Interpretation*, trans. D. Savage (New Haven: Yale University Press, 1970).

2 Paul Ricoeur, "Intellectual Autobiography," in *The Philosophy of Paul Ricoeur*, ed. Lewis E. Hahn (Carbondale: Southern Illinois University Press, 1995), 21; E. Roudinesco, *Jacques Lacan and Company: A History of Psychoanalysis in France*, trans. J. Mehlmann (Chicago: University of Chicago Press, 1990), 394-8.

3 Paul Ricoeur, "Reply to Thelma Z. Levine," *The Philosophy of Paul Ricoeur*, 191.

4 Paul Ricoeur, *The Symbolism of Evil* (*Philosophy of the Will*, II, Part 2), trans. E. Buchanan (Boston: Beacon Press, 1967).

5 Michael Polanyi, *Personal Knowledge: Towards a Post-Critical Philosophy* (London: Routledge & Kegan Paul, 1958), 264-72.

6 Hans-Georg Gadamer, *Philosophical Apprenticeships*, trans. Robert R. Sullivan (Cambridge, MA: MIT Press, 1985), 23-25.

7 Paul Ricoeur, "History as Narrative and Practice," Peter Kemp talks to Paul Ricoeur in Copenhagen, *Philosophy Today* 29, 3/4 (Fall 1985): 213-22.

8 Paul Ricoeur, *The Philosophy of Paul Ricoeur*, 191.

9 Paul Ricoeur, *The Conflict of Interpretations, Essays in Hermeneutics* (Evanston: Northwestern University Press, 1974).

10 Paul Ricoeur, *Oneself as Another*, trans. K. Blamey (Chicago: University of Chicago Press, 1992).

11 Paul Ricoeur, *The Rule of Metaphor, Multi-disciplinary Studies of the Creation of Meaning in Language*, trans. R. Czerny with K. McLaughlin and R. Costello (London: Routledge & Kegan Paul, 1978).

12 Paul Ricoeur, *Time and Narrative*, I–III, trans. K. McLaughlin and David Pellauer (Chicago: University of Chicago Press, 1984).

13 Ricoeur, *Oneself as Another*, 16-23.

14 Ricoeur, *Oneself as Another*, 297-376.

15 Paul Ricoeur, *Lectures I: Autour du politique* (Paris: Seuil, 1991); *Lectures III: Aux Frontières de la philosophie* (Paris: Seuil, 1994).

16 Ricoeur, "Intellectual Autobiography," 51

17 Ricoeur, *Freud and Philosophy*, 3.

18 Paul Ricoeur, "The Question of Proof in Freud's Psychoanalytic Writings," in *The Philosophy of Paul Ricoeur. An Anthology of his Work*, ed. C. E. Reagan and D. Stewart (Boston: Beacon Press, 1978).

19 Paul Ricoeur, "Consciousness and the Unconscious," in *The Conflict of Interpretations*, 99-120.

20 Roudinesco, *Jacques Lacan and Company*, 398.

21 Sigmund Freud, *Project for a Scientific Psychology*, in *The Standard Edition of the Complete Psychological Works of Sigmund Freud*, ed. James Strachey, vol. 1 (London: Hogarth Press, 1966), 283-398.

22 Ricoeur, *Freud and Philosophy*, 338.

23 Ricoeur, *Freud and Philosophy*, xi-xii.

24 Ricoeur, *Freud and Philosophy*, 3.

25 Ricoeur, *Freud and Philosophy*, 5.

26 Ricoeur, *Freud and Philosophy*, 375.

27 Ricoeur, *Freud and Philosophy*, 6.

28 Ricoeur, *Freud and Philosophy*, 417.

29 Ricoeur, *Freud and Philosophy*, 3.

30 Ricoeur, *Freud and Philosophy*, 59.

31 Ricoeur, *Freud and Philosophy*, 4.

32 Ricoeur, *Freud and Philosophy*, 8.

33 Ricoeur, *Freud and Philosophy*, 56.

34 Ricoeur, *Freud and Philosophy*, 66.

35 Adolf Grunbaum, *The Foundations of Psychoanalysis: A Philosophical Critique* (Berkeley: University of California Press, 1984).

36 Ricoeur, *Freud and Philosophy*, 375.

37 Ricoeur, *Freud and Philosophy*, 375.

38 Hans-Georg Gadamer, *Philosophical Apprenticeships*, 49-51.

39 Ricoeur, *Freud and Philosophy*, 116.

40 Ricoeur, *Freud and Philosophy*, 367.

41 Ricoeur, *Freud and Philosophy*, 408.

42 Ricoeur, *Freud and Philosophy*, 432.

43 Ricoeur, *Freud and Philosophy*, 516.

44 Ricoeur, *Freud and Philosophy*, 517.

45 Ricoeur, *Freud and Philosophy*, 419.

46 Ricoeur, *Freud and Philosophy*, 459.

47 Martha Nussbaum, *The Therapy of Desire, Theory and Practice in Hellenistic Ethics* (Princeton: Princeton University Press, 1994), 3.

48 Ricoeur, *Freud and Philosophy*, 196.

49 Ricoeur, *Freud and Philosophy*, 323-4.

50 Ricoeur, *Freud and Philosophy*, 547.

51 Ricoeur, *Freud and Philosophy*, 4.

52 Ricoeur, *Freud and Philosophy*, 548.

53 Ricoeur, *Freud and Philosophy*, 550.

54 Ricoeur, *Freud and Philosophy*, 32-3.

55 Ricoeur, *Freud and Philosophy*, 551.

56 Ricoeur, "Intellectual Biography," 23.

57 Ricoeur, "Psychoanalysis and the Work of Art," in *Psychoanalysis and Language*, ed. Joseph H. Smith, *Psychiatry and the Humanities*, I (New Haven: Yale University Press, 1976), and Ricoeur, "Image and Language in Psychoanalysis," in *Psychoanalysis and Language*, ed. Joseph H. Smith, *Psychiatry and the Humanities*, III (New Haven: Yale University Press, 1978).

58 Ricoeur, *Freud and Philosophy*, 550.

59 David Carr, "Discussion: Ricoeur on Narrative," *Narrative and Interpretation*, ed. D. Wood (London: Routledge, 1991), 160-74.

60 Charles Taylor, "Discussion: Ricoeur on Narrative," 174-9.

61 Hayden White, "The Metaphysics of Narrativity: Time and Symbol in Ricoeur's Philosophy of History," *Narrative and Interpretation*.

Dietrich Bonhoeffer, *Letters and Papers from Prison* and Paul Ricoeur's "Hermeneutics of Testimony"

JAMIE S. SCOTT

Introduction

On 5 April 1945, German dictator Adolf Hitler issued one of the many annihilation orders which characterized the last vindictive days of the Third Reich. Before dawn on 9 April, Dietrich Bonhoeffer was tried in a summary court-martial, charged with complicity in the von Stauffenberg assassination plot on Hitler. Later that morning, Bonhoeffer and several other victims were led to the woods behind Flossenbürg concentration camp and ordered to strip. Their hands were tied behind their backs and they were hanged. Bonhoeffer's last words were: "For me, this is the end – the beginning of life."[1] The studied ambiguity of this state-ment embodies the sort of irony of necessity often associated with such deadly conflicts between political and religious loyalties. On the one hand, we now know that Hitler's suspicions of Bonhoeffer and his fel-low conspirators were accurate, and that therefore, within terms of the harsh exigencies of wartime law, Bonhoeffer's execution was in some sense justified. On the other hand, the influential ecumenicist, Dr. G.K.A. Bell, expressed a much more agreeable view when he pro-claimed Bonhoeffer "one of a noble company of martyrs of differing traditions."[2] More recently, Clifford Green has elaborated upon Bell's judgment, locating Bonhoeffer within that "noble lineage in Christian theology in which an intimate relationship exists between the thinking of the theologian and his personal experience as a Christian man."[3] The fact that he was willing to die for his beliefs testifies to his sense of self-justification. But as Bonhoeffer awaited death in prison, he attempted to flesh out this sense of self-justification in writing. These efforts resulted in a classic of Christian prison testimony: *Letters and Papers from Prison*. The marked inseparability between Bonhoeffer's actions and thoughts is most obvious in this text. This paper attempts to articulate the relationship between life and writing in terms of the dialectics of literal and literary testimony. The literal self-offering of martyrdom and the literary self-offering of autobiographical narrative are mediated in and through what Paul Ricoeur and others have called the "hermeneutics of testimony." What follows is an exploratory archaeology and application of this philosophy of testimony to the case of Bonhoeffer, and by implication, to any narrative arising out of conflicts between allegiances experienced as equally irresistible.

Christian Testimony as a Literal Act

Bonhoeffer's story recapitulates a larger story. In popular parlance, a martyr is someone who suffers for some cause. But this requirement of suffering is not part of the original meaning of the term. The Greek term "*martus*," from which we derive "martyr," means "witness," and the cognate noun "*marturia*," means "testimony." A martyr is someone who bears testimony to something. In the New Testament *marturein* means "bearing testimony to the reality of the divine presence in the world." Jesus says, "these very works which I am doing, bear me witness that the Father has sent me" (John 5:30-37). So also the disciples bear testimony to Jesus; the risen Christ says, "you shall be my witnesses in Jerusalem and in all Judaea and Samaria and to the end of the earth" (Acts 1:8). With second-century Christians like Polycarp and Ignatius of Antioch, martyrdom comes to mean perfect Christian confession.

The Christian martyr's situation is thus a liminal situation. Poised on the boundary between this world and the next, the Christian martyr is torn between worldly authority and commitment to God. In the words of liberation theologian Leonardo Boff:

> Martyrs are those who suffer violent death for the sake of God or Christ, or for the sake of actions derived from faith in God or in Christ; or, finally, for the sake of what constitutes the true content of the words God or Christ: truth and justice.

Bonhoeffer's literal act of testimony bears witness to such a transcendent sense of truth and justice. Like the early Christian martyrs, Bonhoeffer was caught between competing demands upon his allegiance. Like the early Christian martyrs, he had to identify where worldly authority ends and the authority of God begins. The point of identification becomes the altar upon which he sacrifices himself. Simply to be called a Christian is not enough. As Theofried Baumeister has put it, the final proof lies in action, for "through action [one] is able once again to become a word with power to speak to others."[4]

Christian Testimony as Literary Act

Because the Christian martyr is a liminal figure, the circumstances of martyrdom are necessarily ambiguous. Such ambiguity calls for judgment, but judgment in turn calls for evidence. As Boff has observed, "[w]e need ways of surely identifying real truth and justice from the mechanisms of ideology (illusion), fanaticism (exacerbation of subjectivity) and idolatry (erroneous identification of God)."[5] Texts help us make such distinctions, and certain Christian martyrs have left writings testifying to their own self-sacrifice. This literary tradition includes certain Pauline epistles, the letters of Ignatius of Antioch, Justin Martyr's *First Apology*, Origen's exhortation to martyrdom, Cyprian's *On the Lapsed* and *On the Unity of the Church*, Perpetua's letter from prison, Boethius's *Consolation of Philosophy* and Thomas More's *Dialogue of Comfort against Tribulation*. Bonhoeffer's *Letters and Papers* belongs to this literary tradition – a tradition of Christian literary testimony. Those martyrs who write such literary testimonies all write as Christians, but their acts of literary testimony reflect distinct and differing historical circumstances. We must take account of the circumstantial differences among these texts as surely as we invoke generic similarities among them in our efforts to identify a tradition of Christian literary testimony.

Such an approach is an exercise in literary thematics. Three critical terms help us here – *Motiv*, *Stoff*, and *Thema*.[6] The term *Motiv* serves as a metonymy for the fundamental human situation at the heart of a work of literature. This fundamental human situation permeates a work of literature in the same way that the molecular structure of a cell permeates a living organism. We may express the *Motiv* at the heart of literary testimony in the form of the question: How do I resolve a dilemma in my life which seems to pit irresistible worldly authority against my absolute commitment to God? Some celebrated phrases from *Letters and Papers* epitomize the *Motiv* of this literary testimony. Bonhoeffer's sense of having "to hold out in this boundary situation" reflects the liminality of the martyr's dilemma, and his understanding of the times as a "great masquerade of evil" expresses the ambiguities of this liminality. Bonhoeffer has to make a choice. He chooses actively to resist the worldly authority of Hitler. Yet this resistance issues not in heroic acts of military valour, carried out in the public arena of national and international conflict. Rather, Bonhoeffer's resistance lies secret, only to be revealed long after he himself has died, in the correspondence between Bonhoeffer and foes, family and friends, especially the correspondence with his former student, who later became his nephew and friend, Eberhard

Bethge. Bonhoeffer's struggle to justify the stance he has taken in and through the epistolary exchanges contained in *Letters and Papers* exemplifies what Tzvetan Todorov calls "exotopy" -- "finding oneself outside."[7] We now read this correspondence as *Letters and Papers*, a Christian literary testimony embodying a *Motiv* of exotopy, of a human being finding himself in and through a process of having to choose between allegiances experienced as opposed, but equally irresistible.

Peculiarities in every writer's situation are necessarily reflected in the raw material – *der Stoff* – out of which a work is constructed. Just as the Christian martyr's literal act of testimony is the ultimate expression of Christian confession, so Christian literary testimony may be understood as a kind of Christian confessional writing. For Northrop Frye, confessional writing is a major form of prose writing, related to, but distinct from, the novel, the anatomy and romance. More specifically, "[n]early always some theoretical and intellectual interest in religion, politics or art plays a leading role in the confession."[8] Because confessional writers address themselves to "an audience that will validate [them], toward a community that is not merely an aesthetic relationship but a moral order as well," the confessional text is at once "introverted" and "intellectualized in content."[9] In this sense, Bonhoeffer's *Letters and Papers* display the general characteristics of confessional writing. More specifically, we read Bonhoeffer's literary testimony as confessional writing in the form of postmodern epistolary fiction. Autobiographical, insofar as it is rooted in Bonhoeffer's experience, *Letters and Papers* is not autobiography, at least, not in any narrow, positivistic sense. The epistolary form of much of *Letters and Papers* undermines the self-referentiality of autobiography. Rather, *Letters and Papers* reads as fiction because Bethge has edited the letters and other historical documents into an historical sequence: "Time of Interrogation, April to July, 1943," "Waiting for the Trial, August, 1943 to April, 1944," "Holding out until the Overthrow, April to July, 1944," and "After the Failure, July, 1944 to February, 1945." This arrangement gives the text a plot, with a beginning, a middle and an end. Because Bonhoeffer rejects the old language of theology, yet cannot or will not prescribe new understandings of Christian truth and justice, *Letters and Papers* enacts the postmodernist's urge to "keep talking, even though he may be conscious of the fact that he cannot do more than recycle petrified meanings."[10] The absolute certainties of a metaphysical or modernist Good no longer obtain. "God as a working hypothesis in morals, politics, or science, has been surmounted and abolished; and the same thing has happened in philosophy and religion," writes Bonhoeffer.[11] In place of this surmounted and abolished God, such celebrated notions as "religionless Christianity" and Jesus as "the man for others" suggest traces of theology, but Bonhoeffer leaves the "world come of age," only an "Outline for a Book."[12] The creed, "[b]efore God and with God we live without God," encapsulates these postmodern ambiguities.[13]

Finally, by *"Thema"* we may understand that interpretive resolution of a work's *Motiv* and *Stoff* which governs our reception of it as readers. *Letters and Papers* suggests interpretive resolutions to the conflict between worldly authority and commitment to God. Such interpretive resolutions are never easily accomplished, even when, as in this case, we might know beforehand that the author of the text with which we are about to try to come to grips died as a Christian martyr. We have no way of knowing, for example, whether or not Bonhoeffer's final remarks about his death being a beginning betray some egotistical urge deep within to perpetuate his life beyond the hangman's noose. *Letters and Papers* might be read as offering evidence that Bonhoeffer did entertain such intimations of immortality. At one point, he actually suggests that Bethge "will be called to write my biography."[14] But whatever the ambiguities surrounding the motives of the historical Bonhoeffer, the Bonhoeffer implied in *Letters and Papers* clearly undergoes a transformation in personality from conditions of despair to conditions of resolve.[15]

At first, Bonhoeffer seems suicidal in prison.[16] But the failure of the plot to assassinate Hitler reveals the full meaning of *metanoia* not as some sort of otherworldly translation, but as "this-worldliness" – a faith which entails "living unreservedly in life's duties, problems, successes and failures, experiences and perplexities."[17] At the same time, *Letters and Papers* invites its readers to rework such a this-worldly transformation in their own lives.[18] The dominant voice of *Letters and Papers* "speaks to the reader in the form of an 'I' that demands to be recognized, that wants or needs to stake a claim on our attention."[19] *Letters and Papers* perpetually challenges us to be "responsible people," to be "plain, honest, straightforward men."[20] Fully to participate in the reading of *Letters and Papers* is to rewrite in one's own life a certain resolution to meet this challenge.[21] To rewrite *Letters and Papers* as readers is to reaffirm the struggle against the kinds of economic, social and political values espoused by Hitler and the Nazis. In this respect, Bonhoeffer's Christian literary testimony, like all literary testimony, "represents an affirmation of the individual subject," as John Beverley has put it, "even of individual growth and transformation, but in connection with a group or class situation marked by marginalization, oppression, and struggle."[22]

The Discourse of Loyalty and the Hermeneutics of Testimony

Drawing upon the work of Jean Nabert, Paul Ricoeur has articulated the question at the heart of testimony: "Does one have the right to invest a moment of history with an absolute character?"[23] Pursuing the origins of Ricoeur's hermeneutics of testimony, we may say that the dialectic between literal acts of Christian testimony and literary acts of Christian testimony expresses a discourse of loyalty. As we have seen, the Christian martyr is caught between loyalty to political realities claiming absolute authority and loyalty to the absolute demands of transcendent truth and justice. Remembering that martyrs are witnesses, we may follow Max Scheler and say that, in moral terms, witnesses may reserve freedom of conscience, but at the same time they must look to "principles of authority and the contents of tradition."[24] This ambiguous intersection between freedom of conscience and the contents of tradition marks the point at which the Christian martyr must resolve the moral conflict between the competing claims of earthly authority and divine authority.

In this situation, the Christian martyr asks the question: "How do I know this or that ideal to be true and just?" Answering such a question involves translating an ideal understood as true and just into a course of action. Understood in ethical terms, to undertake such a course of action is to pursue a cause. The discourse of loyalty thus embodies a philosophy of loyalty. If the discourse of loyalty revolves around the question of moral authority, the philosophy of loyalty is rooted in the issue of the true and just cause. Josiah Royce has articulated this idea of the true and just cause within the context of a philosophy of loyalty. The philosophy of loyalty is a practical philosophy; it has to do with learning why one should choose one course of action instead of another. "The art of learning how to choose, and what to choose, and how to carry out my will, is for me, since I am gregarious, imitative, and conventionalized, a social art."[25] At the same time, however, "no social art that I ordinarily learn is sufficient either to teach me my whole purpose in life, or to make a consistent self of me, or to lead me out of that chaos of self-thwarting efforts wherein so many men pass their lives."[26]

The question thus arises: "How may I discover a principle of life which I may follow without any fear of regret?" This question is not an unreasonable one, since we are all familiar with people in many walks of life whom we admire for their apparently effortless, yet total commitment to a particular way of life. "It would be wrong to say, as some do," Royce argues, "that they are characterized by mere 'altruism,' by 'utter self-forgetfulness,' by 'living solely for others'."[27] One experiences rewards or regrets only in and through service to a cause. Only the willingness so to devote oneself will reveal the truth and justice of the cause. "Your cause you take, then," Royce continues, "to be something objective – something that is not your private self."[28] For Royce, loyalty marks the intersection of two principles. The first principle is simply: "Be loyal."[29] The second principle, however, locates individual loyalty to a cause within a transcendent context. This principle is: "So be loyal to your own cause as thereby to serve the advancement of the cause of universal loyalty."[30] In sum, "Be ... loyal to loyalty."[31]

At the same time, however, to locate loyalty in some transcendent context is not to remove the cause to which one is devoted from the temporal and spatial spheres of human existence. According to Royce, a true and just cause may only be found "in human shape."[32] "A cause ... means something that is conceived by its loyal servant as unifying the lives of various human beings into one life."[33] Loyalty is not self-assertion; it is the realization of one's own selfhood in and through service to a cause which will benefit one's fellow human beings. "In such service one finds self-expression even in and through self-surrender," argues Royce, "and is more of a self even because one gives one's self."[34] Loyalty thus defines the moral life. Loyalty to a true and just cause acknowledges conscience "as rational and universal in its authority, and yet as individual in its expression in the life of each man."[35] Such considerations involve the "metaphysical aspects" of a philosophy of loyalty.[36] "That union of self-sacrifice with self-assertion which loyalty expresses," Royce writes, "becomes a consciousness of our genuine relations to a higher social unity of consciousness in which we all have our being."[37] We experience such a higher social unity of consciousness in and through the practice of loyalty in word and deed. Echoing William James, Royce argues that in the last analysis, "loyalty is the Will to Believe in something eternal, and to express that belief in the practical life of a human being."[38] If this idealist stance seems to run the risk of divorcing the idea of a true and just cause from its practice in the arenas of everyday life, Royce asserts that there is "no merely theoretical truth, and there is no reality foreign, in its nature, to experience."[39]

In the last analysis, testimony is able to mediate between Royce's categories of "theoretical truth" and "experience." "The witness's belief is not the truth of his belief."[40] At the same time, however, to commit oneself to a cause is not to possess certainty about the truth and justice of that cause. In Gabriel Marcel's words, "[w]e are concerned here with a certainty which I *am* rather than with a certainty which I *have*."[41] It is impossible to bear witness to a true and just cause unless one is involved in it, and it is impossible to bear witness to a community of one's fellow human beings without considering oneself in some sense a participant in that community. "But how can I *be* a certainty, if not in as much as I am a living testimony?"[42] It is only possible to testify to an idea, "that is to say to something which is in itself beyond time," only insofar as "the idea has been embodied."[43] To commit oneself to a true and just cause is to make a trial of one's life. One's own life assumes significance insofar as it serves as an arena in which one pursues the cause to which one is loyal, in solidarity with those who also believe in the truth and justice of one's cause, and in combat with those whose lives embody alternative causes. Even the risk of losing one's life serves to extend its significance, insofar as one dies for a cause which survives in the memory of one's self-sacrifice. "The witness ... is not just he who observes or makes a statement; that is not what he really is," Marcel argues, "but he is one who testifies and his testimony is not a mere echo, it is a participation and a confirmation; to bear witness is to contribute to the growth or coming of that for which one testifies."[44]

We are now at the point at which we can introduce Paul Ricoeur's hermeneutics of testimony. The philosophy of loyalty embodied in the discourse of loyalty issues in an interpretive process. When loyalties conflict, an interpretative process is set into motion. This interpretative process we may call the "hermeneutics of testimony." As Ricoeur has noted, such an interpretative process mediates between "an *experience* of the absolute" and "the *idea* of the absolute."[45] In this respect, Ricoeur continues, "the term testimony should be applied to words, works, actions, and to lives which attest to an intention, an inspiration, an idea at the heart of experience and history which nonetheless transcend experience and history."[46] The existential structure of testimony differs from that of mere observation. Testimony testifies to something absolutely and objectively other, yet involves the willed, inward commitment of the individual's "entire being as a person who is answerable for my assertions and for myself."[47]

Certainly, such single-minded commitment may involve a deep-seated desire to slough off feelings of fault, failure, and solitude in a search for value and meaning through the exercise of duty and responsibility in the world. In fact, to be thus committed to a purpose may betray a need to experience the special attention bestowed by one's fellow human beings upon those who sacrifice themselves for a cause. With unequivocal approval, Ricoeur draws upon the insight of fellow Frenchman Jean Nabert, that "[w]hen absolute actions imply willingness to lose one's life, they arouse our highest veneration."[48] But in the last analysis, Ricoeur continues, again citing Nabert, the martyr's literal act of testimony constitutes "*le désir de Dieu*" – with all the wonderfully ambiguous overtones of the word "*de*" – the possessive "of," and attributive "from."[49]

Conclusion

Finally, let me bring together Bonhoeffer's story and the interpretive strategy for understanding such narratives suggested by a discourse of loyalty articulated as a hermeneutics of testimony. As an interpretative expression of the circumstances of political and religious conflict in which Bonhoeffer found himself, *Letters and Papers* is not just fond observations on the course that Bonhoeffer's life took. As a text which embodies, yet survives the special pleading of its author, this act of literary testimony expresses Bonhoeffer's desire for God in terms which bear witness to the desire of God to bestow the perfection of divine truth and justice upon all his creatures. The Bonhoeffer implied in *Letters and Papers* supersedes the residual self-interest of Bonhoeffer the historical autobiographer. If Bonhoeffer seems to be pleading the causes of his own martyrdom in *Letters and Papers*, this literary testimony perpetuates the self-sacrifice of its author by textualizing the ambiguities involved in the philosophical issue of the true and just cause which characterizes the martyr's situation. As a literary act of testimony, *Letters and Papers* recapitulates the loyalty to loyalty of its author. Transcendent principles of truth and justice are refigured in the life of every reader who rewrites Bonhoeffer's literary testimony in and through the dialogical act of reading *Letters and Papers*.

In the last analysis, literal acts of testimony and their re-enactment in literary acts of testimony circulate the double *"dépouillement"* (literally, "divestment") that Ricoeur, again following Nabert, identifies at the heart of all testimony. Those martyrs who bear witness in deed as word, in word as deed, purify their understanding of their own lives, as well as their understanding of the ambiguous reality of that transcendent truth and justice to which their deaths testify. Witnesses refine their own motives for testifying in terms of the absolute reality to which they bear witness. At the same time, they refine their understanding of the nature of transcendent truth and justice, as they are revealed in life and in history. This interpretative circulation is not only a reciprocal process of purification; it is also a reciprocal process of judgment. "Testimony wants to justify," Ricoeur argues, "to prove the good basis of an assertion which, beyond the fact, claims to attain its meaning."[50] The testimony of witnesses, in deed as word, in word as deed, puts on trial their understanding of their own experience, as well as their understanding of the nature of the transcendent truth and justice for which they are willing to sacrifice themselves. This sense of complete commitment is not rooted in a "philosophy of absolute knowledge," but in an interpretative process which correlates two acts: "the act of a self-consciousness which divests (*se dépouille*) itself and tries to understand itself," and "the act of testifying by which the absolute is revealed in its signs and works."[51]

If we understand absolute commitment to the truth and justice of a cause as an interpretive process of purifying trial, we may assert, along with Ricoeur, that "to triumph in the trial is to maintain oneself as soul, to save one's soul."[52] As far as the case of Bonhoeffer is concerned, we may say that the memorialization of Bonhoeffer as a Christian martyr refigures his courage in the lives of later generations. In the words of Donald Evans, "[w]itness is behaviour which so expresses love towards other men that it can be for other men an occasion for cosmic disclosure."[53] In this sense, as mysteriously disclosive of transcendent principles of truth and justice, the blood of Christian martyrs is indeed the seed of loyal congregation. But this shed blood is also a writing in blood of the lives of Christian martyrs. Thus written in blood, the history of Christian martyrdom is a history of literal acts of testimony, and the death of every Christian martyr marks a moment of closure in the history of the presence of transcendent principles of truth and justice in the lives of humankind. Yet the inscription of the literal testimony of Christian martyrs in literary acts of Christian testimony opens another history of witnessing to the reality of these transcendent principles of truth and justice. This other history of witnessing perpetuates the ambiguous presence of the absolute among humankind with every writerly rereading of every work of Christian literary testimony, of every dialogical refiguring of the reality of transcendent truth and justice. Like Bonhoeffer's act of self-sacrifice, *Letters and Papers* testifies in the world and to the world against the powers of the world, including, ironically, in the last analysis, the powers of its author. In Ricoeur's words, "[t]here is therefore no witness of the absolute who is not a witness of historic signs, no confessor of absolute meaning who is not a narrator of the acts of deliverance."[54]

Notes

1 See Eberhard Bethge, *Dietrich Bonhoeffer: Man of Vision, Man of Courage*, trans. Eric Mosbacher, ed. Edwin Robertson (New York: Harper & Row, 1970), 830.

2 These are the words of Dr. G.K.A. Bell, Bishop of Chichester. They are part of a sermon he delivered at a memorial service for Bonhoeffer on 27 July, 1945, in Holy Trinity Church, Kingsway, London. See Bethge, *Dietrich Bonhoeffer*, 833. On Bonhoeffer as martyr, see also, Eberhard Bethge, *Bonhoeffer: Exile and Martyr*, ed. and intro. John W. de Gruchy (New York: Seabury Press, 1975).

3 Clifford J. Green, *The Sociality of Christ and Humanity: Dietrich Bonhoeffer's Early Theology, 1927-1933* (Missoula: Scholars Press, 1972), 145.

4   For a fuller analysis of these issues, see Jamie S. Scott, *Christians and Tyrants: The Prison Testimonies of Boethius, Thomas More and Dietrich Bonhoeffer* (New York: Peter Lang, 1995).

5   Leonardo Boff, "Martyrdom: An Attempt at Systematic Reflection," in *Concilium: Martyrdom Today*, ed. Johannes-Baptist Metz and Edward Schillebeeckx (New York: Seabury Press, 1983), 16. Boff refers to M.-L. Gubler, *Die frühesten Deutungen des Todes Jesu* (Göttingen: n.p., 1977), 10-94, 203-5.

6   Theofried Baumeister, "Martyrdom and Persecution in Early Christianity," in *Concilium*, ed. Metz and Schillebeeckx, 4.

7   Boff, "Martyrdom," 16.

8   Theodore Ziolkowski, *Varieties of Literary Thematics* (Princeton: Princeton University Press, 1983), ix.

9   Elizabeth Frenzel, *Vom Inhalt der Literatur* (Freiburg: Verlag Herder, 1980).

10 Dietrich Bonhoeffer, *Letters and Papers from Prison*, ed. E. Bethge (London: SCM Press, 1953), 129, 4.

11 Quoted in Giles Gunn, *The Culture of Criticism and the Criticism of Culture* (New York: Oxford University Press, 1987), 136.

12 Northrop Frye, *Anatomy of Criticism: Four Essays* (Princeton: Princeton University Press, 1957), 312.

13 Frye, *Anatomy*, 308.

14 Terrence Doody, *Confession and Community in the Novel* (Baton Rouge: Louisiana University Press, 1980); and Frye, *Anatomy*, 307.

15 Douwe W. Fokkema, *Literary History, Modernism, and Postmodernism* (Philadelphia: John Benjamins, 1984), 45.

16 Bonhoeffer, *Letters and Papers*, 360.

17 Bonhoeffer, *Letters and Papers*, 280, 326, 382, 380-83.

18 Bonhoeffer, *Letters and Papers*, 360.

19 Bonhoeffer, *Letters and Papers*, 202.

20 On the notion of the implied author, see Wayne Booth, *The Rhetoric of Fiction* (Chicago: University of Chicago Press, 1961), 71-75, 211-21.

21 Bonhoeffer, *Letters and Papers*, 35. Certainly, suicide was on his mind, for Bonhoeffer writes: "Suicide, not because of consciousness of guilt but because basically I am already dead."

22 Bonhoeffer, *Letters and Papers*, 370.

23 On the notion of the implied reader, see Wolfgang Iser, *The Implied Reader* (Baltimore: Johns Hopkins University Press, 1974), passim..

24 Iser, *The Implied Reader*, 16.

25 *Letters and Papers*, 5, 17.

26 On the notion of participatory reading as rewriting, see Roland Barthes, *S/Z*, trans. R. Miller (New York: Hill and Wang, 1975), passim; and Terence Hawkes, *Structuralism and Semiotics* (London: Methuen, 1977), 112-20.

27 John Beverley, "The Margin at the Center: On *Testimonio* (Testimonial Narrative)," *Modern Fiction Studies* 35 (1989): 23.

28 Jean Nabert, *Essai sur le mal* (Paris: Presses Universitaires de France, 1955), 148.

29 Max Scheler, *Formalism in Ethics and Non-Formal Ethics of Values*, trans. Manfred S. Frings and Roger L. Funk (Evanston: Northwestern University Press, 1973), 322-23.

30 Josiah Royce, *The Philosophy of Loyalty* (New York: Macmillan, 1908), 128-39.

31 Josiah Royce, *The Sources of Religious Insight* (New York: Octagon Books, 1977), 186.

32 Royce, *Sources of Religious Insight*, 186.

33 Royce, *Sources of Religious Insight*, 197.

34 Royce, *Philosophy of Loyalty*, 19.

35 Royce, *Sources of Religious Insight*, 202.

36 Royce, *Sources of Religious Insight*, 203.

37 Royce, *Philosophy of Loyalty*, 121.

38 Royce, *Sources of Religious Insight*, 206.

39 Royce, *Philosophy of Loyalty*, 252.

40 Royce, *Sources of Religious Insight*, 200-01.

41 Gabriel Marcel, *The Mystery of Being*, Vol. II, *Faith and Reality*, trans. René Hague (Chicago: Henry Regnery, 1960), 144.

42 Marcel, *The Mystery of Being*, 144.

43 Marcel, *The Mystery of Being*, 146.

44 Gabriel Marcel, *Homo Viator*, trans. Emma Craufurd (Chicago: Henry Regnery, 1951), 213.

45 Paul Ricoeur, "The Hermeneutics of Testimony," in *Essays on Biblical Interpretation*, ed. and trans. Lewis S. Mudge (Philadelphia: Fortress Press, 1980), 119.

46 Ricoeur, "Hermeneutics of Testimony," 119-20.

47 Gabriel Marcel, *The Philosophy of Existence*, trans. Manya Harari (London: Harvill Press, 1948), 70.

48 Jean Nabert, *Elements for an Ethic*, trans. W.J. Petrek (Evanston: Northwestern University Press, 1969), 191.

49 Jean Nabert, *Le Désir de Dieu* (Paris: Aubier-Montaigne, 1966).

50 Ricoeur, "Hermeneutics of Testimony," 120.

51 Ricoeur, "Hermeneutics of Testimony," 124.

52 Ricoeur, "Hermeneutics of Testimony," 153, 151.

53 Donald Evans, *Faith, Authenticity, and Morality* (Toronto: University of Toronto Press, 1980), 42.

54 Ricoeur, "Hermeneutics of Testimony," 134.

The Role of Figure in Metaphor, Narrative and Architecture

GRAHAM LIVESEY

The work of architects tends to concentrate on the formal and the constructed, often neglecting the intangible and the elusive, or the way in which people inhabit and use buildings and the spaces they encompass. As Paul Ricoeur points out "life has to do with narration."[1] Therefore, to gain a greater understanding of the reciprocal relationship between human actions and architecture, the following will explore Ricoeur's theories of metaphor and narrative as they pertain to architecture. Here architecture can be understood as works of human making, which are designed, constructed, inhabited and interpreted; architecture shapes spaces in which human actions unfold.

Ricoeur states in the preface to the first volume of *Time and Narrative*, that "whereas metaphorical description reigns in the field of sensory, emotional, aesthetic, and axiological values, which make the world a habitable world, the mimetic function of plots takes place by preference in the field of action and its temporal values."[2] In his earlier text, *The Rule of Metaphor*, Ricoeur explores metaphor in rhetorical, structural and hermeneutical terms moving from the figural aspects of metaphor contained in a discussion of Aristotle to the existential implications of metaphor and "the power to 'redescribe' reality."[3] It is in the realm of metaphor that architecture more typically operates. Ricoeur's work on narrative addresses primarily questions of time with reference to discourse and texts. In his writings, there is little discussion of the world or of those human works that contribute to the shaping of the spatial world.

The way to unite a discussion of architecture and narrative, I would suggest, is to concentrate on Ricoeur's use of figure as derived from Aristotle, both with regard to metaphor as a "figure of speech" and to his use of figure as shaping, which is central to his analysis of narrative and time. The word "figure" may be either a noun or verb. As a noun, it has a variety of meanings: a shape, a form, the human form, a likeness,

25

a diagram, a symbol, a metaphor. A figure may be a geometrical or bodily shape or representation thereof, and it can also refer to a diagram
that is drawn or traced out by the movements of dancer, skater or musi-
cian. "Figure" as a verb means "to bring into shape, to represent, to imagine, to portray, to perform a figure."[4] The word "figural," or
"figurative," particularly in light of modernist representation, can be
opposed to "abstract," or "abstraction." In this case, "abstraction" can
imply the use of purely formal or structural terms, the ideal or the intellectual. There is an essential phenomenology in Ricoeur's use of the term
in that it connotes an embodied form, as he notes in his discussion of the
figural nature of metaphor: "Figures are to discourse what contours,
characteristics, and exterior form are to the body."[5]

In the first volume of *Time and Narrative*, Ricoeur presents his theory
of emplotment based largely on a reading of Augustine's *Confessions*
and Aristotle's *Poetics*, in which he introduces the notion that the work
of a poet is to make plots, to imitate in a mimetic manner human actions; to make a plot is "to make the intelligible spring from the accidental, the universal from the singular, the necessary or the probable from
the episodic."[6] Here, Ricoeur also introduces the core to his monumental exploration of narrative and time, his notion of a "threefold" understanding of mimesis in which the idea of figuration is fundamental.

The first part of the model, Ricoeur labels as mimesis$_1$; he suggests
that the "composition of the plot is grounded in a pre-understanding of
the world of action, its meaningful structures, its symbolic resources,
and its temporal character."[7] This refers to the practical world of everyday action, which Ricoeur describes as the realm in which stories or
narratives are prefigured; narratives are based on actions that have motives, agents, and take place in the world and in time. As Ricoeur implies, architecture and spatiality can be considered as part of the world
that prefigures narratives, as both meaningful structure and as symbolic
systems. This prenarrative condition is affirmed when he writes that
"literature would be incomprehensible if it did not give a configuration
to what was already a figure in human action."[8] This statement, which
concludes his discussion of the prefigurational aspect of narrative, confirms that action is figural and points forward to his discussion of the
second, and central, part of his model.

Mimesis$_2$ is the configurational aspect of Ricoeur's theory of
emplotment, which he suggests functions in three ways. Firstly, it mediates between individual events and a story or narrative as a whole, it
gives shape to a succession of events. Secondly, "emplotment brings together factors as heterogeneous as agents, goals, means, interactions,
circumstances, unexpected results."[9] Thirdly, it unites the temporal char-

acteristics of the plot. The configurational role of emplotment is the "grasping together" of heterogeneous factors into a meaningful story that possesses shape (or figure) and a "sense of ending." In Ricoeur's model, this is the action of the poet, the production or making of stories or plots. It is also the aspect that coincides most closely with other forms of creative production such as design.

Mimesis$_3$ completes the circular nature of the model and "marks the intersection of the world of the text and the world of the hearer or reader."[10] This third part of the model is the interpretative aspect, which reaffirms Ricoeur's ongoing exploration of hermeneutics and the "conflict of interpretations." We, as readers, gain understanding of our lives and of our world by engaging in what a work (text, artifact, building, city) reveals; that which is prefigured and configured is thus refigured. The act of interpretation reveals worlds that might be inhabited and contributes to our inhabitation of the material world. Presumably, this does not only apply to reading, but also to our physical engagement with the world.

Anthony Paul Kerby sums up Ricoeur's model of emplotment and his use of various modes of figuration in the following words:

> Emplotment, in histories and fictions, takes a prefigured world of events and actions and draws out or proposes a configuration that serves to organize worldly events into meaningful sequences and purposes. This textual structure is in turn the mediating cause of the reader refiguring his or her own world in light of the possibilities offered by experiencing the world of the text [work].[11]

I would like to extend Ricoeur's three stages of mimesis as prefiguration, configuration and refiguration into aspects of architecture. The cyclical and continuous nature of the model presents a vital and timely way of considering human creativity and production. When an architect is asked to design a building, usually by a client, the practical world of everyday action shapes to a certain extent the building that will emerge. The design of a building takes place within a dense cultural context, or web of constraints, which determines methods of construction, uses of space, symbolic systems, economic parameters, languages of architecture, etc. For an architect, this world is also shaped by buildings that already exist. The design of a building and its subsequent inhabitation are also predetermined to a degree by the site, the program (the design brief or functional requirements) and budget. This coincides with Ricoeur's proposition that the world is prefigured by narrative, that stories are latent in the world and that narration and life are intertwined. It can be suggested that architecture is both part of and emerges from a prefigured world.

The configurational aspect that is proposed in the second part of Ricoeur's model is vital as it is the intentional shaping of, or giving structure to, the narrative. This is akin to the process undertaken by architects in the design and execution of a work of architecture (both in drawings and in actual construction). Normally this is an activity that takes some time to accomplish and involves many individuals. The giving of architectural form or structure to a disparate range of elements and requirements is very similar to Ricoeur's description of narrative emplotment. Out of this heterogeneous wealth of factors a project emerges, or is "grasped" together – the poetic act of the "productive imagination." The events (meetings, decisions, discoveries, etc.) that configure the design of a project have a structure in time very similar to Ricoeur's notion of emplotment. It is a grasping together of the significant events or decisions into a comprehensible work, a poetic act. Peter G. Rowe, in his book *Design Thinking*, has used accounts of design projects by a number of architects as one form of evidence for understanding the workings of design. He maintains that the design process "assumes a distinctly episodic structure, which we might characterize as a series of skirmishes with various aspects of the problem at hand."[12] Rowe is describing a process analogous to Ricoeur's notions of configuration as described in the second part of his mimetic model. A figure gradually emerges out of what may begin as a random series of events or episodes. This is not necessarily a linear, sequential or continuous activity but usually has a structure based on the prefigured context. However, Ricoeur's model challenges modernist notions of creativity as originality, firmly reestablishing that making is part of a historical and cultural context, it is to a large extent an interpretation of that which is given, or prefigured.

The third part of Ricoeur's mimetic model addresses what happens to a work when it is given to the world to be read, interpreted or inhabited. Examining the relationship between the world of a work and that of a reader, Ricoeur proposes that "hermeneutics takes hold of the hinge between the (internal) configuration of a work and the (external) refiguration of a life."[13] Architecture, like any other work, contains an intentional world that emerges from that which is prefigured (given) and that configured (the poetic act). All works participate in this "fusion of horizons" that occurs between the world of the work and the world of the reader or inhabitant. The relationship between building and inhabiting is reciprocal as architecture exists as part of the context that prefigures narrative and architecture itself.

Many of the ideas alluded to above are suggested by the contemporary British architect Nigel Coates, who describes the use of various narrative strategies in the design of a large urban project for the Isle of Dogs area of London:

> The first [narrative] is drawn out of the place itself – its barren landscapes, broken buildings and empty docks. Then a video narrative explores the possible mixing up of work and home without ever referring to buildings directly. Thirdly, each piece of the island ... develops its own industrial process to mark a narrative of movement, process and sequence. The final narrative occurs when the experience of the place – living on the island, riding the bus, settling into the work/home landscape – puts all these layers together.[14]

This quotation closely matches the mimetic model employed by Ricoeur as the architect gives shape to form based on an interpretation of the context and by creating narratives. From this comes a potential for the emergence of new unforeseen narratives.

Much of twentieth-century architecture has revolved around the on-going debate over the dialectical relationship between function and form. This relationship was codified by late nineteenth-century architects, most famously by Louis Sullivan who wrote that "form ever follows function."[15] This proposition insists that the form of a building is a direct expression of the function or use of the building. Derived from the natural sciences and the analysis of the form and functions of biological specimens, this scientistic model relates to our discussion of the correlation between architecture and the narrative use of space. The preceding discussion of figure can shed light on this debate, as it encompasses both physical form and human action. The formal qualities of architecture have a metaphorical dimension, while the so-called functional aspects are implicitly narrative.

Architectural historian and critic Alan Colquhoun, in an essay entitled "Form and Figure,"[16] discusses the formal question in light of postmodern efforts to revive a figural understanding of architecture. He argues that the modernist emphasis on form and function was consistent with a seeming rejection of history by such architectural luminaries as Walter Gropius and Le Corbusier: a searching for abstract and mechanistic architectural form as a direct expression of function. This rejection of history, according to Colquhoun, was also the rejection of the figural, or that given by culture or history. The use of figure, rather than form, as the basis for understanding architecture implies a history of shared meaning, a set of conventions or a comprehended language. Consistent with Ricoeur's discussion of metaphor in *The Rule of Metaphor*, he notes that the origins of metaphorical figure date back to classical rhetoric. In Western architectural culture, this inevitably means the classical language of architecture, a language of construction full of metaphor. Beginning in the 1960s, a revival of classical architecture occurred. Architects such as Robert Venturi, Charles Moore, Aldo Rossi, and Leon Krier argued for the continuing historical relevance of this language deeply embedded in the memories and traditions of Western culture. As Colquhoun notes, this is in the postmodern context the revival of "fragments" of this history, and much of the subsequent work was an architectural pastiche of classical elements.

Architectural historian Anthony Vidler has described three ways in which architecture has used the human body, or figure, as the metaphorical basis for building.[17] In Vitruvian and Renaissance classicism, the body provided an authority by which a building could be ordered. In the eighteenth century the emergence of the sublime emphasized physical and mental states of being. Recently, there has been a shift to a more general animism. We have also reached a stage where the use of inanimate metaphors, such as machinery, information technology, and preoccupations with the absent body, means that metaphor can shift to the non-figural or non-existent.

The relationship between the form and its function has been examined by many contemporary architects. The Italian architect Aldo Rossi rejects empiricist notions that suggest that form is a direct result of the function or use of spaces. He stresses that, while architectural archetypes have continuity and establish a permanency, the use of the space evolves over time, and is therefore fluid. Rossi has employed methods of drawing as a way of mediating between a detailed examination of human action and architecture. Using the historical analogy that architecture is theatrical he suggests that people are like actors acting against the backdrop of buildings "involved in an event with which they are probably unfamiliar."[18]

Rossi has long been interested in the potential for spaces to create meaningful and memorable events, events of a proto-narrative significance. Inspired by Giorgio di Chirico's paintings, Rossi has worked to understand the event that is both prefigured and refigured by his architecture. He writes: "In some of my recent projects, or ideas for projects, I try to stop the event before it occurs, as if the architect could foresee – and in a certain sense does foresee – the unfolding of a life in the house [building, urban space]."[19] Rossi's buildings are formally simple, the spaces he creates are defined and comprehensible, architecture provides a fixed and stable definition of space for the multiplicity of human actions that take place within space and time. As Colquhoun notes, Rossi's work, while preoccupied with archetypal form, rejects the merely formal, embracing the figurative history of an interpreted classicism.

This debate has similarities with discussions between figure and abstraction as found in twentieth-century painting. The suggestion that describing architectural form in figural terms implies only the historicist revival of the classical language is erroneous. As Colquhoun himself suggests:

> The effectiveness of figures or tropes resides in their synthetic power. They draw together and crystallize a series of complex experiences, which are diffuse and imperceptible. The figure, therefore, is a condensation, the immediate effect of which is to suggest the richness and complexity of reality.[20]

Here, I would like to shift from a discussion of the figural qualities of form, or the constructed world, to the figural inhabitation of space as defined by form, implied in Ricoeur's work. What Michel Butor has called "trajectories"[21] and architect Christopher Alexander has labelled "patterns"[22] can here be described as figures. This figural engagement with space and time is consistent with the movements of a dancer or skater. As Sondra Horton Fraleigh writes: "In dance, leaping and turning are actually single figures of movement having specific shapes in time and space. The dance work as a whole is the gestalt that emerges from the integration of single figures."[23] Human actions trace out figures, or series of movements that can be comprehended, reinforcing Kerby's claim that "each human life traces out a complex figure that necessarily intersects and interacts with the figures of others."[24] This statement affirms that our movements or journeys in the world, and in time, are figural and carry the latent potential, through intersections with other figures, for contributing to a plot. The patterns or figures we make in space and time as we inhabit the world, are potentially metaphorical and narrative. A figurative intersection occurs between a figural definition of space, as determined by architecture, and the figural actions of human engagement with the world. This idea has been explored by a number of contemporary architects who have focused on the event, the constitutive element of a narrative and the correlation between movements and spaces.

The questioning of functionalist definitions of space has also been embraced by architects such as Bernard Tschumi and Nigel Coates who are more overtly interested in the narrative potential of space. Tschumi has also explored aspects of narrative and architecture with particular emphasis placed on the events that occur in space. This is captured in Tschumi's statement that "there is no space without event, no architecture without programme,"[25] and by his definition of the program as "a combination of events."[26] Rather than presenting the components of a program as a list of spaces with fixed functions, a more continuous sense of space is proposed which concentrates on the potential for human action, or the making of events. During the 1970s and early 1980s, Tschumi and Coates initiated a series of studio experiments at the Architectural Association School of Architecture in London, in which literature, cinema and dance movement notation systems were actively used to understand and design spaces and buildings. The work of Bernard Tschumi and Nigel Coates has indicated a range of new possibilities for understanding the relationship between architectural space and human action, with a de-emphasis of the functionalist concerns typical of much of modernist architecture.

Architects do often engage the prefigured and refigured aspects of narrative in their work, but normally revert to architectural means (drawing, models, construction, etc.) to execute the configurational aspects of design. However, there are noteworthy examples of architects and designers using actual narratives or stories, either written by them or by others, to structure a design. One tradition that employed this technique is eighteenth-century English garden design, the so-called "picturesque" tradition. A famous example is the garden at Stourhead by Henry and Richard Hoare, which was organized according to Virgil's epic poem *The Aeneid*. Some of the events in this story are used to loosely structure a linear journey that visitors follow around the artificial lake that forms the heart of the design. As one progresses around the lake, one encounters a series of constructed and textual events – temples, grottoes, statues, inscriptions, etc. – that allude to the ancient poem and to contemporary renditions of it. Following the path reveals a story, the elements comprising the garden "are woven into a complex narrative that calls for exegesis. This is not merely a matter of uncovering Hoare's intentions or revealing his prototypes ... for Stourhead certainly means more than its creator intended, and has significance beyond that. It seduces by offering the subtle pleasures of hermeneutics."[27] This technique, while not often used, has been revived in the postmodern era by a number of contemporary architects, including Rem Koolhaas and Peter Eisenman.

In a number of "Masque" projects, American architect and educator John Hejduk has explored the metaphorical and narrative aspects of architecture. These projects have affinities with the masques performances staged for the English court in the sixteenth and seventeenth centuries. For his project entitled the "Lancaster/Hanover Masque" Hejduk's design derives from

> the space of a Rural Farm Community and the process of "spell-binding" the space (as in a ritual dance) by means of a number of "subjects" and corresponding "objects" which denote this imaginary habitat.... As such, the Masque can be seen as a configuration of intertwining, interacting parts; a dynamic whole consisting of "objects" and "subjects" in continuous, unpredictable, self-determined movement.[28]

In the project, Hejduk devises a diverse range of characters, each with his or her corresponding dwelling. The design of the individual pieces of the project are metaphorically linked to the character that they house. These are placed on the site, along with complementary instructions, in such a way as to set up a complex and mysterious matrix of narrative possibilities. It is a strange and unusual game that is established, one that touches on many themes related to the role of architecture in the contemporary world.

There is much in Ricoeur's "threefold" mimetic model that lends itself to a renewed understanding of the design and inhabitation of buildings. The figurative, as Ricoeur suggests, is prefigured in our symbolic systems and in the multiplicity of languages that we comprehend, configured by our productive or poetic tendencies, and refigured through interpretation and inhabitation. The figural qualities of form and human action, and their relationship to the spatial world and narrative is a vital source of thinking for architects. The question remains as to what is the nature of the figures being described, whether the references are abstract, anthropomorphic, mechanistic, textual or informational. The shapes of contemporary structures in many cases tend towards amorphousness or fragmentation. Do they need to be comprehensible in traditional terms?

While Ricoeur falls short of stating that we are the authors of our own life stories, he nevertheless affirms that narrative is essential to our human existence in time and space. Generally, architects tend to concentrate on the configurational aspects of design, neglecting a rigorous exploration of that which is prefigured and how their work allows for refiguration. By using Ricoeur's discussion of metaphor as figural discourse and the figurational aspects of emplotment in the structuring of human narratives, it can be concluded that architecture is both metaphorical and participates in narrative. Architecture figures the spaces in which we dwell or move figuratively. Our actions trace figures that can be retold in the narrative ordering of our life stories. Intersections between humans and their world (architecture), between each other and with ourselves, create the events that plot our journeys in time and space.

Notes

1 Paul Ricoeur, "Life: A Story in Search of a Narrator," in *Facts and Values: Philosophical Reflections from Western and Non-Western Perspectives*, ed. M.C. Doeser and J.N. Kraay (Dordrecht: Martinus Nijhoff, 1986), 121.

2 Paul Ricoeur, *Time and Narrative*, I, trans. Kathleen McLaughlin and David Pellauer (Chicago: University of Chicago Press, 1984), xi.

3 Paul Ricoeur, *The Rule of Metaphor*, trans. Robert Czerny (Toronto: University of Toronto Press, 1977), 6.

4 "Figure," *The Oxford English Dictionary*, Vol. V (Oxford: Clarendon Press, 1989), 896-99.

5 Paul Ricoeur, *The Rule of Metaphor*, 52.

6 Ricoeur, *Time and Narrative*, I, 41.

7 Ricoeur, *Time and Narrative*, I, 54.

8 Ricoeur, *Time and Narrative*, I, 64.

9 Ricoeur, *Time and Narrative*, I, 65.

10 Ricoeur, *Time and Narrative*, I, 71.

11 Anthony Paul Kerby, *Narrative and the Self* (Bloomington: Indiana University Press, 1991), 43.

12 Peter G. Rowe, *Design Thinking* (Cambridge, MA: MIT Press, 1987), 34.

13 Ricoeur, "Life; A Story in Search of a Narrator," 127.

14 Nigel Coates, "Narrative Break-up," in *Themes 3: The Discourse of Events* (London: Architectural Association, 1983), 17.

15 Louis Sullivan, "The Tall Office Building Artistically Considered," in *Kindergarten Chats and Other Writings* (New York: Dover, 1979), 208.

16 Alan Colquhoun, "Figure and Form," in *Essays in Architectural Criticism: Modern Architecture and Historical Change* (Cambridge, MA: MIT Press, 1981).

17 Anthony Vidler, "The Building in Pain: The Body and Architecture in Post-Modern Culture," *AA Files* 19 (Spring 1990): 3-10.

18 Aldo Rossi, *A Scientific Autobiography* (Cambridge, MA: MIT Press, 1981), 50.

19 Rossi, *A Scientific Autobiography* , 6.

20 Colquhoun, "Figure and Form," 191.

21 See Michel Butor, "The Space of the Novel," in *Inventory: Essays by Michel Butor*, ed. Richard Howard (New York: Simon and Schuster, 1968).

22 See Christopher Alexander, *The Timeless Way of Building* (New York: Oxford University Press, 1979).

23 Sondra Horton Fraleigh, *Dance and the Lived Body* (Pittsburgh: University of Pittsburgh Press, 1987), 88.

24 Kerby, *Narrative and the Self*, 52.

25 Bernard Tschumi, "Spaces and Events," in *Themes 3: The Discourse of Events* (London: Architectural Association, 1983), 6.

26 Bernard Tschumi, "Index of Architecture," in *Questions of Space: Lectures on Architecture* (London: AA Publications, 1990), 104.

27 C.W. Moore, W.J. Mitchell and W. Turnbull, Jr., *The Poetics of Gardens* (Cambridge, MA: MIT Press, 1993), 137-141.

28 Wim van den Bergh, "Icarus' Amazement, or the Matrix of Crossed Destinies," in John Hedjuk, *The Lancaster/Hanover Masque* (London, Architectural Association, 1992), 83.

Writing as Repossession:
The Narratives of Incest Victims

MORNY JOY

It has now become something of a commonplace to remark that just when it seemed women were discovering what it was to have a self, to take responsibility for self-definition, to assume some form of autonomy, along came postmodernism and declared that there was no such thing as a self. So women's fledgling attempts to claim a measure of self-confidence in how they organized and understood their identities seem to have suffered a major setback. Suffice it to say that the dispute still rages between proponents of postmodernism, who declare that its model of displacement aptly portrays the fragmented and peripheral role of women, and advocates of self-determination, who believe it is time for women to take charge of their lives.

Literary critic Patricia Waugh voices discontent with both of these projects, stating that both characterize situations where the identity or role of woman is being dictated by the prevailing paradigms of a masculine-oriented matrix:

> How can they [women] long for, reject, or synthesize a new mode of being from a thesis which has never contained or expressed what they felt their historical experience to be? ... Postmodernism expresses nostalgia for, but loss of, belief in the concept of the human subject as an agent effectively intervening in history, through its fragmentation of discourses, language games, and decentering of subjectivity.... Despite common concerns the postmodern deconstruction of subjectivity is as problematic for women as the liberal construction of self.[1]

Perhaps nowhere has this struggle been exemplified more than in the current theoretical discussions of women's autobiography. In recent years, there has been a plethora of books, with both theoretical and substantive essays, that seek to delineate the place/space from which a woman can speak and in what manner she can be considered accountable for these depictions.[2] Central to the debate are the notions of self and subject. Basically, the former liberal ideal of autonomy and authorial control in the portrayal of a homogeneous self has been put into question.[3] In this perspective, it appears to be the male individual who, in autobiography, related his imposition of order on the flux of experience, primarily in the public realm, while women's more informal narratives were generally excluded from the canon of autobiographical writings. But as the artifices of universality and impartiality of the predominantly male approach have become apparent, and the fictive self so constructed has been revealed in all its pretensions, women have been reluctant to adopt such blatant self-aggrandizement. It is one thing, however, to demonstrate the deceptions of such an approach, but it is another to seek solace in its diametric opposite of fragmentation. Yet this is how postmodern challenge and its application to women appears to have been interpreted.

Michel Foucault, in his acclaimed piece, "What is an Author?", questions the ideological presumptions of any author.[4] On Foucault's reading, this does not necessarily lead to the immediate dissolution of the self, but of the accepted notion of individuality that has supported traditional claims to identity. The latter is depicted by Foucault as the result of social and historical influences. Rather than a unique self, there is instead a subject that is the locus of forces over which one cannot assume control. An author, for Foucault, marks the nexus of the proliferation of influences on him/her. As a result, perhaps the best one can hope for is awareness of these limitations; and cautionary provisos are then attached to whatever claims regarding subjectivity are made. Such qualified self-locations are being cautiously adopted by certain women theorists, particularly regarding political strategies.[5] There are others who would dispute such a tactic, arguing that women have never had easy access to the dominant discourse of society, and admonitions against authorial hubris do not ring true for them.

There is, however, another format of postmodernism, exemplified by the early work of Julia Kristeva, that has also received a sympathetic ear. Kristeva advocated the demise of any notion of self in the name of a type of polymorphous perversity that delights in its own indeterminacy: "I myself, at the deepest level of my wants and desires, am unsure, centerless, and divided. This does not eliminate my capacities for commitment and trust but makes them, literally and in no other way, playable."[6]

If there is a resonance of certain women with this proclamation, it is probably because they can recognize themselves in this profile of a decentered subject.[7] But what if the adoption of Kristeva's position entails that the best a woman can hope for is to perceive her marginal status? As a result, she can write only in a reactive fashion, even if Kristeva views this as a disruptive and destabilizing tactic that serves to unsettle the establishment. Such a strategy would only leave the prevailing norms and values securely entrenched, while women merely register protest, but do not effect change.

Shari Benstock, in comparison, seems to have arrived at a more complex approach, involving a constructive, if simultaneously suspicious, stance in her adaptation of postmodernism:

> Post-structuralism has taught us to read the politics of every element in narrative strategy: representation; tone; perspective; figures of speech; even the shift between first-, second-, and third-person pronouns. In identifying the "fissures of female discontinuity" in a text, for example, we also point toward a relation between the psychic and the political, the personal and the social, in the linguistic fabric. [8]

Benstock's awareness of the disjunctures of female identity does not lead simply to indulgence in such discrepancies, but rather to investigation of the very processes that have contributed to such a situation. Such explorations need not result in any absolute answers or definitive solution to the problem of how women are to constitute identity, but they point in a direction that interrogates the conditions of the construction of any identity. This approach mitigates the extreme dissipation suggested by some adherents of postmodernism and thus the fact of accepting the self as a construct should not lead to an indeterminate relativism, but rather an informed awareness of the specific details operating in a given context.

So what type of option is left for a woman who seeks to write an autobiography today? What sense of self can she claim if she is not to succumb to the temptations of either an idealized univocal self or to any number of heterogeneous guises in the name of an unstable postmodern subject? Following Benstock's lead, I would like to focus on the idea of a narrative or strategic identity, and on a certain genre of autobiographical narratives, as indicating a possible way out of this impasse.

In recent works, Paul Ricoeur has commented on a thematic modality he has named "narrative identity." Because of its past associations, the term "narrative" seems to be associated with predominantly linear and logical procedures, and thus I would prefer to use the term "strategic identity." This term alludes to the fact that to narrate one's life is always an interpretation, situated at the confluence of many influences. It thus makes provision for the fact that a life can be viewed as a composite of many plots, not just as one major theme in the service of a master plot or ideal. At any one time, then, I could be trying to grasp or make sense of a particular episode that has affected my life, in relation to other plots, rather than writing an all-embracing panorama that incorporates every facet of my existence. I believe that it is in this way of partial, contextual or relative insight (in a larger context of shifting frames) that Ricoeur can say "we learn to become the narrator of our own story without becoming the author of our life."[9]

From this perspective, it is possible to entertain an appreciation of a strategic identity as a construct that allows for movements of change and that also provides for a form of critical self-awareness. Each plot lends cohesion and coherence to the manifold influences that ceaselessly threaten to overwhelm us. So it is that a particular plot is constructed by a person in response to a particular situation or experience that needs clarification. This plot can help a person establish a bridgehead from which he/she can thematize a set of events that may otherwise be either too chaotic or too distressing. It can also assist in the expression of strategic actions of a political or ethical kind in response to the same situation. As Ricoeur affirms:

> Unlike the abstract identity of the Same, this narrative identity, constitutive of self-constancy, can include change, mutability, within the cohesion of one lifetime. The subject then appears both as a reader and the writer of its own life, as Proust would have it. As the literary analysis of autobiography confirms, the story of a life continues to be refigured by all the truthful or fictive stories a subject tells about himself or herself. This refiguration makes this life itself a cloth woven of stories told.[10]

In his latest work, *Oneself as Another*,[11] Ricoeur has expanded and qualified this earlier formulation of "narrative identity," for he had become aware that the dilemma of delineating identity in time brought into stark relief an ambiguity in the meaning of the term "identity." In one sense, "identity" refers to the idea of similarity that implies repetition in time. For this aspect of identity, Ricoeur uses the term *"idem."* The other meaning of "identity" is that of selfhood which conveys an idea of constancy as in perduration in time. It has reflexive and existential connotations, and Ricoeur employs the term *"ipse"* to indicate this aspect. It is the failure to distinguish between these two aspects that, on Ricoeur's account, has led to many misunderstandings in contemporary discussions on the nature of identity. But this is not to say that Ricoeur's clarification will lead to an immediate resolution of the problem, for it is not as simple as that. Ricoeur will argue that though these meanings are indeed discrete, and need to be so acknowledged, it is in fact their very interplay that constitutes the richness and complexity of identity. And so it is this very affinity, yet distinctness of the two forms of identity, *idem* and *ipse*, against the backdrop of a "timescape," that generates the dynamics that provide the construct of narrative, or as I prefer to name it, "strategic identity."

Attention to such subtleties, which make more modest rather than grandiose claims for identity, would seem to be particularly apt for contemporary women who are acutely sensitive to the fact of their difference, to their exclusions from the dominant order, yet at the same time do not wish to be viewed as making definitive counterclaims on the part of all women. In addition, they do not wish to be confined to ineffectual peripheral resistance. The model proposed allows that the construction of any form of identity will always be circumscribed by the specific elements that imbue any event or episode with its distinctive intensity and relevance. Identity is thus understood as a constantly negotiated process, which is never complete. There are multiple possibilities of self-definition, which reflect the diverse influences at work – that range from those that would impose conformity and control to those that can induce disintegration.

As an illustration of this sense of strategic self, I would like to discuss three contemporary autobiographical narratives that deal with the topic of incest. This is a highly charged area, and I chose these three depictions only because the woman concerned have gone public with their books in the explicit hope of helping others. For these women, writing was also a form of therapy and so a way of coming to deal with experiences that otherwise could have left them wounded beings whose lives seemed, in some measure, out of control. Indeed such retelling of the experience and its influences are encouraged, for those so disposed, as a form of recuperation.[12]

These women, as incest victims, are doubly disadvantaged. On the one hand, as it has been observed, women until recently have not had access to the public realm to voice their complaints, but rather have been confined to the domestic arena. Here, however, women who are victims of family violence are also estranged in the private realm. Perhaps, it could be said that they have been doubly deprived of a "sense of self." Yet though these women have been manipulated and violated so that their lives may be considered damaged and decentered, in no way could their condition be invoked in support of the postmodern move to indeterminate, fragmented subjects. The first priority of these women would seem to be a reclaiming, a retrieval of a sense of identity that does not succumb to either nominalist or idealist tendencies. It is to locate, disclose, and confront a traumatic series of events that has tragically distorted their lives. The focus in their autobiographical narratives is to investigate this trauma and its influences to the exclusion of all else. In their narratives and their search for meaning, they would appear, in the very act of confronting their past in writing, to be constituting an identity.

This specific or contextually dependent sense of self is an exemplar of what I would call a "strategic identity."

The three books I will discuss are: *Don't: A Woman's Word*, by Elly Danica,[13] *Daddy's Girl*, by Charlotte Vale Allen,[14] and *My Father's House*, by Sylvia Fraser.[15] For better or worse, all of the scenarios are located in Canada. These are disturbing, profoundly anguishing books. There is hate and rage against the perpetrators. There is grief, fear, even desolation, for these victims who struggle with what must be the most perverse violation of trust, the most debased expression of love human beings can inflict on each other. All of the experiences were recorded many years after the event. One victim, Sylvia Fraser, had even repressed all memory of the abuse and her life story is told in thinly disguised fictional form, punctuated by subliminal flashes as she gradually moves towards the moment of recognition that actually occurred when she was in her forties.

For all these women their need to write eventually prevails over their doubts, terror, and sorrow. As Danica writes, her putting pen to paper constituted "Survival. Dreaming with a pen in my hand. Writing. Writing. Who will hear me?"[16] It was also a tenuous hope. For Vale Allen, writing is therapeutic and a mode of self-understanding, of facing the demons that had dominated her life:

> I sat down to write about it and pried the scab off my life. It was excruciating to have to go backward, in detail, and minutely examine what happened, and why, and how it had all conspired to see me into adulthood flawed, not really an adult but a frightened, hate-filled, angry child with strong antisocial tendencies, a head filled with dreams and fantasies, and a grinding determination to emerge at the far end of my life as a *good* person.[17]

For Fraser, it was not only a cathartic experience, but the reintegration of a part of herself and of her life that she had banished from consciousness:

> Mine was a story of early loss – of innocence, of childhood, of love, of magic, of illusion. It was a hazardous life, which began in guilt and self-hate, requiring me to learn self-forgiveness. This meant discovering the difference between fixing blame and taking responsibility. The guilty child was me, though I didn't know of her existence. Her actions were mine, for which I must assume responsibility.
>
> My life was structured on the uncovering of a mystery. As a child, I survived by forgetting. Later, the amnesia became a problem as large as the one it was meant to conceal.[18]

The emotions revealed, as anticipated, are destructive, and each victim had specific repercussions that she had to come to terms with. Madness and suicide are constant temptations for all three women:

> Life as a void. Life as a black hole in space. All memory, all craziness, stored in a closet at the back of my head. I'll never let it out. I promise. I don't want anybody to know how crazy I really am.[19]

For Vale Allen, death is an option that still remains:

> Always, in the back of my mind, was the knowledge that if I failed, I could open the door marked EXIT and walked through it via pills, or razor blades, gas ovens, or a slow walk into deep water. That EXIT was my secret, long-made reservation with death and if things got too bad, if I proved too unacceptable on too many levels, I could present myself to the *maître d'* and make my way over to the door. My feelings on this matter haven't changed in the least. I like knowing I have one irrevocable option at my disposal. It somehow provides me with the courage to take another step, to face the empty house and The Man with the Knife one more time.[20]

There is nonetheless affirmation involved in these recountings, even healing. Each woman realizes that she is negotiating a distressing and painful journey – and that just doing this is an accomplishment. To do so, they have had to overcome what was at times overwhelming guilt and feelings of utter helplessness and inferiority.

> Looking at my life from one vantage point, I see nothing but devastation. A blasted childhood, an even worse adolescence, betrayal, divorce, craziness, professional stalemate, financial uncertainty and always, always a secret eating like dry rot at my psyche. That is the dark side, the story I have told in this book. Yet, like the moon, my life has another side, one with some luminosity.[21]

Yet moments of quiet happiness, of radiance even, are not an irrevocable achievement. Their insights come by a conscious process of psychological archaeology that often threatens to founder, punctuated as it is by moments of clarity that churn destructive primitive emotions.

> Forty. I sit here shivering. I want to throw up. What is wrong with me? Why am I so nauseated? What brings so much fear? I write about the past. Almost thirty years ago. Why do I feel so sick writing this? Why am I so cold?[22]

Insidiously, these emotions have a way of undermining whatever fragile sense of identity has been formulated; of reversing the tables. Hate of the other can all too easily flip into self-hatred.

> My thoughts sail off the edge of my known world, leaving me with a bitter after-taste of guilt. Guilt for what? For father-hate. It is a serpent that turns back on me, infecting me with the poison of self-loathing.[23]

These women realize that theirs is not a permanent peace, a solid self that is impervious to further emotional turmoil. But a measure of calm and understanding has been achieved. Their writing has enabled them to recuperate a part of their lives that was lost or relegated to an inaccessible file, because it was so indescribably painful. Their insight into the repercussions of this episode on their lives has permitted them to feel and experience life in ways that were previously impossible. Tentative affirmations are possible.

> Always I was travelling from darkness into the light. In such journeys, time is our ally, not our enemy. We can grow wise. As the arteries harden, the spirit can lighten. As the legs fail, the soul can take wing. Things do add up. Life does have shape and maybe even purpose. Or so it seems to me.[24]

Vale Allen has continued to write, to appreciate of the nebulous distinction between fiction and reality and its recuperative value. But she has also come to appreciate the power of words, not just as therapy, but as advocacy, as stating one's case. Her happiness in this sense of achievement is wonderfully palpable:

> I'm very happy writing. I'm able to live out every dream, every fantasy I've ever had. I can deal with injustice, unfairness, the problems women face; I can say, on paper, what I think. It's illuminating, and almost illicitly pleasurable. I have a home, a career, a child, and a large measure of peace.[25]

It is Danica, however, in her elliptical style, who fashions and polishes words until they glow, until they convey in single utterances the power and terrible beauty of the insights she has gleaned:

> Woman. Dreaming. The mind. Freedom. Bestowed from within. Self. This night. No longer dark. Star messages. Silver and gold. Blessings. I dream. I love. I am.[26]

These are not cautionary tales. They are exemplifications of the dynamic of reclamation, but one where the process can never be complete, for many reasons. As a result, I would hesitate to say that these women have recovered the self that was denied them. Rather, through an exercise, both lengthy and intense, to the point of desperation, they have been able to piece together fragments of their past which, in a sense, had never been theirs to claim.

It is not as if they are also accepting responsibility for these incidents. Indeed, they come to understand how responsibility had been all too rudely wrested away from them. But in naming the experience, in finding the words to contain the original devastation, it is as if they protect themselves (though never completely) from further uninvited psychic and emotional assault. By naming the experience, they achieve a measure of distance, of a fragile hold on the present.

Yet a confusion of emotions remains, exerting disruptive powers because their source is virtually too intimidating, too powerful, to be eradicated entirely. It was a mesmerizing interference in their lives that nonetheless needs to be faced and exorcised. Their achievement is, by their writing, to confront the forces that have and could continue to dominate their lives. This is not absolute mastery, for a residue will always remain, but a space has been cleared where each woman can integrate into her life a measure of disengagement by a narrative retelling of a pivotal and potentially destructive experience. A further thread has been incorporated into the weaving of a life, giving a measure of proportion to the pattern. And the process will continue – never complete, yet never totally out of control.

In this sense I feel that neither a theory of ideal types nor one of totally dislocated subjects is appropriate. What is conveyed by these narratives is the need for a sense of coherence, however provisional, in these women's lives. On reflection, patterns emerge that reflect the diverse aspects and influences of the past. There is never a comprehensive viewpoint or an integrated conclusion. Instead there are multifaceted crisscrossing threads that constitute the texture of our lives. Narrative is a schema for delineating such perspectives. These manoeuvers are not omniscient in the service of a master plot, neither are they totally chaotic, or irredeemable as formative episodes. I believe it is the charting of these various roles and experiences as plots (albeit not those of an orthodox sequential variety) that provide the basis for what I would call a strategic or narrative sense of identity. Narrative is, in this form, a mediation that allows us to name and claim aspects of our lives, perhaps, as for these women, for the first time.

From a philosophical perspective, the basic issue concerns the viability of this composite of a narrative or strategic self, born, as Ricoeur would say, of the dialectic of *idem* and *ipse*. In what way is it a mediation between the deflated pretensions of an essentialist or egocentric self, on one hand, and alternately, the indeterminacies of the decentered postmodern subject?

My ruminations on this subject have been greatly aided by movements in contemporary feminist thought, in this particular instance by the work of Jane Flax, "Thinking Fragments: Psychoanalysis, Feminism and Postmodernism in the Contemporary West."[27] Flax's work mirrors the growing unease that many feminists have with a unilateral modern rejection of subjectivity, with its concomitant wariness of notions of agency. At the same time, however, Flax is suspicious of any assumption of immediate access to a self that is authoritative and has pretensions to atemporal stability. This leads her to a re-examination of postmodern thinkers, such as Derrida and Foucault. She arrives at an awareness that their thoroughgoing distrust of subjective presumptions does not utterly abolish a possible recuperation of a chastened format of subjectivity. Indeed, inherent in the work of both Derrida and Foucault, Flax detects an unthematized notion of subjectivity that operates along aesthetic rather than conceptual lines. As Flax observes: "For, though they denounce any essentialist or universalist notion of human nature, their work also incorporates a profoundly romantic/aesthetic dimension."[28] This aesthetic aspect of subjectivity features as a participant in a movement in which it both constructs yet suspects itself simultaneously. Thus, initially, both Derrida and Foucault seemed to advocate the construction of a playing field where the game of identity is deployed in a fast and loose fashion. What can be observed in this game is that there is nonetheless (though not immediately apparent) a sense of continuity, that in fact cultivates and is cultivated by the game. Their later work, however, clarifies certain misconceptions and points respectively to more deliberate articulations of the conditions of possibility for the emergence of subjectivity.[29]

Flax's own observation on the type of subjectivity employed here reflects her work as a psychotherapist, which she conducts in tandem with her academic research as a political scientist. Flax comments: "Those who celebrate or call for a decentered self seem self-deceptively naive and unaware of the basic cohesion within themselves that makes the fragmentation of experiences something other than a terrifying slide into psychosis."[30]

Flax's work with psychotic patients, whose every effort is to try to establish some tenuous toehold on a configuration of self, illuminates the gratuitously assumed self-cohesion on the part of certain postmodernists who can so cavalierly dispense with other semblances of the self. In this apparent inconsistency, Flax discerns a failure to distinguish between two different understandings of self or identity:

> Postmodernists seem to confuse two different and logically distinct concepts of the self: a "unitary" one and a "core" one. All possible forms of self are confounded with the unitary, mentalist, deeroticized, masterful and positional selves they rightfully criticize.[31]

And it is this core sense of self (as distinct from the unitary one), that Flax is trying to help her psychotic patients reclaim – that Flax feels is particularly pertinent for contemporary feminists who are trying to delineate an appropriate sense of identity. And this is where I believe that Ricoeur's and Flax's diagnosis of the situation have similar reverberations for depicting a modified sense of identity. For it could be said that Flax's *unitary* sense of self closely approximates Ricoeur's sense of *idem*, while the *core* sense has existential implications that are similar to those of *ipse*. It is in their applied therapeutics, however, that the emphasis varies. (Ricoeur depicts a constant interplay that is both theoretical and practical between the two forms of identity, whereas Flax appeals to life experience and therapeutic intervention to help establish a stabilized, if provisional, sense of self.)

Such a process would also imply a continuous movement from theory to praxis, so that the strategic self is firmly grounded in lived experience. For Ricoeur, it is this practical engagement that prevents his construct of the "narrative self" from being absorbed into the interminable dislocations that mark the postmodern position. In this connection, for Ricoeur the conventional conflation of *idem* and *ipse* in the definition of identity can be understood as the indicator of the unitary temptation to abstraction that will haunt all our projects of self-definition. This urge, however, is constantly in need of disruption by critical appreciation of the dynamic oscillations of everyday life, so that the differentiation between *idem* and *ipse* may emerge.

In Ricoeur's model, this disruption is supplied by the non-convergence of *idem* and *ipse* – a non-synthesis that questions any easy congruence of theory and lifeworld. Yet, at the same time, this incompatibility is witness to a type of continuation in identity that subsists and persists in diversity and that is not to be confused with unilateral pronouncements. Ricoeur's work, in this sense, moves beyond the simply disruptive decontextualized devices of deconstruction. His appeal to a sense of self that issues in and through the narrative mode can thus be understood as holding in tension (within a practical setting) the very disparate elements that discourage the formation of any ideal self.

And it is here that more discriminating work needs to be done. In her first book, Flax does not elaborate on what a core sense of self actually is or consists of. This is a highly contentious topic in contemporary psychoanalysis, for its critique argues that the core sense of self remains embedded with assumptions of Western normative ego-psychology and that its notion of agency is both apolitical and ahistorical in its orientation.[32] But I do not think that it is this form of "core" self to which Flax is referring. Flax is in fact using "core" in opposition to the unitary sense of self which she depicts as indebted to the Enlightenment view of reason as objective and homogeneous, and of humans as inherently autonomous in their use of reason to define their identity. Thus, there is a need to refine what Flax intends by "core" as distinct from this contemporary psychoanalytic usage (which in fact seems more in accord with Flax's description of the unitary self). In a more recent work, *Disputed Subjects: Essays on Psychoanalysis, Politics and Philosophy*, Flax gives more indications as to how she understands the notion of "core self." Here she states that:

> Our contingent experiences, for example, how each person is held, nurtured, attended to, or stimulated, may deeply affect how and what we think. Unconscious processes operate outside and by different rules from those of rational thought.[33]

What Flax wants to emphasize by her notion of core self is the contextual aspects of our lives and how these can interfere not just with the presumptions of reason but also with any absolutist or ideal sense of identity. The enlightened Western tradition and much of psychoanalysis, however, continues to project an image of mastery, of rational self-containment. When it is challenged, it often seems to imply that the only alternative is a type of pathological disintegration where all control and standards are abandoned. Flax wants to challenge both these scenarios: firstly, of a monolithic, triumphalist reason with its self-sufficiency, and secondly, of the spectacle of postmodern dissipation which is promoted as the inevitable counterposition. Neither takes into account the constant interplay of an embodied and emotional subject in a lifeworld where constellations of identity are formed and reformed. Identity is not something bestowed or definitively attained. Nor is it infinitely inaccessible or irrevocable. Perhaps Flax comes closest to her definition of a core self in the following statement:

> The task of therapy cannot be the discovery (or construction) of a solid, unitary, pristine, and undistorted self lying somewhere down deep inside. If this is our definition, patients are bound to be disappointed and feel inadequate and defeated. Subjectivity is not an illusion, but the subject *is* a shifting and always changing intersection of complex, contradictory, and unfinished processes.[34]

From this perspective,

> Experience is constantly reworked in conscious and unconscious ways as our cognitive and linguistic skills and intra- inter-subjective worlds and purposes change. Meanings of our experience are affected by and shift within different intra- or inter-subjective contexts. The (temporary) content and endings of our stories about our experiences are partially determined by the questions we and others pose. They are also shaped by the interventions and efforts of outer social structures and bodily changes that occur while we are reconstructing our narratives.[35]

Temporary coherence into seemingly solid characteristics or structures is only one of identity's many possible expressions. When enough strands are woven together, a solid entity may appear to form. Yet the flexibility of the threads and the fabric itself remains. What felt solid and real may subsequently separate and be reintegrated.

In conclusion, I also believe that the opposition of the diverse tendencies towards either changeless uniformity or incessant dissemination need not be tabled under the headings of modernity versus postmodernity, where they appear as mutually exclusive options. They constitute instead the paradox of any consciously lived existence and the always inadequate attempts to depict such vicissitudes in words. At the same time, in acknowledging this and welcoming the contribution of Ricoeur to such an articulation, I am aware that a more critical assessment needs to be undertaken regarding the work of Ricoeur on identity. In a recent article in the *Oxford Literary Review*, Pamela Anderson analyzes Ricoeur's entrenchment in the tradition of Descartes, Kant, and Hegel.[36] Despite Ricoeur's critique of modernist presuppositions, Anderson thinks that he remains within their orbit, virtually to the point of reappropriating a form of transcendental subjectivity. Such allegations need further careful exploration and evaluation, but it needs to be observed that Ricoeur's self-description as a post-Hegelian Kantian is modified considerably by a hermeneutic contextual sensitivity in his theory of narrative, so that he cannot be held to strict conformity with an abstract rationalist tradition.

In the meantime, it can be conceded that Ricoeur and Flax both provide vital insights into this on-going exploration of identity in a way that does justice to the intricacies of existence, without leaving us stranded with hypothetical intangibles that bear no relation to the aspirations or limitations of our lives. In this sense, a strategic identity can also be understood as a more realistic attempt to reflect the components of a mutable lifeworld, and to provide a base from which concrete responses to contemporary political and social challenges can be organized. This poetic resolution to the problematic of identity is thus intimately connected to a practical and critical commitment to change, not just with regard to one's perception of oneself, but with regard to that of the world.[37] There is no implication that this undertaking is an easy one, for it is fraught with the dissonance/consonance variables of time, place, and other contingencies that delimit the realization or our ownmost possibilities.

The dialectic, or rather dialogical, model that Ricoeur promotes and that I have qualified, allows for a constant interaction of both terms, and of participants, in all their modulations of heterogeneity. These exchanges of divergent views occur in a social context where life is never held hostage to theory. There is a dynamic process, where a range of variables, both theoretical and practical, is taken into consideration. In such a setting, feminist as well as other contemporary discussions of identity need not remain fixated in an antithetical posturing, but can explore the innovative insights that an open-ended conversation in a plurivocal mode encourages.

Notes

1 Patricia Waugh, *Feminine Fictions: Revisiting the Postmodern* (London: Routledge, 1989), 9.

2 Bella Brodzki and Celeste M. Schenck ed., *Theorizing Women's Autobiography*, (Ithaca: Cornell University Press, 1988); The Personal Narratives Group, ed., *Interpreting Women's Lives: Feminist Theory and Personal Narratives* (Bloomington: Indiana University Press, 1989); Sidonie Smith, *A Poetics of Women's Autobiography* (Bloomington: Indiana University Press, 1987; Shari Benstock, ed., *The Private Self: Theory and Practice of Women's Autobiographical Writings* (Chapel Hill: University of North Carolina, 1988).

3 An exemplar of this attitude to autobiography would be the work of G. Gusdorf, "Conditions and Limits of Autobiography," in James Olney, ed., *Autobiography: Essays Theoretical and Critical* (Princeton: Princeton University Press, 1980), 28-48.

4 Michel Foucault, "What is an Author?", *The Foucault Reader*, ed. P. Rabinow (New York: Pantheon, 1984), 101-120.

5 Judith Butler, "Contingent Foundations," *Feminists Theorize the Political*, ed. Judith Butler and Joan W. Scott (New York: Routledge, 1992), 3-21.

6 Julia Kristeva, *In the Beginning was Love: Psychoanalysis and Faith*, trans. A. Goldhammer (New York: Columbia University Press, 1987), 8.

7 Susan J. Hekman, *Gender and Knowledge: Elements of a Postmodern Feminism* (Boston: Northeastern University Press, 1990).

8 Shari Benstock, "Authorizing the Autobiographical," *The Private Self*, 21.

9 Paul Ricoeur, "Life: A Story in Search of a Narrator," *Facts and Values: Philosophical Reflections from Western and Non-Western Perspectives*, ed. M.C. Doeser and J.N. Kraay, (Dordrecht: Martinus Nijhoff, 1986), 131.

10 Paul Ricoeur, *Time and Narrative*, III, trans. Kathleen Blamey and David Pellauer (Chicago: University of Chicago Press, 1988), 246.

11 Paul Ricoeur, *Oneself as Another*, trans. Kathleen Blamey (Chicago: University of Chicago Press, 1992).

12 *Recollecting Our Lives*, Women's Research Centre (Vancouver: Press Gang Publ., 1989); Carol Poston and Karen Lison, *Reclaiming our Lives* (Boston: Little, Brown and Co., 1989).

13 Elly Danica, *Don't: A Woman's Word* (Charlottetown, P.E.I.: Gynergy Books, 1988).

14 Charlotte Vale Allen, *Daddy's Girl* (New York: Vintage, 1980).

15 Sylvia Fraser, *My Father's House: A Memoir of Incest and Healing* (Toronto: Doubleday, 1987).

16 Danica, *Don't*, 92.

17 Vale Allen, *Daddy's Girl*, 94.

18 Fraser, *My Father's House*, 250.

19 Danica, *Don't*, 70.

20 Vale Allen, *Daddy's Girl*, 94.

21 Fraser, *My Father's House*, 251.

22   Danica, *Don't*, 43.

23   Fraser, *My Father's House*, 77.

24   Fraser, *My Father's House*, 253.

25   Vale Allen, *Daddy's Girl*, 95.

26   Danica, *Don't*, 94.

27   Jane Flax, *Thinking Fragments: Psychoanalysis, Feminism and Postmodernism in the Contemporary West* (Berkeley: University of California Press, 1990).

28   Flax, *Thinking Fragments*, 216.

29   See Jacques Derrida, "'Eating Well,' or the Calculation of the Subject: An Interview with Jacques Derrida," in *Who Comes after the Subject?*, ed. E. Cadava, P. Connor and J.-L. Nancy (New York: Routledge, 1991), and Michel Foucault, "Technologies of the Self," in *Technologies of the Self: A Seminar with Michel Foucault*, ed. Luther H. Martin *et al.* (Amherst: University of Massachusetts Press, 1988), 16-49.

30   Flax, *Thinking Fragments*, 218-9.

31   Flax, *Thinking Fragments*, 218.

32   In this connection, I am thinking of the recent reviews by Philip Cushman, Haim Omer and Carlo Strenger. See, in particular, Philip Cushman, "Ideology Obscured: Political Uses of the Self in Daniel Stern's Infant," *American Psychologist* 46/3(March, 1991): 206-19.

33   Jane Flax, *Disputed Subjects: Essays on Psychoanalysis, Politics and Philosophy* (New York: Routledge, 1993), 83.

34   Flax, *Disputed Subjects*, 107-8.

35   Flax, *Disputed Subjects*, 108.

36   Pamela Anderson, "Having it Both Ways: Ricoeur's Hermeneutics of the Self," *Oxford Literary Review* 15/1-2 (1993): 227-52.

37   Paul Ricoeur's argument is that narrative can offer a "poetic" resolution to the aporias that result from trying to define both time and identity according to strictly rational categories. See *Time and Narrative*, III, trans. Kathleen McLaughlin and David Pellauer (Chicago: University of Chicago Press, 1984), 66.

Re-reading Myth in Philosophy: Hegel, Ricoeur and Irigaray Reading *Antigone*

PAMELA ANDERSON

I. Introduction

I am not a classicist, nor am I an authority on the philosophy of G.W.F. Hegel or the feminism of Luce Irigaray. However, recently, my interest in reading the figure, Antigone, in Sophocles' ancient tragedy has been aroused – first – by Paul Ricoeur's "Interlude" in *Oneself as Another*.[1]

Ricoeur offers a brief reading of this figure of woman from Sophocles' play. This is the mythical woman who, according to Ricoeur's narrative, "acts in the service of spiritual powers" when she defies the king, her uncle, in order to fulfill her familial duty as sister to give a proper burial to her brother, even though he has become an enemy of the city and she will, consequently, be forced to face her own death alone with no friends nor family to mourn her. But, perhaps surprisingly, in Ricoeur's judgment Antigone's moral failure is also due to her lack of knowledge of a "political distinction," which results in a tragic liaison with the god/ goddesses of death.[2] In his words:

> The bond between sister and brother, which knows nothing of the political distinction between friend and enemy, is inseparable from the service of divinities of the underworld and transforms the family bond into a sinister pact with death.[3]

Following this judgment on the supposedly blind single-mindedness of Antigone's familial bond, Ricoeur directs readers to Hegel,[4] as well as to more contemporary readings of *Antigone* by George Steiner and Martha Nussbaum. And with this direction, my interest is aroused – second – by the impressive variety of readings of the same myth in philosophy and, especially, readings of *Antigone* by such feminist philosopher-critics as Luce Irigaray.[5]

Reflection in an indirect manner upon *Antigone* leads to thinking about philosophical interpretations of women in myth and about the way in which (male) philosophers in particular have formulated, perhaps unconsciously, these interpretations of women by reading myth. And, at risk of a platitude, it does seem remarkable that specific myths of women and of femininity continue to have a consistent hold on individuals and cultures, male and female. Yet there is always the *possibility* of different interpretations of women in these enduring myths.

By "myth," let us agree minimally with Hans Blumenberg that

> Myths are stories [which] are distinguished by a high degree of constancy in their narrative core and by an equally pronounced capacity for marginal variation. These two characteristics make myths transmissible by tradition: their constancy produces the attraction of recognizing them in artistic or ritual representation as well [as recital], and their variability produces the attraction of trying out new and personal means of presenting them. It is the relationship of "theme and variations," whose attractiveness for both composers and listeners is familiar from music. So myths are not like "holy texts," which cannot be altered by one iota.[6]

A comparison of myth with music is also implicit in the title, "Interlude," of Ricoeur's section on *Antigone*. The "Interlude" (*L'interlude*) constitutes a short piece which is presented between the parts of a more sustained argument. Moreover, concerning myth, Ricoeur would agree to the existence of a core of narrative constancy as well as to myth's marginal variability; but he stresses that myth is irreducible to secular history insofar as myth invokes the spiritual powers of divinities (or, as we might say, of gods and goddesses) which point to the inevitable limit of human institutions.

In the case of *tragedy*, myth develops out of the spectacle of unmerited suffering which both provokes and purifies enduring human passions. So Ricoeur would seem to connect the constancy of mythical narrative with a generic understanding of "the human" and, in particular, the limitations pointed to by the deliberation of the tragic hero or heroine who suffers unjustly but with – apparently blind – steadfastness. And, in the particular case of Antigone, the tragic heroine's steadfastness has been interpreted by Nussbaum and Ricoeur, at least, as a blind single-mindedness. According to Nussbaum, this sort of blindness is apparent in Antigone's deliberation which simplifies the motives for action in becoming single-minded and so removing the difficulty of internal moral conflicts. Nussbaum also calls this simplification of motives "a strategy of avoidance" (of moral conflicts).[7]

However, concerning Antigone's steadfastness, we will read other (female) philosophers who insist over and against Hegel (and so by implication Ricoeur) upon Antigone's tough-minded, not blind devotion to what is both noble and just. Antigone's steadfastness is not, according to this other interpretation, an unconscious intuition of familial duty nor an unreflective position defined by her gender, but a courageous stance, consciously taken and held, in the light of clear moral alternatives.[8]

To crystallize this issue of conflicting interpretations, it needs to be recognized that different readings of Antigone's steadfastness raise a crucial, critical question concerning the nature of women's action(s). Specifically, does Antigone's steadfastness imply single-mindedness? One alternative is to agree, as Ricoeur does, that Antigone's action reflects, in Nussbaum's terms, "a strategy of simplification"[9] in the one-sidedness of motive. But, if this is accepted as an appropriate reading, is the one-sidedness of Antigone a "tragic flaw"? According to Ricoeur, the answer seems to be "yes." The one-sidedness of equal, but opposite principles and characters is determined by three factors which constitute *tragedy*: (*i*) fate which goes beyond any deliberate choice; (*ii*) spiritual powers which in some sense determine morality/immorality; and (*iii*) human passions.

Alternatively, it has been argued that the tragedy of Antigone's actions is not marked by the flaw of being one-sided or single-minded. Rather the tragedy is connected with the all-too-common fragmentation of women's identities.[10] We will return to this argument later on.

What is not clear in Ricoeur's "Interlude," but is of critical interest in this context, are the implications of gender in the suffering of Antigone, the tragic heroine. Is gender part of the narrative core which remains constant, e.g., the role and intuition of women in family life? Or is it part of that which is variable? Conflicting answers can be – and have been – given to such questions. Yet what is clear in Ricoeur and of interest remains (in his recent as well as earlier writings) myth's variability. This variability makes myth irreducible to its narrative core and so allows for innovative interpretations of mythical characters, in Ricoeurian terms, opening up actual and possible worlds.[11]

II. Questions of Gender: Myth or Philosophy?

In the light of the preceding introductory section, two relevant questions can be raised for further reflection: (*i*) Why might interpretations of women in myth, with both its narrative constancy and marginal variability, be especially significant for feminist as well as non-feminist philosophy? (*ii*) Philosophers could ask, do the specific characteristics of myth offer certain possibilities for interpretations of gendered action in mythical narratives which, otherwise, do not exist or have not existed for interpretations of philosophical texts? That is, it may be that in contrast to myth, philosophy has been held to be closer to those "holy texts," mentioned above by Blumenberg, which cannot be altered by one iota, especially when it comes to either (female) gender or "the human." It would, then, seem to be significant for those concerned with our inescapably genderized intellectual tradition that Antigone remains a mythical figure of woman/women who can be read either as an archetypal woman or as resistant to male and female stereotypes.

To illustrate this point of significance, at the very same time as Antigone seems to defy any univocal reading, she has been eulogized by male philosophers, artists, poets, etc., as the highest embodiment of femininity. In Hegel's own words, "Antigone is the most beautiful description of femininity; she holds fast to the bond of the family against the [state's] law."[12] And in the words of translator and critical commentator, Richard Jebb,

> It is not without reason that moderns have recognized that figure as the noblest, and the most profoundly tender, embodiment of woman's heroism which ancient literature can show; but it is also distinctively a work of Greek art at the highest. It is marked by the singleness of motive, and the self-restraint, which belonged to such art; it deserves to be studied sympathetically, and as a whole; for there could be no better example of ideal beauty attained by truth to human nature.[13]

Yet Ricoeur queries,

> Finally, the company of the dead will leave [Antigone] without any fellow citizens, robbed of the help of the gods of the city, without husband and without offspring, and even without friends to mourn her (ll. 880-82). The figure that walks away into the distance is not simply a person who suffers but Suffering itself (ll. 892-928).
>
> Why, nevertheless, does our preference go to Antigone? Is it the woman's vulnerability in her that moves us? Is it because, as an extreme figure of nonviolence in the face of power, she alone has done no violence to anyone? Is it because her "sisterhood" reveals a quality of *philia* that is not altered by *eros*? Is it because the ritual of burial attests to a bond between the living and the dead, which reveals the limit of politics – more precisely, the limit of the relation of domination which, itself, does not exhaust the political tie?[14]

From the preceding line of questions, Ricoeur chooses to answer the last question only in the affirmative. He insists that tragedy instructs ethical life concerning the limit of every human law, of every human institution; and this answer does not seem to depend upon reading Antigone as a woman (nor, with some critics, as a woman who acts politically as a man). Yet what intrigues is that, in the context of a dense and difficult account of selfhood, Ricoeur singles out *Antigone* for his "Interlude." And this means singling out both the myth and the female figure by distinguishing them from philosophy and so indirectly raising an issue of Antigone's gender role or transcendence of that role. Ricoeur claims that his "Interlude," in reading myth, interrupts his sustained *philosophical* argument.[15] But this "untimely irruption" (*"l'irruption intempestive"*) of a myth is justifiable insofar as it allows tragic wisdom to instruct ethical life concerning the inevitability of moral conflicts.[16]

Ricoeur stipulates that ethical life be defined by "the aim of the good life with and for others in just institutions," while morality be defined by the norms or principles of obligation. He insists that the former, like Aristotle's ethics, constitutes a teleological vision and the latter, like Kant's norms of action, works to fulfill deontological principles.[17] Moreover, at the intersection of ethical life and morality – of universal and particular – it is appropriate that he bring in Hegel's attempt to overcome the conflict between city-state (*polis*) and family life, particularity and immediacy.[18] Ricoeur turns to Hegel's reading of women's role as represented by *Antigone* and reads the duties of her gender role as defined by the pagan world.

Thus, if we take Ricoeur and Hegel as exemplary, myth seems to be brought into philosophy and used – however indirectly – for addressing questions of gender.

III. Reading *Antigone* after Hegel

There is no doubt that the main subtext of Ricoeur's "Interlude" is Hegel's reading of *Antigone* in the *Phenomenology of Spirit*. Yet, as also noted, references are made to other critical texts including Steiner's *Antigones* and Nussbaum's reading of *Antigone* in *Fragility of Goodness*. The works of Steiner and Nussbaum color Ricoeur's Hegelian[19] reading of this myth as portraying an intractable conflict. Ricoeur's use of "Interlude" alone is suspiciously similar to Nussbaum's use of short metaphilosophical pieces, which she calls "Interludes" in *Fragility of Goodness*. And Ricoeur follows Steiner by claiming that Antigone's "ineffaceable permanence" has to do with the *content* of the conflicts between woman and man, divine and human, individual and state.[20] Steiner's *Antigones*, as "a study of the interactions between a major text and its interpretations across time," exposes the variety of possible readings of women in myth. At the same time, Steiner's study of the Western reception of *Antigone* suggests its enduring significance.[21]

Ricoeur's privileging of a Hegelian reading of *Antigone* as a clash between equal, but opposite characters and duties is not inconsistent with his reliance upon Nussbaum and Steiner.[22] As Steiner confirms, Hegel has had an immeasurable effect on nineteenth- and twentieth-century readings of Sophocles' play:

> the influence of commentary, particularly where it is of a philosophic or political tenor, also acts indirectly. Not very many general readers will have come across Hegel's *Antigone* interpretations at first hand. But the Hegelian reading of the play as a dialectical conflict of equal opposites has been widely disseminated in the climate of literacy as well as that of theatrical presentation.[23]

And yet it is precisely the Hegelian reading of Antigone's tragedy as a dialectical conflict of equal opposites which, although accepted by Ricoeur at the very least, has been challenged by various other critics. In particular, certain female critics, whether feminist or not, have rejected this influential "Hegelian" reading of *Antigone*, while either recognizing it as Hegel's, or rejecting it as an inadequate and uncritical reading of Hegel.

It might be thought that, insofar as Hegel focuses upon the myth of the daughter and not that of the father/son, his reading of *Antigone* as a sort of feminine heroine could have something to offer feminists. Perhaps, this would mean trying to argue that, in contrast to Sigmund Freud's preoccupation with the *Oedipus* myth, there is certain value for women in Hegel's account of "the everlasting irony [in the life] of the community."[24] The argument, then, would have to be something like the following: Hegel recognizes the crucial role of femininity in natural ethical life, and it was really only long after Hegel that philosophy, influenced by the pervasive Freudian reading of *Oedipus Rex*, turned away from the possibilities of reading women in myth. Freud decisively subordinates matriarchy to patriarchy and, as is well known, after Freud, femininity became an enigma. This argument would assume that Freud decisively shifted modern thinking away from the daughter and maternal line to the notorious son who kills his own father and marries his own mother and, in turn, becomes a father.

However, the counter-argument is that prior to psychoanalytic readings of *Oedipus*, Antigone's story was already read in the light of the incestuous struggles of her father who is also her more-than-half brother and of her father's son who is also her uncle. Interestingly, the implications for women and for "femininity" in Hegel's reading of *Antigone*, as acting publicly in defiance of the king while fulfilling her familial duty (i.e., to the house of Oedipus) are not much better than those in Freud's reading of *Oedipus*. Ultimately, by being read as guardian of her brother (i.e., of her father's son and her father's half-brother) even in his death, Antigone is interpreted as guardian of the paternal, not the maternal line. Moreover, Antigone's action is further subordinated by patriarchy, since in Hegelian terms the act on behalf of her brother cannot be mutual: no one will bury or mourn her in death.

Female and/or feminist critics tend to support this latter critical reading of Hegel. That is, perhaps despite himself, in choosing Antigone, who is daughter of Oedipus, Hegel appears preoccupied with the incestuous nature of family life, as well as with what we might today call a gender privileging of the father/son and, possibly, brother/sister relationships over the mother/daughter or sister/sister. The preoccupation with incest and the privileging of male gender are evident, despite

Hegel's idealized claims concerning the mutual recognition of brother and sister. As Patricia Jagentowicz Mills maintains,

> [the] paradigm of mutual recognition between sister and brother, which is supposed to be devoid of desire [according to Hegel], is rooted in the incestuous origins of the house of Thebes. Antigone's father, Oedipus, is also her brother making Polyneices her uncle as well as her brother and she his aunt as well as his sister. In choosing this seemingly atypical family to represent the family as natural ethical life, Hegel gives significance to the Oedipus myth long before Freud.[25]

Luce Irigaray also rereads the "Hegelian dream" of an unsullied, i.e., supposedly without desire, relationship between brother and sister. Irigaray, informed by the psychoanalytic tradition, develops a richly nuanced and radical rereading of *Antigone after* and *against* Hegel – and, more generally, against Freud and Jacques Lacan.[26] For one thing, she reads Antigone's public act of defiance as a "digestion of the masculine." In her words,

> if Antigone gives proof of a bravery, a tenderness and an anger that free her energies and motivate her to resist that *outside* which the city represents for her, this is certainly because she had digested the masculine. At least partially at least for a moment.[27]

For another thing, Irigaray inverts Hegel's reading of Antigone by demonstrating the significance of the mother/daughter relationship. The daughter identifies with the mother not only in burying her mother's son but in feeling guilty for being born, like her brother, of incestuous embraces. This daughter who remains faithful to her mother must be excluded from the city, from society: "she must be ... deprived of freedom, air, light, love, marriage, children."[28] Jocasta, wife of Oedipus and mother to Antigone, Polynices and Ismene, remains the silent mother's voice in the myth; the relationship of mother and daughter collapses when Antigone acts and grieves as Jocasta would have.[29] Furthermore, on the one hand, the myth of *Antigone* represents the closing off of the possibility of future maternal genealogies or matrilineal readings. Yet, on the other hand, with Antigone there is an attempt to claim the mother's blood tie.[30]

In contrast, Ricoeur's "Interlude" on Antigone's tragic action raises no questions concerning mother/daughter or the maternal blood tie. And he merely asserts that the relationship between sister and brother involves a quality of brotherly love unaltered by *eros*. In following Hegel in his reading of *Antigone* (and not turning to Freud on *Oedipus Rex*), Ricoeur reveals his traditional reliance on ancient and modern western philosophy, in general, as well as on a patriarchal reading of myth in particular, according to which archetypal man acts over and against archetypal woman. Attention is not, in fact, placed centrally upon the brother and sister relationship, nor for that matter upon the mother/ daughter identity, but rather upon the different visions of justice represented by Creon and Antigone, king and non-citizen. Consequently, Ricoeur's Hegelian reading of a patriarchal myth may itself be put in dispute by critics, feminist and non-feminist.

Roughly, three lines of criticism have gradually emerged. First, some philosophers read *Antigone* more or less according to Hegel – as Ricoeur does – as a conflict between intractable sets of (supposed equal) duties and motives.

Second, others (e.g., Mills, above) critically read Hegel's *Antigone* and are more sympathetic to the motives of Antigone than either Ricoeur or Nussbaum are. In particular, cogent arguments are given against reading Antigone as if she represents women's actions as tragically trapped in a conflict of equal opposites. This second sort of critical reading points out what is missing both in Hegel and in readings of Hegel. For instance, the central *conflict* between Antigone and Creon, ruled and ruler, tends to be scrutinized, but there remains more to be assessed in Hegel's proposed ideal *relationship* of mutual recognition between Antigone and Polynices, sister and brother. Also it is noticed that Hegel disregards the sister-sister relationship, yet describes the family as a sphere of womankind without showing any curiosity about the relations between women. But this response still remains a critical reading rather than a disruptive rereading of Hegel.

Third, other feminist philosophers who follow Irigaray (e.g., Chanter and Pritchard) disruptively reread *Antigone*. That is, they read Hegel's Antigone *against* him, seeking to collapse the binary oppositions by playing upon various nuances of gender identities. Notably, there is Antigone's so-called, "digestion of the masculine," in acting publicly as and on behalf of a male. In contrast, the many nuances of gender identities are totally missed when one follows Nussbaum's reading of a strategy of simplification[31] or Ricoeur's reading of (Hegelian) genderized oppositions. Different from either a conflict-of-opposites reading of Hegel or a critical exegesis of Hegel's Antigone, this disruptive rereading aims to subvert strict oppositions of male/female, divine/human, by revealing the various unconscious motives in the actions between brother and sister, of mother and daughter, sister and sister, which are made evident in women's internally and externally fragmented sense of self.

IV. One-sided Motive or Fragmented Identities?

The preceding sections suppose that Hegel gives an account of Antigone in which the motive of her action has been read as one-sided. In line with this reading of Hegel and *Antigone*, Ricoeur states that

> What *Antigone* teaches about the tragic wellspring of action was indeed perceived by Hegel in the *Phenomenology of Spirit* ... namely the narrowness of the angle of commitment of each of the characters.[32]

He, next, continues

> [but] the source of conflict lies not only in the one-sidedness of the *characters* but also in the one-sidedness of the moral *principles* which themselves are confronted with the complexity of life.[33]

Ricoeur, then, finds in Nussbaum's *Fragility of Goodness* a rich resource for preserving the complexity of moral life. But it is Nussbaum as a classicist and moral philosopher who recognizes in the characters of Sophocles' original narrative both a strategy which aims to avoid moral conflict and a strategy which seeks to simplify moral duties with steadfastness to one motive. It should be stressed that Nussbaum does not (first) base her reading of Antigone's motive in action upon Hegel's philosophical reading of myth, but upon the original tragic play.

Besides considering Nussbaum's reading of the one-sided motive in *Antigone*, Ricoeur reads the resulting conflict of opposite principles in terms of Steiner's reading. In particular, he recalls Steiner's description of the *agonistic* ground of human experience, which constitutes the interminable confrontations of man and woman, living and dead, society and family, human and divine. Yet, in contrast with Nussbaum, Steiner counsels against trying to read the original play, since the *Ur-Antigone* is irretrievable.[34]

Still different from any in the trio of Ricoeur, Nussbaum and Steiner, Patricia Jagentowicz Mills represents a second line of criticism. In "Hegel's *Antigone*," Mills presents a lucid exposition which may confirm that Hegel reads the myth as a conflict between equal and contrary principles. However, Mills's different line of criticism emerges in arguing cogently that Hegel's reading is a gross oversimplification of the women's actions in the myth.[35] It is Mills who points to Hegel's failure to consider Antigone in contrast to her sister, Ismene. This contrast would have demonstrated that Antigone does not in fact display the "natural ethical orientation," which, according to Hegel, is required of her sex. The ethical orientation of womankind is to remain within the realm of the family, i.e., of private life, and so to follow "first nature." However, Antigone directs her action towards the *polis* and so threatens to follow a "second nature" – something which is not a natural characteristic of her sex.

Finally, as already recognized, the third line of criticism ultimately aims to subvert Hegel and Hegelian readings of *Antigone*. This line may agree to a certain degree with the preceding interpretation, but it is further influenced by Irigaray's "The Eternal Irony of the Community," in *Speculum of the Other Women*. Following Irigaray, Tina Chanter, for instance, reads Antigone's dilemmas against Hegel and maintains that Antigone is successful in subverting the relationship between family and city-state:

> In *taking on* her brother's death, in performing the burial rights denied him by the polis, Antigone is precisely taking on a male role. Insofar as she puts his honor before her fulfillment as a woman, she is not acting as a woman, but, in the courage that it takes to defy the king's command, she acts as if she were a man ... subverting the relationship between family and polis ... she crosses the boundary between private and public. She elevates her duty to her brother above the political significance of his public action ... and thereby transforms her familial duty into an act of political defiance.[36]

Chanter reflects Irigaray's account of Antigone's "digestion of the masculine." That is, in her fulfillment of familial duties, Antigone acts publicly in the place of, as well as for her brother. And this is only one way in which Antigone's identity as a woman is reinterpreted as fragmented between public and private lives, between male and female roles. By emphasizing this fragmentation, readings of Antigone's actions influenced by Irigaray suggest a breakdown in the distinction between masculine and feminine gender. The act of defying the king is a public action and as such divides Antigone against herself as a woman, since in the ancient Greek *polis* all public action is reserved for men. In addition, Antigone's actions in burying and grieving her dead brother are thought to collapse the relationship of mother and daughter: in publicly expressing her feelings at the death of her brother and her own imminent death, Antigone represents the voice of her dead mother, Jocasta, who suffers the loss of her son and her daughter. Thus, Antigone's consciousness is both split as maternal sister and divided against herself as a female who acts as a male agent. Her fragmentation brings into question any sharp distinction between private and public identities. Moreover, she both undermines any neat division of gender roles, of masculinity and femininity and breaks down such hierarchical, binary oppositions as male over female, public over private sexual identities. Put roughly, the mythical configurations of Antigone's actions can help us rethink the sex/gender system that has become most apparent in the late twentieth century.[37]

This third line of criticism works with the multiple ways in which the myth continues to be interpreted and reinterpreted by philosophers today, male and female. That *Antigone* is still one of our most powerful western myths is due (in part) to the way in which its tragedy emerges along with various images of female identity. To rephrase my introductory point, the images – like the myth – exhibit both a constancy and a variability.

But a choice between the questions of two different readings still remains for the critical philosopher:

i. Do the images and characters in the myth confirm both the one-sidedness of women who are locked into intractable, genderized conflicts and the domination of men over women, *or*

ii. Do the mythical images and actions offer the possibility of reading women against the genderized tradition insofar as they seem to be fragmented by complex, conflicting duties and desires, e.g., duties to and/or desires for brother, mother, family, goddesses of the earth and the underworld, even duties to the State as guardians of the family?

An affirmative answer to the first question would basically reflect the dilemma of the modern woman who seeks to step out of her private role in the family (which is "natural" for a patriarchal society), but finds that such uncharacteristic action of her sex only ends a conflict with the opposite sex. A negative answer to the first question and an affirmative answer to the second would roughly suggest the dilemma of the postmodern woman who wants to assert her lack of a unified identity, yet has to wonder whether or not acknowledgment of a fragmented self will only render her actions meaningless and her agency impotent.

If we turn to interpret the myth, we do find rich images of women as goddess of birth and death, guardian of passing in and out of life. There are also images which connect women and nature. These include images of women as wildness, as blind to political law, as uncultivated, as a field to be ploughed and so on. Essentially, such images have sustained patriarchy with the belief that both women and nature must be subordinated by the ordering power of male reason.

In the light of this patriarchal affiliation of ideas and images, it is also necessary to consider the dangers and possibilities for women reading myth in philosophy with examples of passages that connect nature and women. This connection can be illustrated by a reading of the Chorus's famous "Ode to Man" in Sophocles' play.[38] The Ode is sung before Antigone's capture for having defied the king and buried her brother Polynices. And, essentially, it is concerned with the taming of a wild nature in order to aid the progress of man (sic). The images of domination and particularly the rape of nature (which will be picked up in association with women) that pervade this lyric ode underscore the fact that women must also be overcome for the greater advance of patriarchy. That is, the images of nature as female can be read as indicating the necessity of (male) reason to control the irrational defined as nature, as well as indicating the superiority of the laws of the city as male (i.e., as patriarchal). Later, when Creon speaks, he connects the Chorus's images of nature with women – implying that both women and nature need to be dominated. This is particularly noticeable where Creon states metaphorically that when Antigone is dead, "there are other fields for [Haemon] to plough."[39] Thus, the "Ode to Man" centers on the ambiguously *creative/destructive* aspects of human (sic male) beings, enabling them to take the "brute" matter of nature – which includes women – and mold it. Arguably, such patriarchal images seem to constitute a "natural" basis for the oppression of women by denying them rationality. (Further illustration of this basis is apparent in the number of times Antigone's actions are called "mad" or "irrational"!)

So, finally, let us return to the crucial choice between the reading of mythical configurations either (*i*) to confirm the intractable, genderized conflicts under patriarchy, or (*ii*) to allow fragmented identities to be refigured so that we move beyond that which has been intractable in traditional interpretations. It is my contention that, notwithstanding philosophical disputes over whether or not the narrative of *Antigone* configures the one-sidedness of a woman's actions, one could interpret Antigone's actions in terms of her multiple identities. This would resist simplification to a single motive of familial duty preserving divine law – as opposed to male political or civil law. But, admittedly, there will always remain the danger of a univocal reading (whether patriarchal or matriarchal!) to suppress the fragile multiplicity of male/female identities. Strong univocity can constitute the power to control and oppress, while ambiguity and fragmentation may weaken self-identity, yet widen our horizons. Re-reading women and myth in philosophy exposes the power of images and narrative to be either exclusive or inclusive in its configurations of identity. Crucial to these alternatives is the possibility that myth's marginal variability could allow reading new visions, playing new variations on an old theme.

Some philosophers may not accept or believe in a utopian vision. Yet, in highly Ricoeurian terms and with reference to Irigaray's distinctive refiguring, Drucilla Cornell urges the utopian moment in feminism:

> We are trying to discover the possibility of the "way out" from our current system of gender identity in which "her" specificity opens up the unknown, in which sexual difference would not be re-appropriated. Through Irigaray's mimesis,[40] we move

within what has been prefigured so as to continually transfigure [refigure] it. We not only affirm Woman, we continually re-metaphorize her through the "as if."
The necessary utopian moment in feminism lies precisely in our opening up the possible through metaphoric transformation.[41]

The above language recalls Ricoeur's account of the way in which metaphor may "rule" the literal, as well as the way in which mimesis prefigures and refigures [transfigures] action.[42] But Irigaray employs *mimesis* in a unique and non-Ricoeurian sense. It does not include a configuration of reality, nor a prefiguration. Instead hers is a refiguring that aims to disrupt traditional discourse, to transform gender hierarchy.

V. Conclusion: Reading Women and Myth

The preceding sections have aimed to uncover certain possibilities in reading myth and reading women that do not (often) exist for philosophy and women. Here the inflexibility of philosophy is exemplified by a certain Hegelian dialectical reasoning which can distort and reduce Antigone's motives, since it inhibits reading the nuances of the characters' identities in myth. To reiterate, the possibility in reading women and myth lies in the marginal variability of myth which could, in turn, suggest potentially either creative or destructive aspects in the variability of women's fragmented identities.

Yet, if the general possibility of reading myth and women in ways which could contribute to debates concerning gender equality and difference is granted, there remain three specific questions for the particular case of *Antigone*. First, is Antigone the archetypal woman? Or second, in contrast to her sister, Ismene, is Antigone a rebel against her own sex – and so closer to being "male" in her actions? Third, is Antigone – as suggested by Irigaray and contended by other scholars – "digesting the masculine,"[43] even while remaining guardian of the (maternal) blood tie, sacrificing/resisting the role of wife,[44] and so transcending any homogeneous gender identity? Positive answers to this third question would probably give content to the utopian vision proposed by Cornell (as quoted above) and give reason to reformulate the possibilities of using Ricoeur's three forms of narrative *mimesis* to discover the "way out" from a rigid system of gender identity.

However, in order to explore such possibilities, it would be necessary to turn to the actual narrative, especially specific passages from Sophocles' play (although admittedly in translation) which provoke debatable readings. These can be read either with or against Hegel, according to the lines of criticism outlined in the previous two sections of this paper. Ultimately, informed by both Ricoeur and Irigaray, the task would seem to be to recognize the constancy of a narrative core and the variability of a mythical margin. What continues to seem problematical is Ricoeur's clear alliance with Hegel in his "Interlude" (an alliance which does not appear before or after this brief section). This alliance means that, for instance, "the human" – which includes human passions, human limitations, human fate and so on – remains part of the narrative core of tragic action. This would suggest that gender identity is not brought into question, instead "the human" is marked by the inevitable conflict of equal, but opposite gendered characters. In the end, the question remains: can gender identity be read as part of the variability on the margins of myth? When we turn to certain lines of the translated text of Sophocles' *Antigone*, gender identity does seem to be open to question – even to the refiguration of actual and possible worlds.

For example, consider the words spoken by Antigone,

> how many griefs our father Oedipus handed down!
> ... our lives are pain – no private shame, no public disgrace, nothing I haven't seen.[45]

These lines could indicate that the fate of the two sisters has been determined by their identity under patriarchy as daughters of Oedipus: they will die suffering for his guilt. Alternatively, these words could forecast Antigone's challenge to this paternal line as guardian of the maternal blood tie, even in death.

For a further example, consider the words of Ismene,

> we *must* be sensible. Remember we are women, we're not born to contend with men. Then too, we're underlings, ruled by much stronger hands, so we *must* submit in this.[46]

These lines could recall that the assumed gender role of women in a city-state of ancient Greece is represented by Ismene, Antigone's sister, but not by Antigone herself. Alternatively, the words of Ismene show, by contrast with Antigone's other actions, that female characters suffer the consequences of male action and of their own multiple identities; and so women's motives can *never* be *un*ambiguous.

To conclude, I would like to direct the reader back to the myths of women in philosophy. By rereading lines from a recent translation of Sophocles' *Antigone*, we may be able to recognize both the narrative's constancy and myth's variability. Ultimately, it is left to each of us to attempt the task of narrative refiguration. Using Ricoeur's threefold account of *mimesis*, we may be able to challenge the rigid gender identities that result in narratives of inevitable and tragic conflicts. Of course, this might mean that Ricoeur's mimetic form of narrative refiguration is turned back upon his own configuration of Antigone's tragic action in the "Interlude."

My final word is merely to stress the urgency of a *mythical* transformation. Such a transformation would have as its task to refigure, for instance, the highly genderized prefiguration of Antigone as spoken by Creon: "I am not the man, not now; she is the man if this victory goes to her and she goes free!"[47]

Notes

1 Paul Ricoeur, *Oneself as Another*, trans. Kathleen Blamey (Chicago: Chicago University Press, 1992), 241-9, 256.

2 Antigone herself and the Chorus in Sophocles' play both make references to Dionysus (or Bacchus), the god of ecstatic self-destruction, and to Persephone/Demeter, the goddess(es) of death. The Chorus's lyric ode to Dionysus reflects the ambivalent nature of this god as jubilant protector and menacing inhumanity, born (monstrously) of Zeus's lightning and dark earth, i.e., Semele's womb. See Sophocles, *The Three Theban Plays: Antigone, Oedipus the King, Oedipus at Colonus*, trans. Robert Fagles, with introduction by Bernard Knox (Oxford: Penguin Classics, 1984), lines 981-2, 1054, 1239-72.

3 Ricoeur, *Oneself as Another*, 242.

4 Ricoeur's judgment on Antigone's moral failure or culpability has a philosophical precedent. Within the framework of Hegel's *Phenomenology of Spirit*, Antigone remains "criminal" in that she upholds only the law of the family and does not recognize the law of the *polis*. In fact, despite suggesting that the laws of Creon and Antigone represent a conflict of equal opposites, Creon appears to be the real *hero* for Hegel. Antigone wittingly commits a "crime" but does not admit her "guilt." In contrast, Creon admits guilt for his crime and so, by self-recognition, achieves a higher ethical consciousness. See *Phenomenology of Spirit*, trans. A.V. Miller (Oxford: Oxford University Press, 1977), 276-7, 281-4, paragraphs 460-1, 468-70, respectively.

5 In particular, in her most recently translated reading of Antigone, Luce Irigaray objects to contemporary readings that present Antigone's actions as either anarchist or suicidal, as determined strictly by familial and religious *pathos*. See Irigaray, *Thinking the Difference: For a Peaceful Revolution*, trans. Karin Montin (London: The Athlone Press, 1994), 67-73, 85-6.

6 Hans Blumenberg, *Work on Myth*, trans. Robert M. Wallace (Cambridge, MA: MIT Press, 1985), 34.

7 Ricoeur recognizes Antigone's *steadfastness* but describes it as "one-sided" (*Oneself as Another*, 244-245). Here Ricoeur relies on Martha Nussbaum's account of *deliberation*, including the numerous Greek words used for deliberating in *Antigone*. See *Fragility of Goodness: Luck and Ethics in Greek Tragedy and Philosophy* (Cambridge: Cambridge University Press, 1986), 51f. Bernard Knox also describes Antigone's steadfastness, with glowing terms of "heroic individualism," in his "Introduction to *Antigone*," Sophocles, *The Three Theban Plays*, 53; cf. Richard Jebb, ed. and trans., "Preface," *Sophocles: The Plays and Fragments*, with critical notes, commentary and translation in English prose (Cambridge: Cambridge University Press, 1900), v-vi.

8 Patricia Jagentowicz Mills, "Hegel's *Antigone*," *The Owl of Minerva* (Spring 1986): 141.

9   Nussbaum, *Fragility of Goodness*, 63-5, 67.

10 Annie Pritchard, "Antigone's Mirrors: Reflections on Moral Madness," *Hypatia* 7/3 (Summer 1992): 81.

11 According to Ricoeur, the human imagination in its narrative activity – in its myth-making – opens up actual and possible worlds; so he seems to assume that a mythico-poetic nucleus of meaning resides at the center of human experience. See Paul Ricoeur, "Myth as the Bearer of Possible Worlds," in Richard Kearney (ed.), *Dialogues with Contemporary Continental Thinkers: The Phenomenological Heritage* (Manchester: Manchester University Press, 1984), 36-45; and my "Narrative Identity and the Mythico-poetic Imagination," in David Klemm and William Schweiker (ed.), *Meanings in Texts and Actions: Questioning Paul Ricoeur* (Charlottesville: University Press of Virginia, 1993), 195-204. For a feminist reading indebted to Ricoeur (and other contemporary French philosophers, including Jacques Derrida and Luce Irigaray) on the imagination, metaphor and myth/mimesis opening up of new worlds, i.e., a certain utopian vision, see Drucilla Cornell, *Beyond Accommodation: Ethical Feminism, Deconstruction and the Law* (London: Routledge, 1991), 167-72, 224.

12 G.W.F. Hegel, *Elements of a Philosophy of Right*, trans. H. B. Nisbet, with an introduction by Allen Wood (Cambridge: Cambridge University Press, 1991), 439 (also see paragraph 166); and Hegel, *Phenomenology of Spirit*, 266-289, paragraphs 444-76. Cf. George Steiner, *Antigones: The Antigone Myth in Western Literature, Art and Thought* (Oxford: Oxford University Press, 1984), 4, 19; Allen Wood, *Hegel's Ethical Thought* (Cambridge: Cambridge University Press, 1990), 245.

13 Jebb, "Preface," *Sophocles*, v-vi.

14 Ricoeur, *Oneself as Another*, 244-5.

15 Ricoeur, *Oneself as Another*, 241.

16 Ricoeur, *Oneself as Another*, 241, 247, 249.

17 Ricoeur, *Oneself as Another*, 170-1, 249.

18 Here I assume that Hegel gives two readings of *Antigone* – one, of women's role in the *pagan* world, which appears in the *Phenomenology of Spirit* and the other, of women's role in the *modern* (i.e., Christian) world in the *Philosophy of Right*; in the latter, but not the former, particular and universal can be reconciled in the State. For a helpful discussion, see Patricia Jagentowicz Mills, "Hegel's *Antigone*," 131-52. As Mills explains: "In the *Philosophy of Right* we learn that the bifurcation of reason in the pagan world is *aufgehoben* in Spirit's movement toward universal self-knowledge with the development of the modern Christian world into a triad consisting of the family, civil society and the state. The bourgeois family is the sphere of the universal as undifferentiated unity or immediacy; civil society represents the moment of particularity; and the state is the sphere of universality in which the universal and particular are reconciled. The aim of the *Philosophy of Right* is to resolve the relationship between desire, morality and ethical life; the analysis begins with a discussion of sexual desire within marriage, shifts to a focus on the generalized desire of civil society and the abstract morality of that sphere, and ends with a consideration of the concrete ethical life or *Sittlichkeit* of the state" (147-8). Cf. Ricoeur, *Oneself as Another*, 250-6.

19 In numerous places in his writings, Ricoeur distances himself from Hegel and often claims to be a "post-Hegelian Kantian." However, in the "Interlude," Ricoeur explicitly compares himself with Hegel in his reading of *Antigone*; see *Oneself as Another*, 241, 243, 244, 248.

20   Ricoeur, *Oneself as Another*, 243, 247.

21   George Steiner, "Preface," *Antigones: The Antigone Myth in Western Literature, Art and Thought* (Oxford: Oxford University Press, 1984).

22   Ricoeur even claims that Nussbaum is "not as anti-Hegelian as she seems to think." Ricoeur, *Oneself as Another*, 243.

23   Steiner, *Antigones*, 295.

24   For Hegel, Antigone embodies the fact that "womankind" is at once essential and threatening to the community; she represents, "womankind – the everlasting irony [in the life] of the community" (*Phenomenology of Spirit*, 288).

25   Mills, "Hegel's *Antigone*," 137n19.

26   To understand fully Irigaray's texts, it is essential to know Jacques Lacan's psycho-analytic reading of *Antigone* in which Creon is the inhibitor of desire. This reading has implications for Irigaray's critical re-readings of Hegel and of Antigone. Very roughly, in focusing upon Creon, Lacan's reading marginalizes the figure of woman, while Irigaray and other feminists challenge this marginalization. Unfortunately, a more detailed analysis of Lacan is beyond the scope of this chapter. But, once again, Steiner can also offer us his male reading that "Jacques Lacan's remarks on *Antigone* (in the seminar sequence entitled *L'Ethique de la psychanalyse*) may not, as yet, be generally accessible. But his view of Creon as the "denier of desire," as one whose refusal of the *discours du désir* entails the choice of death, will, by osmosis of fashion, be diffused," 295.

27   Luce Irigaray, *Speculum of the Other Woman*, trans. Gillian Gill (New York: Cornell University Press, 1985), 220-1, 225; cf. Patricia Jagentowicz Mills, *Woman, Nature and Psyche* (London: Yale University Press, 1987), 27.

28   Irigaray, "The Necessity of Sexuate Rights," in *The Irigaray Reader*, edited Margaret Whitford (Oxford: Blackwell, 1991), 199.

29   This collapse is most apparent in the myth where Antigone's grieving recalls the mother/daughter goddess, Demeter/Persephone; see Sophocles, *The Three Theban Plays*, lines 470-1, 978-82.

30   Pritchard, "Antigone's Mirrors," 83; cf. Irigaray, *Speculum of the Other Woman*, 216, 218.

31   It should be noted that Nussbaum does not read all other Greek women in myth in terms of strategies of simplification and of avoidance. In fact, she eulogizes Euripides' *Hecuba* for representing the inevitability of moral conflict and the fragil-ity of goodness in the very same work where she condemns Antigone. (Yet it was Hecuba who, as a result of her vengeful action, is metamorphosed into a dog!)

32   Ricoeur, *Oneself as Another*, 243. Also, in a long footnote, Ricoeur elaborates his reading of Hegel: "In the *Phenomenology of Spirit*, tragedy is that moment of mind when the harmonious unity of the beautiful city is disrupted by an action (*Handlung*), the action of particular individualities, from which the conflict between the charac-ters stems. The effect of this *Entzweiung* – this dividing in two – is to split the ethical powers that dominate them: the divine against the human, the city against the fam-ily, man against woman. Here, the finest pages are those that assign to the sister – the woman who is not daughter, mother, or spouse – the responsibility of guarding the family bond that links the living and the dead. By giving her brother a tomb, Antigone elevates death above natural contingency. But if there is a sense to all this, it is not 'for them' but 'for us.' 'For them,' disappearance in death; 'for us,' the

indirect lesson of this disaster. The calm reconciliation sung by the chorus cannot take the place of pardon. The one-sidedness of each of the characters, including Antigone, excludes any such mutual recognition" (248n13).

33   Ricoeur, *Oneself as Another*, 249.

34   Steiner, *Antigones*, 296; his exact claim is: "But no Ur-Antigone can exist for us. No stripping of interpretative accretions can take us back to the premiere of the drama, to the phenomenology of its purpose and impact in the 440s BC."

35   Mills, "Hegel's *Antigone*," 137, 145.

36   Tina Chanter, "Antigone's Dilemma," in Robert Bernasconi and Simon Critchley (ed.), *Re-reading Levinas* (Indianapolis: Indiana University Press, 1991), 140. Cf. Irigaray, *Speculum of the Other Woman*, 220-1.

37   Cf. Sandra Harding, "Why has the Sex/Gender System Become Visible Only Now?" in Sandra Harding and Merrill Hintikka (ed.), *Discovering Reality: Feminist Perspectives on Epistemology, Metaphysics, Methodology, and Philosophy of Science* (Dordrecht: Reidel, 1983), 311-324; and Judith Butler, "Gender Trouble, Feminist Theory and Psychoanalytic Discourse" in Linda J. Nicholson (ed.), *Feminism/ Postmodernism* (London: Routledge, 1990), 324-40.

38   Sophocles, *The Theban Plays*, 76, lines 383ff.

39   Sophocles, *The Theban Plays*, 89, line 643.

40   Earlier in her text, Cornell has argued that Irigaray uses *mimesis* in a specific, technical sense (cf. *Beyond Accommodation*, 147-52). Roughly, Irigaray's *mimesis* is the way in which we move within a gender hierarchy and give its metaphors new meaning. It is not an artistic representation or configuration which simply mirrors the real. Her use of *mimesis* seems to be closest to the third form of Ricoeur's threefold *mimesis*, i.e. refiguration. See note 42 below.

41   Cornell, *Beyond Accommodation*, 169.

42   Cf. Paul Ricoeur, *The Rule of Metaphor*, trans. Robert Czerny (Toronto: University of Toronto Press, 1977); *Time and Narrative*, I, trans. Kathleen McLaughlin and David Pellauer (Chicago: University of Chicago Press, 1984), 53; and *Time and Narrative*, III, trans. Kathleen Blamey and David Pellauer (Chicago: University of Chicago Press, 1986), 4, 158-9.

43   Irigaray, *Speculum*, 220; cf. Chanter, "Antigone's Dilemma," 140, 145n20.

44   If genuine and accurate in translation, the following lines support reading Antigone's identity as guardian of the maternal blood tie, and possibly as a "digestion of the masculine": "*Antigone*: ... if I had been the mother of children or if my husband died, exposed and rotting – I'd never have taken this ordeal upon myself, never defied our people's will. What law, you ask, do I satisfy with what I say? A husband dead, there might have been another. A child by another too.... But mother and father both lost in the halls of Death, no brother could ever spring to light again" (Sophocles, *The Theban Plays*, 105, lines 995ff).

45   Sophocles, *The Theban Plays*, 59, lines 2, 6-7.

46   Sophocles, *The Theban Plays*, 62, lines 74-5; emphasis added.

47   Sophocles, *The Theban Plays*, 83, lines 541-2.

Narration and Life: On the Possibilities of a Narrative Psychology

HENDERIKUS J. STAM AND LORI EGGER

A "standard view" among many students of narrative, argues David Carr, is one that poses a schism between narrative and life. "It is the view that real events do not have the character of those we find in stories, and if we treat them as if they did have such a character, we are not being true to them."[1] Although Carr disagrees with the view, he implies that expressions of it can be found in authors as divergent as Barthes and Mink, White, and Foucault. More importantly, on Carr's reading, Ricoeur's *Time and Narrative* is unclear on this question. He argues first that Ricoeur is right to distinguish between the episodic and configurational dimensions of narrative since the latter is itself temporal in a complex way. The account of mimesis$_1$ however leaves enough unsaid on the question of life and narrative that it is in danger of slipping into Carr's notion of the standard view. In particular, Ricoeur's account of literary texts leaves a gap between an intelligible text and unformed life, even if they each give form to one another. We will return to this discussion, and to Ricoeur's response, at the conclusion of this paper. However, if Carr had been commenting on selected versions of "narrative" in the social sciences, and in particular, those that pass for a "narrative psychology," then he could not have been more correct.[2]

Narrative Psychology and Psychoanalysis

In psychology, narrative has come to be taken either as a "root metaphor" (in Pepper's sense),[3] as a social construction,[4] or as an "assimilating structure."[5] Narrative is conceived of as story, loosely speaking, and psychological functions of thinking, perceiving, imagining, and so on, all take place within a "narrative structure." By arguing that narrative can take on the burden of a "root metaphor," Theodore Sarbin conflates the narrative structure of psychological life with the metaphorical description of that life as narrative. Other versions of narratives are even more literal; according to Ken and Mary Gergen's account, narratives must develop an evaluative endpoint or goal. Furthermore, the selection and arrangement of events in a narrative must be such that the goal stated is rendered probable and the events are tied together in a dependent form and the overall narrative must have a dramatic impact. Such considerations provide the framework within which to evaluate the rhetorical power of psychological theories, their realist or "scientific" credibility being no longer at issue. Nevertheless, the psychologist remains to say whether a narrative indeed has intelligibility, a judgment retained by one who inspects "from above" rather than within the "narrative" itself.

In their arguments with the positivist tradition, narrative psychologists have unwittingly incorporated this scientistic stance ("the view from nowhere") into their accounts. For the Gergens, the criteria for assessing the value of psychological narratives are based on "aesthetic forms" rendering the problem of observational grounding as one of the selection of appropriate rhetorical devices. Alternatively, James Mancuso conceives the development of narrative as a kind of Piagetian super-task which requires the development of an over-arching narrative structure. This structure becomes the new psychological universal category, not unlike other structures of mind. In each of these cases, there is a deep confusion between the narrative *articulated* by actual persons and the one *ascribed* to persons by the social scientist. Sometimes narrative is just a property of being human, at other times a characteristic of human life "discovered" by the social scientist. In the first case, narrative functions to give "structure" to a life lived pre-narratively; in the second, narrative is a way of "doing" psychology. In either case, narrative takes on the decontextualized and formal character of the representational cognitive accounts of human action they were meant to replace.[6]

Ricoeur's essay on Freud, on the other hand, remains the foundation for a narrative approach to psychoanalysis.[7] Some adherents of this approach in the analytic community have tended to minimize his *hermeneutic* interpretation of Freud. Narration in psychoanalysis is still psychoanalysis[8] or on Donald Spence's account, a kind of narrative psychology.[9] Of course, Ricoeur's essay was never meant to serve as a working guide for the practising analyst, and the narrative turn in psychology and psychoanalysis has never fully appropriated this work for reasons which may have more to do with institutional than intellectual factors. Psychoanalysis is a language of the consulting room and, notwithstanding its widespread use as a cultural resource, retains its legitimacy by referring back to its origins as a foundation for the helping professions. The antagonism between the "already narrated, examined life" of the developmental theory in psychoa-

nalysis and the "always potential life implied by the idea of the unconscious" is, on Adam Phillips's account, no less than "the conflict between
knowing what a life is and the sense that a life contains within it something that makes such knowing impossible."[10]

Ricoeur posits a "dialectic of archeology and teleology" in Freud and
proposes to counter the regressive movement of psychoanalytic theory
with the progression analytic practice puts in operation. This dialectic,
posed by reflective thought, "says that only a subject with a *telos* can
have an *arché*. The appropriation of meaning constituted in the past presupposes the movement of a subject drawn ahead of itself by a succession of 'figures' ... each of which finds its meaning in those to follow."[11]
This interplay between regression and progression finds its identity in
symbol. But symbols take their meaning from concrete reflection, and
Ricoeur saw clearly that this would return psychoanalysis to language,
"reflection passes into the fullness of speech simply heard and understood."[12] This makes psychoanalysis a "transitional language," if you
will, "one possible bridge to a more personal, less compliant idiom."[13]
But it also displaces the professional authority of the psychoanalyst, a
lesson perhaps not lost on the institution of psychoanalysis.

In a later essay, Ricoeur places his work on Freud in a more deliberate
narrative context. "Psychoanalytic reports are kinds of biographies and
auto-biographies," he claims, and their "literary history is part of the
long tradition emerging from the oral epic tradition of the Greeks, the
Celts, and the Germans."[14] This tradition of storytelling "provides a relative autonomy to the criterion of narrative intelligibility," not only for
the "consistency of interpretive procedures, but also the efficacy of the
change in the balance of libidinal energies."[15] On this view, narrative
intelligibility places psychoanalysis in culture or in the broader temporal background of human experience.[16]

In a corollary to his theorem of intentionality in the work on Freud,
Ricoeur argues that "Every enacted meaning is a meaning caught within
the body; every praxis involved in meaning is a signifying or intention
made flesh."[17] The intentional takes primacy over the reflective; "a meaning that exists is a meaning caught up within a body."[18] Ricoeur wants
to establish the ontic basis for a Freudian unconscious with this claim
and to create a link with phenomenology through Merleau-Ponty. But
the claim has wider implications for psychology and narrative.

Personal narratives emerge out of a pre-rational, pre-reflective but
intentional embodiment, or what Ricoeur has called elsewhere the "pre-
narrative quality of human experience."[19] They are first encapsulated in
"joint action," wherein participants in everyday conversations have so-

cially shared identities of *feeling*.[20] These are what Vico called "sensory topics," which give rise to the possibility of common reference in the moment by moment movement of social activity. They are sensory in that they create shared feelings for already shared circumstances. Joint action requires "knowledge" from within a social situation and is akin to knowledge of a practical-moral kind.[21]

It is interesting in this regard that Ricoeur associates the Aristotelian *phronesis* (practical judgment) with narrative understanding.[22] However, there is more at stake than *just* the making of narrative or finding *that* "narrative identity which constitutes us."[23] Let us take Carr's critique seriously for a moment and ask what is to be gained by those who posit "life" as different from narrative. Outside of narrative our task is frequently simply rendering our actions intelligible, "that is, capable of being grasped, reflectively and intellectually, as meaningful within an order of things."[24] Not all of life is narrated, just as *phronesis* is not just a narrative understanding but primarily *practical*. We not only know *about* the world ("knowing what") or how to do things in it, as in the skills we possess ("knowing how"), but we also have knowledge of particular and concrete situations that is prior to both and has its origins in our relations to others (or "knowing from," as Shotter claims). This is knowledge of a moral kind, "for it depends on the judgment of others as to whether its expression or its use is ethically proper or not – one cannot just have it or express it on one's own, or wholly within one's self." Hence, knowledge arises from within a social situation and is responsive to those others in that context.[25] "Knowing from" is derived from the particular situations of one's life for its content allows us to determine what these situations will "afford" or "permit," and as such it is always embodied knowledge.[26] Bernstein, incidentally, associates *this* form of "practical-moral" knowledge with Aristotle's *phronesis*.[27]

The cognitive function of narrative form, on Louis Mink's account, is not simply to relate a succession of events but to "body forth an ensemble of interrelationships of many different kinds as a single whole."[28] Historical narratives claim truth as a criterion of their coherence but, as Mink notes, they are always the product of imaginative construction; they are "cognitive instruments." Evidence, wherever we might find it, does not dictate the form of the narrative. Self-narratives are equally, if not more so, referential to events which occur on some description. Thus, it is not that we live *in* a narrative or even multiple narratives. We live within cultures, at least in the Western tradition, which make available to us multiple resources from a tradition (or traditions). Alasdair MacIntyre has argued, however, that any tradition which is to count as a living tradition consists of not only an argument that brings the past to the present in a socially embodied manner but is also about the very goods which constitute that tradition.[29] The narratives of tradition must be reappropriated and argued before they can, in any sense, be called a living tradition. As both Michael Billig and John Shotter have noted, in order to be a participant in any sphere of life, the mastery of some one side or other in conflictual traditions is necessary, even if one means to overthrow them.[30] Nevertheless, as Mink argues, our actions and our "selves" need not be, and cannot be, narrated as if we were simply narrating a story waiting to be told. The theoretical audacity of such an enterprise does violence to the very lives that are the object of the narrative. The appearance of narrative structure is the consequence of the intentional interest of the narrator and the audience to which the narrative is addressed.

Precisely because life is lived in a disjointed manner, our actions are frequently *not* narrated. The intelligibility that narratives provide in locating actions does indeed render invisible the local and immediate meaning of those actions.[31] A crucial question for a narrative psychology then becomes: "whose narrative is being articulated?" Narratives can seduce us to view them as the measure of truth, allowing us to specify the degree to which actions meet the requirements set out in the story. For when we require that all action be narrated, as MacIntyre surely does, we must by necessity impose a narrative on the disorderly forms of embodied activity which go to make up a life. There are, of course, narratives that pre-figure the life we live in this disorderly sense, and we are capable of, if not frequently required to, give an accounting of our own lives in narrative terms. Our actions nevertheless remain intelligible at the practical-moral-local level without being articulated in or as narrative. The terms that we use to narrate when we do so are thus negotiable and therefore are not in any way intrinsic or automatic.

Psychotherapeutic Narratives

On some occasions narrative intelligibility is crucial to personal and social life. One such location is the psychotherapeutic conversation where it is intelligibility that is sought, not in action but in talk about actions. Even here the notions of narrative promulgated by otherwise effective psychotherapists retain the notion of the requirement of the "story" as the determinant of meaning, the selector of experience, the source of expression of those experiences and the future of experience itself.[32] Although self-narratives are acknowledged as indeterminate, the provision of some one "better" or "cohesive" story remains the goal of the therapeutic encounter. Therapy here acts as a cultural agent, forming narratives that are socially, if not acceptable, at least intelligible.

According to Ken Gergen and John Kaye,[33] both traditional therapy approaches (what they call "modernist") and many of the postmodernist approaches to narrative in therapy share an emphasis on replacing a client's narrative with one which is considered "better." Within modernist therapy, the client's self-narrative is judged inaccurate and dysfunctional, a distortion of reality. The therapist is viewed as a scientist of sorts, with access to an empirically based (nominally at least) professional discourse. It is the therapist's task to replace the client's flawed account with this improved narrative and thereby supply the client with a version of reality which is more accurate and more functional. In postmodern approaches to therapy, the therapist is not limited to a single, fixed, pre-formulated narrative, nor does the therapist work toward replacing the client's narrative with a professional discourse. Instead, the therapist and client are said to jointly construct an alternative narrative and have available to them multiple narratives from which to draw. The therapist's narratives represent only some of the many culturally available narratives that participants might use. The goal of therapy, however, remains the construction of a single overarching narrative that guides the client's understanding of life, action and the world.

While Gergen and Kaye favor the turn towards postmodern approaches to narrative in therapy, they reject the notion that therapy is simply about replacing or reconstructing a client's dysfunctional narrative with a "better" one. They advocate the need to embed narrative and narrative thinking in a "broader concern with the generation of meaning via dialogue." Therapy is a process whereby meaning is "forged" within a "collaborative discourse."[34]

The use of "narrative" here is episodic in Ricoeur's sense. It concerns itself with the ongoing narrative constructions which make up everyday activity but downplays the interactional, dialogic nature of psychotherapy. Psychotherapeutic activity, like all dialogue, is one of joint action. Utterances must be formulated in response to other utterances in a way in which we do not speak out of a clearly formulated plan or representation but into a context that is not entirely our own. The others in the dialogue determine our actions as much as our own internal resources create a developing situation with its own unintended consequences and intentionality.[35] The following two sequences of therapeutic dialogue illustrate this. These sequences, necessarily truncated, are taken from a larger project on the discursive nature of gender in psychotherapy.

I.

In the first sequence, both the client and therapist are women. The client is a university student. They are discussing the client's hesitancy to become involved in a meaningful relationship:

Therapist: Hmhm. And when are you going to be ready to have a relationship

Client: when the next John Kennedy or Robert Kennedy comes along I suppose

T: (laughs)

C: and they're at all pleasant

T: (laughs)

C: ah, no, if there's, I don't know, like I was watching, they had this big special on the Kennedys

T: hmhm

C: very well done actually. No biases at all on either side

T: hmhm

C: and my friend was watching it with me. And I thought – you know, she was still going on about her boyfriend.... But I don't understand how anybody could watch that and still think their boyfriend was the cat's meow and gee I'm going to marry him and live the rest of my life with him. I'd think aghh, get me out (laughs) you know, it's just like a jail sentence. No thank you, I mean, I just don't know anybody that ... really turns my crank. Like I told my mom the other day, I don't think I'm going to get married because my expectations are too high, so I'll probably grow up to be an old maid.

As the therapist and client continue to talk, the therapist resists the client's negative framing of relationships for some time and reminds the client of an earlier conversation in which they discussed her fears of intimacy. In the following excerpt, the therapist introduces a professional narrative of "schemas" to frame the client's concerns as distortions. The client resists this framing, expressing fears about becoming entangled with what she calls a "dodo."

T: remember when we talked about ... schemas

C: schemas? no

T: hmhm. The belief systems from your early chidhood that seem to rule ... how you live your life?

C: I don't know how this

T: do you remember talking about that?

C: well, yeah, kind of

T: ok. Do you remember what they were?

C: oh, the ones that I had

T: hmhm

C: yes, yes, afraid of intimacy and ah I fear that horrible things are going to happen and ... I expect a lot of other is one I think

T: hmhm

C: and I can't remember what the fourth one is off hand

T: ok, the most important ones were unrelenting standards and

C: hmhm

T: expecting so much of self and others

C: oh, it doesn't, in a relationship, I'm sorry, I'm not going to be attracted to some dodo, who doesn't really do much with his life

T: hmhm

C: its just – that's just it

T: but is that an unrelenting standard or that a, just a

C: I don't know

T: healthy expectation

C: I think a healthy expectation

T: yeah. I do too. Where would the unrelenting part maybe come in?

C: I don't know, um, I don't know ... I really don't know

T: (laughs)

C: um

The therapist introduces the possibility that the client might find someone that she might consider acceptable and this elicits from the client some uncertainty and conflicting desires:

T: ok, so say you find a guy that has really high aspirations, who's really ambitious, who really works hard

C: I'll probably run the opposite way

T: hm, why?

C: I don't know, wouldn't it be that if a guy really wants to be with you he'll knock down doors for you and prove you're going to be there tomorrow? Um ... I think , yeah the other thing that worries me lately and I wrote to my sister, is that there hasn't been a hint of a prospect. I mean, I wouldn't mind it. I mean ... I don't want to get involved with anybody right now but it would be nice to know that if I did, there

T: yeah

C: was somebody out there. But I said to mom too

T: right

C: there isn't even ... anybody close

Following this exchange, the therapist suddenly relents and indicates that, perhaps, it is alright after all to be single while a student:

T: maybe you should consider yourself lucky while you're carrying six courses (at university) that there isn't

The client affirms this response:

C: well, that's what I said, that's what I mean

T: (laughs)

C: are you kidding? I don't want a relationship

> T: instead of being disappointed, yeah

What began as a conversation about priorities ends with the therapist framing the client's reluctance as fear. When confronted with the possibility of staying single, the client gives a very different response:

> C: but I think it kind of worries me. My father's always on my case, eh, 'the environment you're in, you have to give yourself a break, you're only 21' and lalala
>
> T: what would be wrong with being an old maid?
>
> C: ... because I personally would like to fall in love some day and have a family
>
> T: ok

The client recognizes that this contradicts her previous stance:

> C: I mean, I mean ... I definitely don't go around telling people that because ... it's, it's a contradictory ... kind of thing with me. Um ... but ah, its very contradictory. I mean ... it's probably one thing I want the most, it's also the thing I'm afraid of the most
>
> T: hm

In this example, various kinds of narratives are being deployed. The therapist resorts to a professional narrative of "schemas" and when this fails to elicit a cooperative utterance on the part of the client, she raises, in turn, the possibility of finding a perfect partner, of being single, and of being an old maid. The multiple resources she draws on eventually elicit the traditional narrative of love and marriage. The outcome of such a therapy session might be construed as a self-narrative of romance, yet in its joint action, it is the joint product of an exchange in the session which may not have been intended by either participant. In the process, various narratives about gender are evoked and discarded as required. The romantic narrative – love and marriage – remains the "final" story. The next excerpt, also about relationships, elicits a different set of therapeutic narratives.

II.

In this example, both the therapist and client are men. Once again, the client is a university student. Earlier, the client had expressed a desire to have a relationship with a woman. In this previous conversation, he worried that the therapist might think he was weird because he was a twenty-one-year-old male who wanted affection. In the following excerpt, the therapist refers back to this earlier conversation:

> T: so a female relationship, that sounds like it's pretty high on the list
>
> C: yeah, I would, I would say so, yeah
>
> T: the shopping list

C: I have ... I ... there's a lot of things I guess that are high on the list and ... of course, you know, this is (laughter) this is the list that's going to have to be moderated or changed because there's nobody that's ever going to fill that perfect bill. And I probably don't think ... I don't think I'd necessarily want her to. I don't know I think a little ... little, ah, im- ... imperfections kind of make you – I wish I could take this approach myself, but I think imperfections kind of, ah, make you appreciate the good.

The therapist moves into what could be called a "problem" narrative about relationships as he points out a number of potential difficulties that could emerge when one becomes involved with women:

T: one of the things about those imperfections, if that's the way that you're looking at it, I don't know if it's an imperfection

C: yeah

T: but certainly differences in people. One of the things that happens I think in relationships is that there is not always a perfect match in terms of the need you are talking about for instance, like affection, and the inclination or ability at that point in time

C: yeah

T: for that person to give, so uh, I may have a very high need for affection, for, ah, nurturance of some kind and my partner, for personal reasons or for relationship reasons at that point in time, is either unable or unwilling to meet my need because she has ah, a need of her own

C: hmhm

T: if not for that, for something else. I mean, relationships are always a matter of sorting these things out

C: yeah

T: which, which brings up not only the affectional issues but also the whole issue of how do people communicate and sort out these different needs they have and the different ... dispositions at a particular

C: yeah

T: point in time. But I think what you're saying is that in a global way, at a global level, you would want to be involved with people, including female people, ah, who are comfortable giving and receiving affection

The client picks up on the therapist's "problem" narrative in discussing his need for affection:

C: yeah ... and in certain ways, its especially, ah, ah, female because it seems, umh, I don't know, but for whatever reason its just more pleasant to be, ah, you know, shown affection by a female than it is, ah, by a male. I've always – in my family it's ... I don't know if this ah, stereotypical or whatever but ah, it's always been important for my mom to show the affection, ah, whereas for my dad to speak it. Like, nonverbal from my mom has been important and, and ah, verbal for my dad – actually it's possibly because my mom gives verbal but not nonverbal and my dad gives, uhm, non-verbal, but he's not – doesn't say, you know, I love you a lot or whatever

T: but your mom does say that?

C: yeah she, she ... not, not a lot, but ah, but that's her expression

T: but you would have liked more nonverbal affection from her?

C: yeah that's

T: right. It starts to hang together a little bit because, uh, as, as ... uh, we grow up we develop sort of attachments to people who are a lot – that are a number of them that are like our parents

C: yeah

The therapist suddenly shifts away from the affection issues and draws on another narrative which emphasizes the sexual aspects of heterosexual relationships:

T: and what happens of course is, is – for heterosexual people, is that somehow or another their female – the female becomes sexualized

C: yeah

T: as well. So there's not only a need for, for closeness and affection, I would think that there's a sexualized aspect to it, so that tends to be in there

C: yeah

T: as well. And it becomes ... not that it's confused with intimacy other ... for other people, its just part of that whole thing maybe ... part of that maybe explaining some of the intensity

C: yeah

T: and, even though you're close friends and everything, there's a ... a special kind of, of need over here with females because there's a sexualized aspect

C: yeah

T: as well

The client takes up and resists the therapist's narrative:

C: I wouldn't think that would be entirely it, but ah, I, definitely a part ... my biggest ... the biggest thing right now is, ah, I'm sure ah, sex would be nice, ah, that aspect would be nice but, uhm I need so much, ah, a companion and somebody that ah, I can ... it's kind of weird but somebody else said that's this mutual fulfilling of needs

T: hmhm

C: because that ... somebody that needs me as well as me needing her? It seems like, uhm ... it's the same way with friends but it ... but it's not? It's ... it's one of these things that's kind of hard to put into words

T: ... but somehow or other you, you seem to be saying that you expect that a relationship with a female to meet needs or to meet them to a degree that other relationships can't....

As with the previous example, a number of narratives are drawn on by the therapy participants. What starts out as a discussion of the value of a relationship with a woman, turns into a narrative emphasizing "problems" in such relationships. What begins as a desire for affection is transformed into a desire for sex. These transformations appear necessary in order to properly define the relationships between women and men and to differentiate such relationships from other possible relationships. What we end up with is not a "love and marriage" narrative, as in the previous example, but a narrative which emphasizes the differences between men and women, constructs women as sexual objects and men as desiring these objects. Again, the outcome of the therapy session is neither the therapist's or the client's alone, but a joint product of both participants as they respond to one another's utterances and speak into a context creating the possibilities for further conversation. In each case, however, the therapist exerts considerable influence by providing terms and allusions to topics (such as love and sex) which then direct the therapeutic discourse. Thus, while engaged in joint activity, presumably aimed at helping the client articulate a self-narrative, by placing certain topics in the talk the therapist sets the overall agenda. By claiming that such talk creates a self-narrative or self-understandings is to miss the dual nature of this construction.

Such episodic narratives are neither configurational nor even fully "narrative" in the sense that they only allude to possible stories which are telescoped into talk and refer back to the potential of narrative available behind the segments themselves. At the same time, they are also not narrative in the traditional sense insofar as they are the creation of not one person but the joint action of two people in conversation. One opens a possible topic, it is taken up or resisted in turn, elements of the topics are utilized to describe the "self" or possible selves of the client which then creates further opportunities for exploring the narrative segments that have been opened and so on. If there is a narrative psychology here, it is not one that requires us to posit the coherence of "storied lives" as much as storied interactions. The requirement of narrative psychology, and in some sense of Ricoeur, that we confront this inchoateness with meaning or that the intelligibility of talk (text) lies in "its potential for fulfillment in the oncoming world of conduct and action," where "texts expose our own actual world to alternative possibilities,"[36] is the hermeneutic imperative. In this sense, we agree with Gerald Bruns that hermeneutics is prophetic rather than nostalgic, for narratives expose not only the limits of our world but exposes "these limits as historical and contingent."[37] In the kind of talk we have presented here, however, such an understanding must be brought to bear upon the activity of the participants. It is neither present in the talk before the talk, nor is there an unrestricted variety of meanings available. Instead, the talk itself is the activity of creating such meanings, which are often partial and fragmented. This is perhaps the nature of the episodic narrative, but most of us spend most of our lives in such inchoateness. We are confronted then not with meaning *per se* but with the work of creating meaning out of the multivocal, multiple and inchoate possibilities which present themselves in talk as well as the constraints on such talk by the activities and social circumstances of our lives. If there is a narrative psychology, then it is not the sort that requires that stories become the psychological substitute for a mental coherence typically assigned to the faculties of mind but, instead, it is the psychology of everyday talk and activity which is frequently corralled into the service of other narratives or is produced in joint action that relies on the partial and episodic narrative possibilities open to us in such talk.[38]

Conclusions

We promised to return to David Carr's notion of the "standard view" and Ricoeur's response, which were part of a Round Table discussion of *Time and Narrative* and were originally published in 1985.[39] Carr takes the standard view to be mistaken, an "expression more of frustration, pessimism and skepticism than of genuine insight into the relation between stories and the real world."[40] What Carr's dispute with the tradition also makes clear, however, is that notions such as "real world" and "life" need some articulation for the standard view to make sense.

Ricoeur responded by saying that "every narrative configuration has a kind of retroactive reference ... because life itself is an inchoate narrative."[41] Only through transformation into what Ricoeur calls "well-made fictions" does refiguration survive. Refiguration is at once "revelatory" and "transformative," but not representational. "Action is already symbolically mediated; literature in the largest sense of the word, including history as well as fiction, tends to reinforce a process of symbolization already at work."[42] Ricoeur is not so much concerned here with the relation of life to history but of the intrusion or circularity of history. After all, "what is prefigured in our life results from refigurations operated by all the other lives of those who taught us," argues Ricoeur.[43] Meaning can nevertheless be extended or progress from the inchoate to the fully determined. What we have argued is that meaning is not only inchoate some of the time, but that the matter of prefiguration, configuration, and refiguration (in psychotherapeutic settings, as well as in life itself) is also a joint activity, not only a narrative one. Just as there is no one narrative to "finally" tell, the question of a narration of the self is also a social activity. However much we may be under the spell of historical and social narrative traditions, everyday life continues to be enacted between people rather than between individuals and traditions. In this sense, perhaps, Carr and Ricoeur are not so far apart since each conceives of narrative as a "container" for life where, in the absence of foundations, philosophical work can be turned back onto traditions to give us an intelligible account of action. But action does not always call out for intelligibility.[44] And, whereas we were critical of narrative psychologists for appropriating narratives to a social science tradition, we feel that so long as narration is taken to be the primary form of understanding human interaction, such cleavage is not only appropriate but inevitable. We have a great deal of respect for the work on narrative both in philosophy and psychology and what they have accomplished against the traditions of foundationalism and positivism, but we also believe that they provide us with an old story for a new psychology.

Notes

1 David Carr, "Discussion: Ricoeur on Narrative," in *On Paul Ricoeur: Narrative and Interpretation*, ed. David Wood (London: Routledge, 1990), 160.

2 Ricoeur too would hardly have much sympathy for the de-chronologized versions of narrative that we will describe briefly below. In this sense, narrative in the social sciences is concerned more with the 'episodic' dimensions of narrative, not the configurational dimensions of literary and historical texts which form the basis of Ricoeur's discussion in *Time and Narrative*.

3 Theodore R. Sarbin, "The Narrative as a Root Metaphor for Psychology," in *Narrative Psychology*, ed. Theodore R. Sarbin (New York: Praeger, 1986). Sarbin is a social psychologist who had made important contributions to alternative conceptions of the discipline over the past forty years.

4 See Kenneth J. Gergen and Mary M. Gergen, "The Social Construction of Narrative Accounts," in *Historical Social Psychology*, ed. Kenneth J. Gergen and Mary M. Gergen (Hillsdale, N.J.: Erlbaum, 1984).

5 See James C. Mancuso, "The Acquisition and Use of Narrative Grammar Structure," in *Narrative Psychology*, ed. Theodore R. Sarbin (New York: Praeger, 1986). Not all of these authors have consistently maintained these positions. In particular, I suspect that the Gergens no longer consider their views on narrative representative of the relational social constructionism they now espouse; see, for example, Kenneth J. Gergen, *Realities and Relationships* (Cambridge: Harvard University Press, 1994) and the discussion of Gergen and Kaye, below; or see James C. Mancuso, "Constructionism, Personal Construct Psychology and Narrative Psychology," *Theory & Psychology*, 6 (1996): 47-70. What these positions *do* have in common is a general concern with finding the structural, story-like elements of psychological life.

6 For example, Mancuso ("The Acquisition and Use of Narrative Grammar Structure," 106) argues "the foregoing overview has been presented to validate the proposition that the typical person who has passed through late childhood imposes story structure on all varieties of input. Current thought can be assembled to create a good story about the motivation of the human psychological system as it undergoes the epigenetic acquisition of a complex narrative grammar." For a general "structural" account of narrative in the social sciences, see Elisabeth Gülich and Uta M. Quasthoff, "Narrative Analysis," in *Handbook of Discourse Analysis*, vol. 2, ed. Teun A. Van Dijk (London: Academic Press, 1985).

7 Paul Ricoeur, *Freud and Philosophy*, trans. Denis Savage (New Haven: Yale, 1970).

8   Roy Schafer, *Retelling a Life* (New York: Basic Books, 1992).

9   Donald P. Spence, *Narrative Truth and Historical Truth* (New York: W.W. Norton, 1982). For a more recent account by Spence see his *The Rhetorical Voice of Psychoanalysis* (Cambridge: Harvard, 1994), wherein he has moved away from a discussion of "narrative" *per se* in order to castigate psychoanalysis for its reliance of rhetoric over evidence. A heavy dose of the latter will, presumably, save psychoanalysis from devolving into mere myth.

10   Adam Phillips, *On Kissing, Tickling, and Being Bored* (Cambridge, MA: Harvard, 1993), 7. Phillips is a practising analyst.

11   Paul Ricoeur, "A Philosophical Interpretation of Freud," in *The Conflict of Interpretations*, trans. Willis Domingo (Evanston: Northwestern University Press, 1974) reprinted in *The Philosophy of Paul Ricoeur*, ed. Charles E. Reagan and David Stewart (Boston: Beacon Press, 1978), 170.

12   Paul Ricoeur, *Freud and Philosophy*, 496.

13   Adam Phillips, *On Kissing*, 8.

14   Paul Ricoeur, "The Question of Proof in Freud's Psychoanalytic Writings," *Journal of the American Psychoanalytic Association* 24 (1977), reprinted in *The Philosophy of Paul Ricoeur*, ed. Charles E. Reagan and David Stewart (Boston: Beacon Press, 1978), 210.

15   Paul Ricoeur, "The Question of Proof in Freud's Psychoanalytic Writings," 210. Note Ricoeur's later self-correction to his account of narrative in *Freud and Philosophy*: "Instead of beginning with an account of the metapsychology, I would begin now by examining the criteria of what counts as a fact in psychoanalysis, as a function of the therapeutic situation itself, and I would subordinate the evaluation of the metapsychology to this first inquiry at the level of case-histories. It is at precisely this level that we must recognize the claim of the narrative component of psychoanalysis." (Paul Ricoeur, "Preface: Response to My Friends and Critics," in *Studies in the Philosophy of Paul Ricoeur*, ed. Charles E. Reagan [Athens: Ohio University Press, 1979], xv.)

16   Paul Ricoeur, "On Interpretation," in *Philosophy in France Today*, ed. Alan Montefiore (Cambridge: Cambridge University Press, 1983).

17   Paul Ricoeur, *Freud and Philosophy*, 382.

18   Paul Ricoeur, *Freud and Philosophy*, 382.

19   Paul Ricoeur, "Life in Quest of Narrative," in *On Paul Ricoeur: Narrative and Interpretation*, ed. David Wood (New York: Routledge, 1991), 29.

20   John Shotter, *Cultural Politics of Everyday Life* (Toronto: University of Toronto Press, 1993).

21   John Shotter, *Cultural Politics*, 3-8.

22   Paul Ricoeur, "Practical Reason," in *From Text to Action*, trans. Kathleen Blamey and John B. Thompson (Evanston: Northwestern University Press, 1991).

23   Paul Ricoeur, "Life in Quest of Narrative," 32.

24   John Shotter, *Cultural Politics*, 197.

25   John Shotter, *Cultural Politics*, 7.

26   John Shotter, *Cultural Politics*, 7.

27 R. J. Bernstein, *Beyond Objectivism and Relativism* (Oxford: Blackwell, 1983). We are aware, however, that Ricoeur's recent works, especially his essays on "Practical Reason" and "Initiative" have significantly added to his earlier notions of the practical sense by incorporating an analysis of the relation between the *present* and *action*. See Paul Ricoeur, *From Text to Action*.

28 Louis O. Mink, "Narrative Form as a Cognitive Instrument," in *The Writing of History*, ed. Robert H. Canary and Henry Kozicki (Madison: University of Wisconsin Press, 1978).

29 Alasdair MacIntyre, *After Virtue* (London: Duckworth, 1981).

30 Michael Billig, Susan Condor, Derek Edwards, Mike Gane, David Middleton and Alan Radley, *Ideological Dilemmas* (London: Sage, 1988). See John Shotter (*Cultural Politics*, Chapter 9) for a critique of MacIntyre's notion of narrative traditions as a public ideal and his failure to grasp the limits of narrative traditions to account for private, ordinary life. Both Billig and Shotter have contributed to the development of discursive approaches to psychology.

31 John Shotter, *Cultural Politics*.

32 David Epston, Michael White and Kevin Murray, "A Proposal for a Re-authoring Therapy: Rose's Revisioning of her Life and a Commentary," in *Therapy as Social Construction*, ed. Sheila McNamee and Kenneth J. Gergen (London: Sage, 1992).

33 Kenneth J. Gergen and John Kaye, "Beyond Narrative in the Negotiation of Therapeutic Meaning," in *Therapy as Social Construction*, ed. Sheila McNamee and Kenneth J. Gergen (London: Sage, 1992).

34 Kenneth J. Gergen and John Kaye, "Beyond Narrative in the Negotiation of Therapeutic Meaning," 181. Missing from all of these discussions, however, is the problem of the unequal nature of psychotherapy – frequently characterized as the dimension of 'power.' Psychotherapy is a contractual relationship and as such never fully approximates relationships in which narrative is forged in the daily activities of social life. Thus theories of narrative in psychotherapy import into their practices ways of talking derived from other kinds of relationships (and theorizing) while obscuring their authority as forms of therapy which *ought* to be applied in a therapeutic context. This issue deserves further comment but is not germane to the remainder of this paper.

35 John Shotter, *Cultural Politics*, 4.

36 Gerald Bruns, "Against Poetry: Heidegger, Ricoeur, and the Originary Scene of Hermeneutics," in *Meanings in Texts and Actions; Questioning Paul Ricoeur*, (Charlottesville: University Press of Virginia, 1993), 38.

37 Gerald Bruns, "Against Poetry: Heidegger, Ricoeur, and the Originary Scene of Hermeneutics," 38.

38 We are in substantial agreement here, of course, with David Carr's views as expressed in his *Time, Narrative and History* (Bloomington: Indiana University Press, 1986). He extends the meaning of narrative to include elements of what we consider here as "talk." The usefulness of employing narrative in such a context is a contestable issue beyond the concerns of this paper, although we anticipate that there are a number of overlaps between his understanding of narrative and various positions in the social sciences which concern themselves with discourse and the social construction of everyday life. Carr's views might find considerable currency in the social sciences were it not for his insistence on retaining the term "narrative" for what more generally goes by the name of "discourse" and "action."

39   In the *Revue de l'Université d'Ottawa/University of Ottawa Quarterly* 55(4) 1985. The quotations here are taken from the reprinted version in Wood, *Ricoeur*, 160-187.

40   Carr, "Ricoeur on Narrative," 162.

41   Ricoeur, "Ricoeur on Narrative," 180.

42   Ricoeur, "Ricoeur on Narrative," 182.

43   Ricoeur, "Ricoeur on Narrative," 182.

44   Like Shotter (*Cultural Politics*) we agree that theories of narrative (and the work of scholars such as Ricoeur) are crucial in helping us understand our own, public traditions. What is at issue is the individualistic agent who underlies the psychology of capturing "life" within a "narrative." We acknowledge, however, that this is far too short an explication of the differences between Carr and Ricoeur and we risk over-simplifying. For another view of the disagreement between these two authors, see David Pellauer, "Limning the Liminal: Carr and Ricoeur on Time and Narrative," *Philosophy Today* 35 (1991):51-62.

Women's Memoirs
and the Embodied Imagination:
The Gendering of Genre that Makes
History and Literature Nervous

HELEN M. BUSS

> We felt a quickening urgency of change drown our sense
> of regular direction, as though something were bound
> to happen soon but not knowing what it would be was
> making history nervous.[1]
>
> Sara Suleri, in *Meatless Days*

In order to answer his question "Can Fictional Narratives be True?", Paul Ricoeur begins by marking certain discourses as most "fictional" (tales, romances, dramas, novels) and others as most "empirical" (histories, biographies and autobiographies).[2] The major difference between the two categories is in terms of their sources, the source for the empirical discourses being "documents and archives,"[3] that of the fictional being the "archive" of the "imagination."[4] Ricoeur asks his question in order to show that each category of discourse shares in the other's world, history by making use of "the logic of narrative possibilities" and fictional narratives through their "mimetic dimension."[5] At the same time, Ricoeur is careful to conclude his essay by emphasizing that the two discourses have separate effects. History, because it is tied to the contingent, is able to "open us to the different," to the possible, and fiction, because it is mimetic – while not tied to contingency, but rather able to make use of the world of action to make "unreal" worlds – is able to address "the universal" and as a result "brings us back to the essential."[6] Thus Ricoeur tends to see the complementarity of the two discourses while maintaining their separate spheres and purposes.

My goal here is not to keep the spheres separate, but to make them (and us) nervous by showing that when we get the two so hopelessly commingled that we may be accused of complete discursive disobedience, of writing a bastardized discourse that cannot "be true," then we may be able to begin to put into words some "truth," that is "poetic

87

truth" (in a revised Ricoeurian sense of that term) concerning the histories, the lived lives of women. It is my experience as a reader of literary texts that this happens in some remarkable uses of the memoir form by women and that Ricoeurian theory can offer points of departure for my project.

My first point of departure is Ricoeur's use of the word "archive" in relation to the imagination. It is this metaphorical turn, by which the word "archive" is pulled from its literal association with actual buildings that are repositories of documents and made to substitute pictorially for what Ricoeur calls, "the imagination as understood in terms of its temporal complexity as the depository of oral and written traditions,"[7] that gives Ricoeur the linguistic pivot which allows him to make the argument of complementarity of historical and literary narratives. Performing a similar "language-game" (a term that Ricoeur uses), or what I call a "willful" feminist reading that revises the father's language by taking him at his word, I want to reliteralize the concept of the imagination as archive, by asserting that the building that houses the archive of the imagination is the body.[8] Thus, until we have a concept of an embodied imagination, we cannot fully read the literary narration of imaginative acts, and since every body has a history, we need to take into account personal historical narratives in order to inscribe the embodied imagination.

Ricoeur himself speaks toward this concept of embodied imagination in "Fictional Narratives," when he asserts in his discussion of the "hermeneutics of historicity" that we can no longer maintain the artificial separation of the subject and object in investigating the structures of historicity:

> The subject-object relationship itself is undermined by the very progression of reflective investigation from the theory of "inner sense" to that of intersubjective historicity. We are part of this field as story-tellers and as story-followers, as historians and as novelists. We *belong-to* history before telling stories or writing histories.[9]

Extending Ricoeur's thought by literalizing it in order to serve a concept of embodied imagination, I would add that we *belong-to* our bodies as well as to history and we belong to our bodies' histories before and while we tell stories and follow stories.

Again, in "Life: A Story in Search of a Narrative," Ricoeur's metaphors encourage me to seek what I call the embodied imagination. He speaks of "pre-narrative quality of human experience," which gives us "the right to speak of life as of an incipient story and thus of life as an activity and a desire in search of a narrative."[10] Ricoeur notes that "before the story is told, the individual seems entangled in the stories that happen to him. This "entanglement" thus appears as a pre-history of the story told in which the beginning is still chosen by the narrator. This pre-history of the story is what connects the latter to a larger whole and provides it with a background. Thus, background is built up into a living continuous overlap of all the lived stories. Thus, the stories told must emerge from this background. In this emergence the story guarantees man."[11]

The process Ricoeur describes here, understood from my strategy of literalizing his metaphor, speaks of a condition of narrative where a disentanglement must occur, where one part of the story must be designated "pre" identity, as background, in order that a "man" may "emerge," be guaranteed as "man." I seek a different "activity," have a different "desire," in that I desire a story that does not emerge, or disentangle, but rather re-*e-merges* , that is, marks itself off, "emerges," only to point to the way it is merged, the way it is entangled, in a way that privileges "background" as a guarantee of the human being.[12] In fact, what I seek is story-making that "guarantees" not a gendering that has a masculine social construction, but a gendering that is socially marked as woman. The process by which I find that alternate story is through a concept of the *embodied imagination*.

To speak here in the discourses of the academy of embodied imagination and its connection with women's use of the memoir form is to risk falling into binary oppositions that allow for the reappropriation of my endeavor into an essentialist universe in which women's imaginations are embodied and men's imaginations are of the spiritual. One does not have to be a philosopher to understand the dangers inherent in my inquiry. This is a risk that all theorizing feminists take at all moments of discourse in the patriarchal language in which we ply our trade. To help me skirt essentialism, undo binaries, I heed the warnings and advice of feminist theorists working to re-entangle the discourses in which we write and speak with the bodies that speak us and our theories. Elizabeth Grosz suggests that in pursuing such a discourse we need to be concerned with the "*lived body*, the body insofar as it is represented and used in specific ways in particular cultures."[13] The group of feminist theorists of embodiment that she refers to map bodiliness that is "neither brute nor passive but is interwoven with and constitutive of systems of meaning, signification and representation. On the one hand, it is a signifying and signified body, and, on the other, it is an object of systems of social coercion, legal inscription, and sexual and economic exchange."[14] In other words, to mark the process of embodied imagination in my reading strategies, I must look for a process by which a history of a life lived in an individual body enables a signifying process that does not separate imagination and body.

I find the beginning of that process in my reading – a reading that is perhaps sometimes with and sometimes against the grain – of Ricoeur. Take, for example, his meditation on metaphor and its function. The work I wish to particularly reread/revise is "The Metaphorical Process as Cognition, Imagination and Feeling,"[15] and I would like to read it in the light of an insight offered me by one of the feminist theorists Grosz cites. In *Bodies That Matter*, Judith Butler points to the importance of ritualization processes in the construction of sexed bodies:

> As a sedimented effect of a reiterative or ritual practice, sex acquires its naturalized effect, and yet it is also by virtue of the reiteration that gaps and fissures are opened up as the constitutive instabilities in such constructions, as that which escapes or exceeds the norm, as that which cannot be wholly defined or fixed by the repetitive labor of that norm. This instability is the *de*constitutive possibility in the very process of repetition, the power that undoes the very effects by which "sex" is stabilized, the possibility to put the consolidation of the norms of "sex" into a potentially productive crisis.[16]

Thus, the social construction of a body, which includes its gendering, is both achieved through repetitiveness that becomes ritualization and is open to change through the performative possibilities that open up during ritual. I would add that part of performance is pictorial metaphorization, an activity which can allow for new readings of old acts. For my purposes, Butler's point about ritual is germane. If the imaginative acts that the embodied imagination yield are the effect of gestures or sets of gestures repeated in a ritualistic way (rituals of the body that through their very performance open up the possibility of new constructions), this permits me to identify those incremental ritualistic embodied gestures so that I can mark moments of the embodied imagination acting to make a new literature and history of women's lives. Since I deal with literary texts, I must find a way of identifying markers of this process in language usage.

Once again I turn to Ricoeur, and to my revisionary reading of "The Metaphorical Process," for my guidance. In this article, Ricoeur, working at what he calls the "boundary between a *semantic* theory of metaphor and a *psychological* theory of imagination and feeling," locates metaphor's ability "to provide untranslatable information and, accordingly ... yield some true insight about reality."[17] It is through bringing together purely semantic operations of metaphor with certain psychological effects of those operations and through locating a metaphorized ritualistic repetition that I will be able to point to acts of embodied imagination. Ricoeur points to the way metaphor operates pictorially:

> The very expression "figure of speech" implies that in metaphor ... discourse assumes the nature of a body by displaying forms and traits which usually character-

ize the human face ...; it is as though the tropes gave to discourse a quasi-bodily externalization.[18]

This pictorial process of metaphor operates to support the substitutional work of metaphor, so that "[t]hings or ideas which were remote appear now as close."[19] Later in "The Metaphorical Process," Ricoeur proposes that imagination "contributes concretely to the *epoché* [suspension] of ordinary reference and the projection of new possibilities of describing the world." Ricoeur further asserts that "in a sense, all *epoché* is the work of the imagination. Imagination is *epoché*."[20] Ricoeur connects the moment of *epoché* with what he calls "poetic feeling":

> this instantaneous grasping of the new congruence [the metaphor] is "felt" as well as "seen." [This] ... underscore[s] the fact that we are included in the process as knowing subjects. If the process can be called ... predicative *assimilation*, it is true that *we* are assimilated, that is, made similar, to what is seen as similar. This self-assimilation is a part of commitment proper to the "illocutionary" force of the metaphor as speech act. We feel *like* what we see *like*.[21]

Ricoeur is careful to deny that such "poetic feelings" are bodily "emotions." In fact, he defines "poetic feelings" as an "*epoché* [suspension] of our bodily emotions."[22] I find the elision of the body by Ricoeur a point of contention. He says:

> feelings [which are not of the body as are emotions] are negative, suspensive experiences in relation to the literal emotions of everyday life. When we read, we do not literally feel fear or anger. Just as poetic language denies the first-order reference of descriptive discourse to ordinary objects of our concern, feelings deny the first-order feelings which tie us to these first-order objects of reference.[23]

In order to have "first-order feelings," instead of just bodily emotions, we must, according to Ricoeur, both deny and transfigure literal emotions.

My willful reading of Ricoeur through Butler goes something like this: To a certain extent we do deny bodily emotions when we have "poetic feelings" because we are constructed to do so. We are so constructed because we lack a language, other than the patriarchal language of transcendence, to describe the complex translation process that is happening. We have no "language-game" (to use Ricoeur's adaptation of Wittgenstein's phrase in a different context) for making sense of them. These emotions that are "suspended" or "denied" do *not go away* but rather are processed differently, are "transfigured" to use Ricoeur's term (once more differently).

I propose that they are trans*figured* (with the emphasis on the dramatic and sight-based nature of "figured") into repeating ritualistic gestures, a performance awaiting decoding by a process of metaphor

(UN)making. If we can recognize what Judith Butler calls the potential for "deconstitutive possibility" in the ritualized gesture, we may, through a metaphoric process, charged with what Ricoeur would call "poetic feeling," trans*figure* the bodily emotion into a more conscious self-construction that does not deny the bodily emotion in its transfiguration. Transfiguration, which I think Ricoeur implies is a disembodiment, I find to be always a further embodiment through the phenomenon of the ritual repetition of gestures not fully transfigured into "poetic feeling" in patriarchal language processes. Since the body begins the process because it is unable to make sense of (therefore "denying") an emotion it cannot construct in language, the body is a participant in the ritualization that occurs as a result. Ritualization embodies the emotion in a realm of performance where it is open to "feeling" – what Ricoeur calls the "poetic feeling" of catharsis.

The process I must use to make new knowledge of the ritualized gesture, the excess left behind by patriarchal theories of transfiguration, is itself embodied. It is the process of metaphor which involves me in pictorial figuration, accompanied by a moment of *epoché* in which I am "assimilated, that is made similar, to what is seen as similar." [24] Thus, while Ricoeur asserts that "this self-assimilation is part of the commitment proper to the 'illocutionary' force of the metaphor as speech act,"[25] I propose that the illocutionary force, the social force, what Butler would call the possibility for "productive crisis," involves an act of embodied imagination, an act in which metaphor made literal, works through bodily experience to make new meanings, and ultimately new language, new generic uses of language.

This metaphorical process, by which acts of the body, and particularly the gendered body, participate in making new meanings is especially foregrounded in women's uses of the memoir form, for the genre, already a bastardized form located between history and literature, borrowing from the genres of the novel and autobiography, is a site where binary oppositions are being deconstructed: binaries of private/public, history/literature, body/mind and male/female. I will briefly illustrate this process by reference to Sara Suleri's *Meatless Days*, the memoir of a postcolonial academic (a teacher of English at Yale) who writes of growing up at the moment of Pakistan's birth in a family that brings together Welsh and Pakistani parents.

In *Meatless Days*, Suleri tells of a number of painful accidents that occur to the bodies of loved ones, events that are not logically related, but which she deliberately makes adjacent in her text, a text where the public story of Pakistan's birth history is paralleled with deeply personal moments: "We felt a quickening urgency of change drown our sense of regular direction, as though something were bound to happen soon but not knowing what it would be was making history nervous. And so we were not really that surprised then, to find ourselves living through the summer of the trials by fire."[26] At this point in her historical narrative, Suleri suddenly switches from the topic of the uneasy and often violent alliance between politics and religion that made Pakistan possible to give examples of the "summer of the trials by fire" not from the national life of Pakistanis, but from the private life of her family. The summer "climaxed when Dadi (her grandmother) went up in a little ball of flames, but somehow sequentially related were my mother's trip to England to tend her dying mother, and the night I beat up Tillat and the evening I nearly castrated my little brother, runt of the litter, serious eyed Irfan."[27]

It is the "somehow related" phrase that needs attention in this quotation, for Suleri is aware that the heap of injuries, battles, deaths and violence, both familial and national, that she builds up in chapter one of her text are not causally or often even chronologically related, yet somehow they are related. The event of her grandmother's accidental burn accident and her slow healing are quite separate, by the narrative patterns of history and literature, from Pakistan's birth, from the mother's return to England to care for a dying mother, and from the night Suleri accidentally pours scalding water on her brother's genitals. And, as well, all these are separate from the night she physically attacks her sister for staying out late with a man. Further removed in time and cause are the later traffic accident deaths of the mother and another sister (the mother killed in a rickshaw accident, the sister by a hit and run driver two years following). Yet all these events are tumbled about in chapter one, highly physical images tumbled amongst and between the history of her father's involvement with the founding of Pakistan. What links these events is their common thread of bodily harm and their incidental occurrence during the events of the engendering of the state of Pakistan.

It is the forcible yoking of private and public, of events adjacent but not related, of narratives of nation and self that alerts me to the need for reading this chapter and, through it, the rest of Suleri's text, as a writing act which is an illustration of how the embodied imagination works. The phenomenon is read through noting the conjunctions of bodily harm, harm that is accidental, random, yet sometimes also angrily intended, but not predictable – some of it painfully healable, some of it never to be healed. These conjunctions act as a kind of language ritualization in this text. The repetition, the juxtaposition of the painful burnings, the senseless deaths, the painful distances between sister and sister, mother and daughter, speak another level of meaning that both informs and intensifies the historical narrative and the literary tropes of the text. They construct a ritualization of bodily harm through repetition and, by doing so, open up the possibility of new meanings, meanings that suggest that the private world of the family's "accidents" and the public world of violent politics and religion, may be related histories.

The act of imagination engaged in here cannot be fully told by Suleri in either discourse, historical or literary, and indeed cannot be fully read by the patriarchal imagination, which must deny and disfigure literal emotion in order to construct first-order feelings, the suspensive experience of the poetic imagination. The *epoché* involved in reading here is not an act of suspensive experience, where one allows some content to be disentangled, leaving a pre-story content neglected and unexamined. The kind of *epoché* demanded by the embodied imagination is an act of reading that never leaves the experience of bodies behind, but insists on their grounding value, their foregrounding in the imaginative act.

I do not wish to imply by my privileging of women's memoirs, and in particular Suleri's text, that the phenomenon of the embodied imagination is not present in other discourses. Once recognized (or readable), it is an ever-present phenomenon. Take a very familiar example: certain pictorial figurations of the crucifixion are acts of embodied imagination because their detail refuses the transcendence of the body of Christ on the cross. An act of the embodied imagination insists on the absolute visual reality of the blood-stained, torn flesh; it insists on the sacrifice, not the transcendence. If this suggests that the embodied imagination is not a very pleasant phenomenon, I think that suggestion is correct. I offer another unfortunate, but very accessible example: much pornography is based on acts of embodied imagination. The visual silencing, binding, flagellation and dismemberment of female bodies that one sees in pornography are meant to act literally, not to deny literal emotions, but rather to include them in the meaning making. As a result, the meaning that is made quite literally expresses the desire and intention of the devotees.

Suleri's text is also not very pleasant at times, but to quite a different intent than a pornographic representation. For the violence and devastation of a country's birth and the attendant history of a family cannot be fairly enacted in language unless we literalize metaphors through a ritually embodied repetition. In Suleri's text, the literalization crosses between the personal and the public discourses as her grandmother always insists on ending the story of Pakistan's creation as a nation with the story of her own conflagration, and Suleri's insists on telling the father's public story of political advocacy as a journalist and historian in the following images marked by the body and the private:

I think we dimly knew we were about to witness Islam's departure from the land of Pakistan. The men would take it to the streets and make it vociferate, but the great romance between religion and the populace, the embrace that engendered Pakistan, was done. So Papa prayed, with the desperate ardor of a lover trying to converse life back into a finished love.[28]

The purpose of this binding together of private and public tells the unwritable story (unwritable in conventional discourses) of the writer's own creation as postcolonial woman being engendered by the quickly lost worlds of her parents, the Welsh world of the mother drowned in an English education and a marriage to a man outside her culture, the Pakistani world lost to the father through the vicissitudes of politics. This is a story that cannot be told directly, through linear narrative or accepted use of tropes, without leaving something out, either the public or the private, the personal or the political, the body or the spirit. The literal pains, displacements and deaths of bodies must be placed on the page for the reader's act, an act which must not transcend, but must stay enmeshed with those bodies.

In her conclusion to chapter one of *Meatless Days*, Suleri observes when explaining the difficulty of locating the third world in discourse: "Trying to find it is like pretending that history and home is real and not located precisely where you're sitting."[29] The reader's act in reading the performance of the embodied imagination must be similarly conscious of the body located precisely where one's own body is sitting, in a conception of the body that is neither "brute nor passive," neither transcendable nor denied, but present and participating, enabling a signifying process which does not separate imagination and body.

Notes

1   Sara Suleri, *Meatless Days* (Chicago: University of Chicago Press, 1987), 10.

2   Paul Ricoeur, "Can Fictional Narratives Be True?", *Analecta Husserliana*, 14, ed. A.T. Tymieniecka (Dordrecht: Reidel, 1983), 3-19.

3   Ricoeur, "Fictional Narratives," 4.

4   Ricoeur, "Fictional Narratives," 5.

5   Ricoeur, "Fictional Narratives," 16.

6   Ricoeur, "Fictional Narratives," 16.

7   Ricoeur, "Fictional Narratives," 5.

8   In *Bearing the Word*, Margaret Homans asserts the centrality of literalization as a women's gendered response to living in patriarchal language: "the shift from figurative to literal and back again is heavily charged with mythic and thematic significance, for if literalization suggests a move in the direction of mother-daughter

language, figuration suggests a return to the paternal symbolic" (Chicago: University of Chicago Press, 1987), 30. I propose that what Homans points to in women's literary texts as a strategy to recreate maternal language through literalizing the father's figurative language can be used as a feminist critical strategy, not to deconstruct and expose the falsity of phallic language, but rather to use it as informant to a necessary theoretical gesture of the re-embodiment of language.

9 Ricoeur, "Fictional Narratives," 14.

10 Paul Ricoeur, "Life: A Story in Search of a Narrative," in *Facts and Values: Philosophical Reflections from Western and Non-Western Perspectives*, ed. M.C. Doeser and J.N. Kraay (Dordrecht: Martinus Nijhoff, 1986), 121-32.

11 Ricoeur, "Fictional Narratives," 13.

12 See my *Mapping Our Selves: Canadian Women's Autobiography in English* (Montreal: McGill-Queen's University Press, 1993), for the connections between re-e-merging as a narrative marker of women's accounts and theories of women's development.

13 Elizabeth Grosz, *Volatile Bodies* (Bloomington: Indiana University Press, 1994), 30.

14 Grosz, *Volatile Bodies*, 30.

15 Paul Ricoeur, "The Metaphorical Process as Cognition, Imagination and Feeling," *Critical Inquiry* 5 (1978-79): 143-59.

16 Judith Butler, *Bodies That Matter: On the Discursive Limits of "Sex"* (New York: Routledge, 1993), 10.

17 Ricoeur, "The Metaphorical Process": 143.

18 Ricoeur, "The Metaphorical Process": 144.

19 Ricoeur, "The Metaphorical Process": 147.

20 Ricoeur, "The Metaphorical Process": 154.

21 Ricoeur, "The Metaphorical Process": 156.

22 Ricoeur, "The Metaphorical Process": 157.

23 Ricoeur, "The Metaphorical Process": 157.

24 Ricoeur, "The Metaphorical Process": 156.

25 Ricoeur, "The Metaphorical Process": 156.

26 Sara Suleri, *Meatless Days*, 10.

27 Sara Suleri, *Meatless Days*, 10.

28 Sara Suleri, *Meatless Days*, 15.

29 Sara Suleri, *Meatless Days*, 28.

Narrative Songs and Identity in Late-Medieval Women's Religious Communities

HERMINA JOLDERSMA

Within the body of manuscripts which constitute our sources for late-medieval vernacular religious song, there are a substantial number, about a dozen or so, which are clearly related and which may, with more intensive exploration, yield important insights into late-medieval spirituality in general and into female spirituality specifically.[1] The manuscripts in question have a number of features in common: they originate geographically from religious communities in the Low Countries and Northern Germany, these communities are all women's communities, and these communities are all ideologically to be situated within the influence of the spiritual renewal emanating from the Modern Devotion.[2] The Modern Devotion was centrally concerned with lay spirituality, and hence institutions influenced by it included the Sister- and Brotherhouses of the Modern Devotion itself, the Tertiary Houses of the established orders, and even some First and Second Order institutions (Post makes the point that institutions did change their official status, usually from less to more cloistered, in the course of time).

The song manuscripts, which all originate from the women's institutions,[3] are clearly religious in intent and purpose. Some contain Latin religious songs, some have brief meditative prose texts, but the main body of all the manuscripts is composed of sacred vernacular songs, between 20 and 100 texts per manuscript, which are mystically lyrical or lyrically mystic: common themes are devotion to Mary, the life and suffering of Christ, the longing of the soul to be united with the bridegroom, and celebration of the anticipated heavenly feast, as well as an awareness of the self as sinner, awed fear of the Lord, death, judgment, and hope for mercy. Our understanding of these manuscripts and the function they may have played in the communities which created them is hampered by the fact that not one of them has been edited in its entirety, but rather that only certain texts have been discussed as individual entities.[4] As a result we have, at the moment, no clear picture of their function. A.M.J. van Buuren has recently argued that the manuscripts were mainly conceived by individuals and used for individual meditation; he bases his conclusions on the small physical size of the manuscripts, the usual absence of musical notation, and the highly personal tone of the songs.[5] Nevertheless, songs differ in this regard from other texts, and van Buuren agrees that it is possible that one person might have read aloud for the group the "passage for the day," after which a song would be sung communally. Indeed, the explicit instructions for group singing in some of the collections, the preference for popular (generally well-known) secular melodies, as well as the frequent occurrence of refrains to the songs, indicate that communal meditation, for example during the completion of manual tasks, may not have been the least of their functions.

Among the many aspects of these manuscripts which would merit further exploration, there is the intriguing phenomenon of the anomalous juxtaposition of sacred and secular texts in so many of them that this cannot be viewed as mere accident. My attention was drawn to this problem some years ago in my work on the late-medieval Tannhäuser ballad, and I would like to anchor my deliberations first of all in this concrete example. The Tannhäuser ballad is a fortuitous text for this purpose, as it illustrates the problem clearly and, through its particular "story," lends itself to some satisfactory interpretations.[6] At the same time, it has led to further inquiry because the answers I can provide for it do not fit as well for the other texts, and it is some of these questions which I would like to raise in this study.

The basic contours of the *Tannhäuser* story as it is transmitted in a large number of late-medieval ballads and short prose narratives are well known. The knight Tannhäuser enjoys many years (most often seven) of carnal delight with Venus in a "Venus mountain." Eventually he repents of his sins; with some effort, he takes leave of Venus and journeys to Rome to ask the Pope for absolution. The Pope, however, does not grant him such absolution immediately. Instead, he gives Tannhäuser a dry stick, telling him that he will be absolved when this stick bears roses. Tannhäuser returns to the mountain – the implication is that he is in despair. Yet, when the stick does bear roses, Tannhäuser is nowhere to be found. Most versions end with a short but biting criticism of the hard-heartedness of the Pope.

Discussion of the ballad tradition of this fascinating tale has always dealt summarily with the fact that one version is to be found in Brussels MS II, 2631, a late-medieval religious song manuscript originating in a women's cloister in Dordrecht, in the Netherlands. In general, scholars have (sometimes gleefully) interpreted the appearance of secular texts in sacred manuscripts as illustrating the irresistible charm which secular literature continued to have for monastics – contrary directives from church authorities notwithstanding. In the case of this version of the Tannhäuser ballad, more attention has been paid to the fact that it is a very "corrupt" text than to the manuscript in which it is found, and the religious woman who entered it into the manuscript has been castigated as semi-literate and/or unfamiliar with the tradition. In my study, however, I examine this version in the light of the manuscript which contains it, and I argue that this text was not "snuck" into the religious manuscript by a naughty and not very literate nun; rather, codicological evidence suggests that it was as deliberately entered into the manuscript similarly to other, more clearly sacred texts, and that, furthermore, it was one of several so-called "secular songs" deliberately so chosen for inclusion in the manuscript. Furthermore, I interpret this particular version in this particular manuscript as a song as "sacred" as all the others, for it continues and amplifies, through dramatic narrative, the themes pervading all of the texts throughout this entire, clearly religious collection. In essence, I redefined the place of this version of the ballad on the continuum of "sacred" to "secular" by interpreting its particular features in the light of this particular manuscript.

Further research revealed, however, that the Tannhäuser ballad was hardly an idiosyncratic entry into a single manuscript, but rather one of a number of similar "secular" texts in similar "sacred" song manuscripts, and there were enough such songs to raise the question of their function in these collections, of their function for these communities and for the individual women in them. Because of the existence of a larger number of examples of texts and manuscripts, it became increasingly clear that although the peculiar version of the Tannhäuser ballad in the Brussels manuscript might be explained by redefining the continuum from "secular" to "sacred" and the place of this version of the ballad on that continuum, this was not a satisfactory solution for all of the texts. What began to seem more interesting was the fact that all of these "secular" texts were "narratives," and, possibly relatedly, that the manuscripts containing them were "women's manuscripts."

The narrative texts themselves, of which any single manuscript might contain between one and six, provide a challenging mixture of "stories." For a better understanding of the way in which the late-medieval religious mind might have perceived them, they might profitably be presented in order on a continuum of what the modern mind might classify as "sacred" and "secular." There are, to begin with, the "Christmas narratives." These might well constitute a distinct group in that they retell, in song form, bits of the central story of Christianity as it is transmitted in the Gospels.[7] On the other hand, they might well be considered in a study on narrative – one longer than the present one – because they also extend the biblical narrative into contemporary contexts. There is, for example, a song which introduces the well-known story of the visit by the three wise men to Bethlehem with a reminder that the relics of these wise men may now be found in the cathedral at Cologne.[8] Moving from Biblical to contemporary stories, two of the texts are legends concerned with the lives of female saints: one tells how the pure love of St. Gertrude thwarts the devil's power over a knight, while the other recounts the tearful farewell of Saint Elisabeth to her husband Ludwig as he departs on a crusade, never to return.[9] In an almost negative counterpoint to pure virtue, two other texts concentrate on episodes in which the eucharist is blasphemed. In one (10 stanzas) a woman steals forty-five pieces of the host, with the result that God sends a mighty storm to visit the region;[10] in the other (19 stanzas) the sexton sells the host to Jews, and their blasphemies are eventually punished by the death of all concerned (146 or 160 persons, depending on the version).[11] On the continuum from sacred to secular, the distance between female saints to queens may not, to the late-medieval imagination, have been very great: two texts depict contemporary queens on their deathbeds.[12] Others, including the Tannhäuser text, are traditional ballads, telling of the trials and tribulations of ordinary mortals in love and death, in tragedy, in misdeed and retribution.[13]

The two specific texts on which I will be concentrating in this study have been chosen because of the challenges that they pose for my central project, which is to gain insight into the lives and minds of the late-medieval women who sang them. At the same time, I will be examining the texts in the light of Paul Ricoeur's narrative theory; in particular, I would like to explore his notion of narratives as "thought experiments," and his position that such thought experiments are essential to the shaping of identity.[14] This is worded another way by Carolyn Heilbrun: "What matters is that lives do not serve as models; only stories do that. And it is a hard thing to make up stories to live by. We can only retell and live by the stories we have read or heard. We live our lives through texts."[15] Heilbrun's particular focus on the debilitating absence of "women's texts," or "women's narratives," may be instructive in our deliberations of the phenomenon I am exploring, as it is peculiar only to late-medieval women's manuscripts.

The two texts I have chosen are not "personal" narratives in a strict sense. Clearly they are not narratives about the women who "told" (sang) them, nor even about women they knew or might have known, as would be the case for other "stories" originating from late-medieval women's religious communities.[16] At the same time, we must remember that the stories in the songs were likely experienced as "true" by the late-medieval imagination; the steps from Biblical stories, to saints lives, to Tannhäuser's folly and the malicious tales circulating about the Jews are incremental and as such not very large. In addition, there are many instances in certain cultures in which impersonal, or general, stories become personalized, particularly in the context of group identity. Ricoeur's notion of "thought experiments" in part addresses this problem; he writes: "It is the function of poetry, in its narrative and dramatic forms, to set before the imagination and meditation situations each of which make up thought experiments by means of which we learn to join the ethical aspect of human behaviour to happiness and unhappiness, to fortune and misfortune."[17] If in fact the "stories" we are considering here, these "thought experiments," are not perceived as "fiction" in the sense of "untrue" but rather "fiction" in the sense of "not issuing out of one's personal life," Ricoeur's notion is very helpful.

The first text to be considered is a very apt, but at the same time a very disturbing demonstration of the function of narrative as "thought experiment." It is the text which so extensively describes the desecration of the sacrament by Jews in Breslau, ostensibly a "real" incident that occurred in 1453. The song seems to have been relatively popular, as it is extant in four different manuscripts from four geographically distant communities. The text is relatively stable, which suggests that it was indeed written by one author, entirely plausibly the "Jacob of Rautingen" mentioned in the last stanza of the poem. Yet, the versions vary enough from one another, for example in the numbers, to suggest oral rather than written transmission; this would in turn indicate that the song had captured the popular imagination.

I find this text, and its existence in the religious song manuscripts in which I have become interested, very troubling, and this troubled feeling is only increased by considering it in the light of the shaping of narrative identity. It must be remarked, first of all, that the text was likely not experienced as fiction in the sense of being "not true," but as a historical event which really happened, materially anchored by a date, a geographical location, an author's name. Nevertheless, since the singers of the song did not experience the actual event, the song is indeed a "thought experiment," and may be seen as exploring "the ethical aspect of human behaviour" within the boundaries of the categories circumscribed by the ethics of medieval Christianity. The song depicts the worst kind of unethical behavior, the rejection of Christ, of which all Jews were by definition guilty through their actions in choosing Barabus over Christ.

The song's first stanza gives a thumbnail sketch of Christ's last days on earth, sketching out Judas' betrayal of Christ to the unbelieving Jews for thirty gold pieces; the rest of the song fleshes out this sketch with the contemporary parallel event. The sexton, explicitly named as Judas' brother, sells the host to the still unbelieving Jews for thirty guilders. Mistreated by the Jews, the Host begins to bleed and cry out, and the culprits are found out. The sexton hangs himself, as Judas did. In contrast to the Biblical example, the Jews are punished immediately with their burning at the stake, prefiguring their eternal fate in the Christian scheme of retribution.[18]

What might such a song have meant for the women in religious communities? At a very simple level, it no doubt served to strengthen the sense of community by establishing a "them" versus an "us." Though this opposition applies particularly to Jews versus Christians, it can go beyond ethnic or religious differences to the simple contrast of "bad them" versus "good us," as illustrated by the thematically similar text in which it is an evil woman who desecrates the host. On another level, this texts parallels the Tannhäuser ballad in that it, too, is a narrative case study of the central concern of these communities, a concern expressed again and again in the lyrical as well as the narrative songs, namely the often bitter and difficult struggle of the soul seeking to escape its earthly confines and move towards its destiny – unification with God. Unlike Tannhäuser, however, who might have been a die-hard sinner but who did repent and presumably was saved, the Jews in this story presented the ultimate negative example of sinners for whom there could be no pardon. And, if a psychological interpretation is not too modern to be valid for literature of an entirely different period, the song might also be seen as providing a vicarious experience of pure evil, as a "thought experiment" in which the most sacred object in the Christian tradition – Christ's body – is reviled and rejected in the most ultimate way. Thus, the action itself and the punishment for such action is vicariously experienced through the dramatic narrative. "The great difference between life and fiction," to quote Ricoeur again, "is in part abolished through our capacity to appropriate in the application to ourselves the intrigues we receive from our culture, and our capacity of thus experimenting with the various roles that the favourite *personae* assume in the stories we love best."[19] These "favourite *personae*," it seems, need not always be positive figures, for in casting the Jews as the ultimate villains in the Christian drama of the soul's acceptance or rejection of, or struggle for, salvation, and in retelling the universal story in this most highly dramatic form, in a specific incident, the individual can safely play out the worst scenario without having to bear the consequences of such an action.

The second text on which I will focus does not, in fact, fit the interpretations for either the Tannhäuser ballad or the Breslau song very well, and I have chosen it precisely for that reason. One of the five "secular" narrative texts in the Brussels manuscript (which also contains the Tannhäuser song) is a popular ballad retelling the tragic story of Hero and Leander, a story which seems to have captured the European imagination from the late-fourteenth century on. Two lovers are prevented from coming together, by a river or, perhaps more precisely, by parents who put them on either side of that river. The girl lights a candle or candles to guide her lover as he swims over to her, but an evil person blows them out. The girl requests parental permission to go down to the river, where she asks a fisherman to bring her beloved up out of the water. Holding the body in her arms, she springs into the water and so ends her own life as well.

As is the case for the Tannhäuser ballad, the Brussels manuscript puts its own stamp on this narrative. It has an extensive preface, which tells us that two royal children loved each other, but that the girl's father put her into a cloister. The boy swam across the sea, guided by the candle the girl caused to be put on the window sill, but an evil nun had it extinguished so that – and the preface is clear about the causal relationship – the boy would drown and not reach the shore.[20] The version in the Brussels manuscript is unique in its telling of the girl's forced entry into the cloister, and in its emphasis on, and condemnation of, the nun who has the candle put out. Left out of the song itself is mention of the girl's lighting the candle; rather, three stanzas are devoted to the actions of the nun, who is depicted as a heartless authoritarian ruling through fear: "Men deder wt die kaersse / Men dorstet laten niet" ("They put out the candle, they were afraid to disobey"). The song also explicitly criticizes the nun for her actions: "Een non god gheef haer al mijn leit" ("A nun – may God send her the harm that I wish her!" or, more colloquially, "I hope God gets her!").

At first reading, and even at second and third reading, there is little in the song that would permit the same religious interpretation which can be given to the other texts. It is, of course, possible to grasp at interpretive straws. Given the preface, the text seems to have been shaped into a criticism of the practice of committing girls or women to a cloistered life against their will. This practice was common at the time, particularly for aristocratic women whose dowries were not sufficient for marriage but might do for the cloistered life.[21] It is of course the case that the religious communities from which these manuscripts originated, influenced as they were by the Devotio Moderna's concern with lay spirituality and its urban roots, were more "democratic" in that women joined them because they wanted to do so, and that members of these communities were not necessarily aristocratic. This might account for the somewhat puzzling condemnation of a nun by women who, though not nuns in the strictest sense, were at least members of a recognized religious community. "Good nuns" are obliquely mentioned in the story as the nuns who extinguish the candle very much against their wills and only because they do not dare to contravene the strict orders of their superior. And yet, it seems unlikely that this text is evidence of inter-institutional nastiness, and that it was included in the manuscript expressly for that purpose.

Another interpretation yields itself when one considers the narrative on a more abstract level. This song is the third in a group of six so-called "secular" songs, and follows two texts which depict contemporary queens on their deathbeds. What all three songs have in common is the unfulfilled longing by a female figure for her male beloved: the queens long for their spouses (who are, as might be expected, doing battle some-where else), the girl for her lover. This longing is expressed more or less erotically, with the girl's kissing of her lover's dead body being the most explicit depiction. Generally speaking, the pervading theme is the sig-nificance of death and unification with the beloved after death. When one looks at these narratives in this more abstract way, one can see that they do, in fact, present concrete examples of the central theme of the manuscript, namely the longing of the soul to be unified with the heav-enly bridegroom after death. In medieval mysticism, whether early or late, the soul is always female, the bridegroom always male, and the erotically charged interaction between the two a standard part of the way in which this interaction was depicted and understood. As such, the ballad of the two lovers becomes a concrete example of the achieve-ment of the unification of soul and bridegroom; the girl's kissing the body (as the song explicitly states, on the mouth more than one hun-dred times), echoes the anointing of Christ's body by female disciples. The unification of the lovers in death, in the same grave bearing sweet-brier roses, provides a tangible analogy for the sweet unification of the soul with God.

One of the (no doubt several) questions which remains, is the one which asks what significance lies in the fact that these manuscripts are all "women's manuscripts." One explanation must certainly lie in the semi-lay character of the institutions involved, that in such institutions its inhabitants had a freer hand (at least collectively) in shaping their meditations and their spirituality. This "freedom" is extended by the fact that women were considered less important than men, and where they were not treated as especially sinful troublemakers who needed stricter controls, women in such semi-lay communities may have enjoyed a certain "benign neglect" in spiritual matters which resulted in greater freedom than was the case for their more important, and hence more controlled, first-order or male counterparts. This does not, however, explain why such clearly earnest women, who deliberately chose a visibly religious life, would have included these texts in their devotional material. If one proceeds from the assumption that these texts were included for sincerely religious purposes, it would seem that their most important feature is their narrativity. Recent feminist theory has suggested that the "literalization" of experience is women's gendered response to the abstract constructs of the dominant culture. In these songs, the narrative may constitute the "literalization" of contemporary abstract spirituality. Even the story of salvation and its significance for one's own daily life, with which these women were so profoundly concerned, was abstract to the extreme, and these contemporary narrative songs seemed to "literalize" the abstraction into a story of human dimensions which could be understood, or, perhaps better, experienced, by the historical individual. One cannot, of course, so simply use modern theory to "explain" a pre-modern phenomenon, and I do so only briefly, knowing that there is much more to be said. At the same time, theories of narrativity cannot confine themselves only to contemporary experience, basically because the phenomenon of narrative is so much older than the theory which examines it.

Let me offer some tentative conclusions about the role and significance of narrative songs in women's manuscripts of the late-medieval/early-modern period. With the qualification that narrative theory may be too "modern," that is, too based on self-conscious subjectivity to be useful for older, especially pre-Renaissance literature, I will venture to suggest that the narrative songs which I have been discussing, in the context which is the central focus of my concern, in fact are "acts of plotting" in Ricoeur's terms. Manifold happenings are transformed into a complete and singular history, and these happenings also contribute to the progress of the story. Once "plotted" in this sense, the individual stories unify widely divergent components, turning "concordant discords" into a single concordant story, where the "how" is ultimately more important than the "what" (we are reminded that these ballads, as part of popular literature, were retold rather than composed). And they introduce into the abstractly temporal story of salvation (for though this story is bounded by time, it is not time which humans can really know, and certainly Ricoeur's notion of infinite succession applies here: "and then?" "and then?") a measured time, a configuration, perhaps, with a culmination and an end. The women who sang these songs, I might remind you, lived in communities in which all of life's "stories" were reduced to one, and they themselves would likely never have "lived" the stories they sang. For them, these stories functioned to make sense of how the very abstract story of salvation might work in the lives of "real" human beings. Many of the narratives in the manuscripts are unique versions of their particular traditions. Thus, between the two poles of servile repetition and calculated deviance, the texts are based on models but constitute an "experimentation in the narrative domain" which can be ascribed to the making of meaning for the individual or the group.

Notes

1 Previous scholarship has alluded to the fact that the manuscripts in question might be related to one another, but little work has been done on them in the context of such a relationship. J.A.N. Knuttel's *Het geestelijk lied in de Nederlanden voor de kerkhervorming* (Rotterdam: W.I. & J. Brusse, 1906) remains a milestone of careful philological attention to late-medieval religious vernacular song in general. Also important are G.G. Wilbrink, *Das geistliche Lied der Devotio moderna. Ein Spiegel niederländisch-deutscher Beziehungen* (Nijmegen: G.J. Thieme, 1930) and Eleonore Benary, *Liedformen der deutschen Mystik im 14. und 15. Jahrhundert* (Greifswald: H. Adler, 1936). See also Walter Salmen, "Das Liederbuch der Anna von Köln und seine Beziehungen zu den Niederlanden" (*Kongress-Bericht, Internationale Gesellschaft für Musikwissenschaft*. Utrecht, 1952), 340-51.

2 The authority on the Modern Devotion is still R.R. Post, *The Modern Devotion. Confrontation with Reformation and Humanism* (Studies in Medieval and Reformation Thought 3. Leiden: E.J. Brill, 1968). Also important is Stephanus Axters, O.P. *De moderne devotie 1380-1550*. Vol. 3 of *Geschiedenis van de vroomheid in de Nederlanden*, 4 vols. (Antwerp: De Sikkel, 1956).

3 The differences which are evident in manuscripts originating from women's versus men's institutions bear further investigation. For our purposes, it might be mentioned that there are fewer "men's" manuscripts, that these contain more Latin and more extensive musical notation, that there is closer adherence to the biblical text, and that the only narratives they contain are songs retelling the life of Christ in a rather orthodox fashion. Three such "men's manuscripts" are discussed in: Walther Lipphardt, "Deutsche Antiphonenlieder des Spätmittelalters in einer Salzburger Handschrift (Michaelbeuern Ms. cart 1). *Jahrbuch für Liturgik und Hymnologie* 27 (1983): 39-82; E. Bruning, OFM, *De Middelnederlandse Liederen van het onlangs ontdekte Handschrift van Tongeren (omstreeks 1480)* (Antwerpen: N.V. Standaard, 1955) [This manuscript is described earlier by Luc Indestege, *Middelnederlandse Geestlijke Gedichten, Liederen, Rijmspreuken en Exempelen. Naar een pas ontdekt handschrift van het einde der 15de eeuw, afkomstig uit het Windesheimer klooster 'Ter Noot Gods,' te Tongeren (met 4 afbeeldingen)* (Antwerpen: N.V. Standaard, 1951)]; and Wilhelm Bäumker, *Ein deutsches geistliches Liederbuch mit Melodien aus dem XV. Jahrhundert nach einer Handschrift des Stiftes Hohenfurt* (Leipzig: Breitkopf & Hartl, 1895).

4 I am in the process of completing an edition of Brussels MS II, 2631, a manuscript which originated in a Tertiary institution in Dordrecht c. 1500. I have also not yet been able to obtain a copy of P.F.J. Obbema, ed. *Die gheestelicke melody. Ms. Leiden, University Library, Ltk. 2058. With an Introduction* (Leiden: 1975).

5 "'Soe wie dit lietdkyn sinct of leest': De functie van de Laatmiddelnederlandse geestelijke lyriek." In *Een zoet akkord. Middeleeuwse lyriek in de Lage Landen.* Ed. F. Willaert *et al.* (Amsterdam: Prometheus, 1992), 234-54.

6 See my article "Appropriating Secular Song for Mystical Devotion in the Late Middle Ages: The *Tannhäuser* Ballad in Brussels MS II, 2631." *Mystics Quarterly* 18 (1992): 16-28. While I would still agree with most of my conclusions in this article, I can see that the inquiry must take into account that the appearance of this ballad in a religious manuscript is not unique, and that it is one of a number of such texts which are better viewed in relation to one another.

7 J.A.N. Knuttel's chapter on "Kerstliederen" gives evidence of the popularity of the Christmas story in song: *Het geestelijk lied in de Nederlanden voor de kerkhervorming* (Rotterdam: W.L & J. Brusse, 1906), 87-147. Subsequent chapters deal with songs on other events in Jesus' life, on events in Mary's life, and on the lives of saints; to the last of these Knuttel comments that there are relatively many, and very "good" ones. A study of these songs from the point of view of narrative theory might yield interesting insights.

8 The text is in W.P. Gerritsen, W.P., and a "werkgroep van Utrechtse Neerlandici," *Het liedboekje van Marigen Remen (Hs. Leiden, U.B., Ltk. 218, F. 62 - F. 78V)* (Utrecht: Ruygh-Bewerp I, 1966), 2-7.

9 The song about St. Gertrude (incipit "Nu wil ich vroelich heven an") is found in a manuscript compiled by "Anna" in Cologne c. 1500; see Walter Salmen und Johannes Koepp, Hrsg. *Liederbuch der Anna von Köln (um 1500),* Denkmäler Rheinischer Musik 4 (Düsseldorf: L. Schwann, 1954), 19-20. A parallel is found in Berlin MG80 185; see the discussion in G.G. Wilbrink, *Das geistliche Lied der Devotio moderna. Ein Spiegel niederländisch-deutscher Beziehungen* (Nijmegen: G.J. Thieme, 1930), 136-46. Only one version of the song about St. Elisabeth has been transmitted; see Paul Alpers, *Das Wienhäuser Liederbuch. Herausgegeben im Auftrage von Gauleiter Oberpräsident Lauterbacher vom Reichspropagandaamt Südhannover-Braunschweig* (Hannover: [1944]), 79-82. That the legend on which the song is based was popular in women's religious institutions is evident in the fact that it is pictured in a number of tapestries, also in the Wienhäuser cloister: see Paul Alpers, "Das Wienhäuser Liederbuch," *Niederdeutsches Jahrbuch. Jahrbuch des Vereins für niederdeutsche Sprachforschung* 69/70 (1939/1947): 30.

10 The text is in Paul Alpers, *Das Wienhäuser Liederbuch. Herausgegeben im Auftrage von Gauleiter Oberpräsident Lauterbacher vom Reichspropagandaamt Südhannover-Braunschweig* (Hannover: [1944]), 36-7.

11 This text seems to have been very well known, as it is extant in four versions; see Paul Alpers, *Das Wienhäuser Liederbuch. Herausgegeben im Auftrage von Gauleiter Oberpräsident Lauterbacher vom Reichspropagandaamt Südhannover-Braunschweig* (Hannover: [1944]), 29-35; Franz Jostes, "Eine Werdener Liederhandschrift aus der Zeit um 1500," *Jahrbuch des Vereins für niederdeutsche Sprachforschung* 14 (1888): 86-8; in Berlin 8o 190, rpt. in Hoffmann von Fallersleben, *Niederländische geistliche Lieder des xv. Jahrhunderts,* Horae Belgicae 10 (Hannover: Carl Rümpler, 1854), 235-238; one further source is given in Paul Alpers, "Das Wienhäuser Liederbuch," *Niederdeutsches Jahrbuch. Jahrbuch des Vereins für niederdeutsche Sprachforschung* 69/70 (1939/1947): 16.

12 Both of these texts are found in Brussels Ms II, 2631, of which I am currently preparing an edition.

13 A number of these, including the Tannhäuser text, are found in Brussels Ms II,

2631, and have been reprinted, not entirely without error, in Robert Priebsch, *Deutsche Handschriften in England*, vol. 1 (Erlangen: Fr. Junge, 1896), 230-8. One particularly interesting text describing how a woman eats the heart of her lover, a text which I will not be considering in this study, is found in W.P. Gerritsen, W.P., *et al.*, *Het liedboekje van Marigen Remen (Hs. Leiden, U.B., Ltk. 218, F. 62 - F. 78V)* (Utrecht: Ruygh-Bewerp I, 1966), 42-7.

14 In particular, I refer to Paul Ricoeur, "Life: A Story in Search of a Narrator," in *Facts and Values: Philosophical Reflections from Western and Non-Western Perspectives*, ed. M.C. Doeser and J.N. Kraay (Dordrecht: Martinus Nijhoff, 1986), 121-32.

15 Carolyn G. Heilbrun, *Writing a Woman's Life* (New York: Ballantine, 1988), 37.

16 I am thinking, for example, of the "biographies" in *Hier beginnen sommige stichtige punten van onsen oelden zusteren* (ed. D. de Man, The Hague: 1919); some of these have been translated by John van Engen in *Devotio Moderna: Basic Writings* (New York: Paulist Press, 1988), 121-136. Such "personal narratives" also form the basis of the work of Carolyn Walker Bynum.

17 Ricoeur, "Life: A Story," 123.

18 Late-twentieth-century hindsight, of course, recognizes that this was not only their eternal fate. Readers must always shudder when they recognize, for example, that this text was reprinted twice during the Nazi period; furthermore, these editions of the Wienhäuser manuscript title the song under discussion "Der Breslauer Judenfrevel," while the song in which it is a woman who desecrates the host is called "Der Blomberger Hostienfrevel" (despite the identical grammatical constructions, the two are not parallel terms). Still, anti-Semitism has no national boundaries; on linguistic grounds Alpers argues that the song is of Netherlandic origin: see "Das Wienhäuser Liederbuch," *Niederdeutsches Jahrbuch. Jahrbuch des Vereins für niederdeutsche Sprachforschung* 69/70 (1939/1947): 16. One of many similar stories about Jewish villainy is told a century earlier, perhaps not coincidentally by a prioress, in Chaucer's Canterbury tales; see "The Prioress's Tale," in Larry D. Benson, ed., The Riverside Chaucer, 3rd ed. (New York: Houghton Mifflin, 1987): 209-12.

19 Ricoeur, "Life: A Story," 131.

20 The text reads: "Ende een quade non lietse wt doen om dat he verdrencken sounden ende niet aen comen."

21 Still the authority on this subject is Eileen Power, *Medieval English Nunneries, c. 1275-1535* (Cambridge: 1922), especially 4-14; her conclusions are repeated, sometimes word for word, in E.W. McDonnell, *The Beguines and Beghards in Medieval Culture* (New York: 1969): 81-91. One further literary example of this practice can be found in the extremely popular "Graf und Nonne" ballad; see my commentary on the Netherlandic version of it in *155. Graf und Nonne (Die Nonne)*, Deutsche Volkslieder mit ihren Melodien 8, ed. O. Holzapfel (Freiburg: Verlag des Deutschen Volksliedarchivs, 1988), 203-5.

On Narrative
and
Belonging

DAVID D. BROWN

In this paper, I present a case study in support of the view that the link-age between personal identity ("I") and collective identity ("we") is a narrative accomplishment. It is proposed that in the course of everyday interaction subjects find in the narrative accounts of others formal par-allels with their own accounts. This line of thought will lead to an inter-pretation of the concept of collective identity as "belonging." One experiences "belonging" to the extent that one is able to interweave inter-pretations of self with the interpretations of others through narrative discourse. Such a notion of belonging sheds light on the phenomena of political consciousness and social movements, and may be a prerequi-site for collective action. I also want to critique the emphasis on categor-ical discourse in identity theory and argue for a view of identification that is agency-centered, and therefore a view with a firmer political foun-dation. My efforts in this regard build in the main on Paul Ricoeur's theory of "narrative identity."

A case study of an ethnic senior's support group is presented as a way of illustrating and exploring these ideas. This study was initiated to gain a clearer understanding of how narrative discourse structured and expressed personal and collective identity. The research followed an ethnographic line of inquiry in keeping with its exploratory nature. In addition to interviews and observations taken during group meet-ings, attention was given to a semi-autobiographical theater production produced and performed by members of the group.

The members of the group have experienced being identified by others and to some extent by themselves in categorical terms as "old." The group is of interest in that they have acted and continue to act to resist the categorical label "old" through an alternate narrative discourse. An examination of this counter-discourse sheds light on the narrative con-stitution of personal and collective identity, especially in terms of human

action and suffering. The group has quite self-consciously named themselves "Primavera" (Spanish for springtime). I name the group with their
consent and indeed their desire to be given acknowledgment. Their
struggle to be acknowledged as capable and multifaceted agents underscores much of their orientation toward their recollected past and
imagined futures.

Theoretical Foundation

Before speaking about my experience with Primavera, let me outline
out a theoretical foundation that has been considerably influenced by
the philosophy of Ricoeur.[1] Relatively little attention has been given in
the social sciences to how reflexive questions of identity are answered
in terms of social agency: the experience of power and domination in
the social world.[2] Rather, the concentration has been on processes of
what I will call "social taxonomy." The implicit logical operation of social
taxonomy is one built upon comparison and contrast, of how subjects
construe basic similarities and differences between one another. What is
at stake here is the distinction between being identified as a member of
a simple general type (for example, "old") and being identified in terms
of one's own lived relational experience. Social taxonomy is biased
toward the former.

The argument being introduced here is not that the study of social
taxonomy is invalid. It is certainly valid to say that identification includes being cognizant of oneself as a member of a given social category
relative to certain referent others. But I am arguing that, even if categorization is a basic mode of social discourse, it is by no means the only
level about which identity work and other processes of social interaction are accomplished. What is understated is how I have knowledge of
myself, not merely relative to others, but in relation to others. This level
of self-interpretation goes beyond differentiation between social types;
self-identification based on relations links the oneself to others in terms
of lived experience. This leads to Ricoeur's concern with the lived interpretation of self as actor and sufferer.

Ricoeur reminds us that the evaluation of action is premised on the
knowledge of subjects in terms of agency, which is in turn premised on
a discursive system that designates certain types of subjects (what I have
called "social taxonomy").[3] Other levels of discourse on human identity,
specifically narrative and ethical discourse, extend identification beyond
a taxonomic foundation. Social taxonomy limits the answer to identity
questions (i.e., "Who am I?", "Who are we?") to the form "I am one of a
certain type of person" (e.g., male/female, young/old, normal/devi-
ant, rich/poor, doctor/lawyer).

For the purpose of this discussion, I will focus mainly on the narrative level of discourse as it is central for constituting the self as an actor in the most significant sense of the term. In Ricoeur's critical hermeneutics, individual consciousness is not pre-given; it is emergent and developmental.[4] Consciousness is accomplished not through unmediated self-reflection, but rather through the ongoing interpretation of cultural texts. Thus hermeneutics directs us toward a de-centered notion of the subject. It assumes a view of selfhood that entails an ongoing dialectic between subject and discourse. We can theorize identity occurring at the point of confrontation between the person as a potential speaker/actor and the system of discourse that enables and constrains speaking/acting. Narrative is that mode of discourse through which human action is interpreted as meaningful agency.

We have seen an increasing interest in the significance of narrative discourse within the fields of history and social sciences.[5] This is evident, for example, in the renaissance of life-history research in sociology, anthropology and psychology.[6] As well, there has been considerable interest recently in forms of discourse analysis that emphasize the accomplishment of narrative in textual works.[7] Narrative is significant as a level of discourse in social life because it has particular properties that distinguish it from other forms of discourse, as Ricoeur has proposed.[8] In particular, narrative discourse enables the representation of self in terms of the affirmation or denial of human action.[9]

Identity and Narrative in Primavera

In the balance of this paper, I will move back and forth between voices from my ethnographic record, on the one hand, and theoretical commentary informed by my interpretation of Ricoeur, on the other. For the present case study of collective narration and identification, I worked with a particular group: approximately thirty female and five male senior citizens from Latin America now living in a major Canadian city. There were a number of reasons for this selection. First, they constituted a distinct ethnic-based collective with already salient features of identity. Second, the size of the group made members relatively accessible in terms of ethnographic research. Moreover, the group was willing to be part of such a study. Since the group is currently involved in certain projects, including the development of a housing co-operative, their experience of history and identity is not simply located in the past; rather, it extends into their imagined future. Finally, and most significant for my theoretical interests, the group has produced and performed a semi-autobiographical play. These characteristics of the group opened the way to explore continuities between individual and collective identity and to examine how identification emerges through the narrative discourse within and surrounding autobiographical productions.

The members of Primavera came together initially because of their common condition of being marginalized by virtue of their language (most speak only Spanish) and their age. In some cases, they have been marginalized as much by their own families as by mainstream Canadian society. Their narrative accounts to me and to each other often focus on the experience of being known, in their words, only as old persons – as people without capabilities or desires. A number of the members also felt alienated from having full relationships with their grandchildren because the Spanish language was often not passed on to the younger generation. In one woman's tearful expression of suffering: "I can only be a babysitter, but not a grandmother."

Primavera was formed within a community where other associations for Latin American seniors already existed. Let me now turn to the ethnographic voices by first recollecting the following account of how the group came to be named.

> The name Primavera ... in Canada first you have spring, then summer, then fall, then winter. So spring is the best season of the year. We are in that season, between heat and cold.

The naming of the group is part of their spoken history, and the name is appropriated by individuals to differentiate themselves from other support groups and from the dominant discourse of their community that, in their view, constrains them with the label: "old" people. They associate the label "old" with the notion of lacking capability, which we might go on to note, following Ricoeur, also implies lacking a story of capability. The symbolic meaning of the name "Primavera" is connected to their age; but specifically as a means of resisting the typification "old people." In poststructural terms, they confront their selves in the symbolic world of their community as an absence. But they appear to go on to collectively resist this absence by striving for a presence through narrative traces – an effort that further strengthens their sense of belonging.[10]

Also included in the spoken history of the group are accounts of its formation and evolving importance for the members. These accounts are important in that they further indicate that group members construct the group as a "we" that has a history.

> Once we built that trust we realized that we could do more things and in spite of our age or illness because some people were sick of different things. And some of them were not really sick. Actually what they had was something else, namely the lack of communication.

When we look further into accounts of the group given by its members, we find statements of an emancipatory nature. People give accounts of themselves as beings in the process of becoming. In other words, identity begins to be connected to agency.

> I came to Canada eight years ago and since I started coming to the group I feel a change in myself. I feel freer and also my family is telling me "What happened to Mom? She seems to be so unleashed." I feel freer now. Before I had to sort of ask them for permission to go here or there because they had to take me. I had to rely on them, but now I feel that I am more myself and freer and I feel much better.

The question to be asked at this point concerns how the group is able to foster such a sense of belonging and actualization, especially in light of the fact that the members are, by their own accounts, quite diverse in terms of political, cultural, national, and religious categories. The answer, I think, lies in the dominant activity of the group meetings: storytelling.

A turn to theory. According to Ricoeur, narrative is the most central level of discourse that structures human identity. Indeed, Ricoeur refers to a "narrative identity." "Subjects recognize themselves in the stories they tell about themselves,"[11] and they do so specifically in terms of their relative agency. Narrative is that form of discourse that represents human action in relation to given problematic situations. To follow a story is to recognize the sequence of events and actions as displaying a particular direction, in which the intentional human response to a situation "brings the story to its conclusion."[12] Ricoeur contends that action is that aspect of human behavior that can be recollected in stories whose function, in turn, is to provide an identity to the actor. Identity is established through an interpretation of who acts in the narrative.

Returning to the meetings of the group: during my visits with Primavera, narrative interaction during the meetings (and other gatherings) sometimes involved the group as a whole, but more often it was based on smaller groups of two or three members. But even if any given storytelling interaction might involve only a few individuals, virtually everyone at the meetings participates in these sort of localized encounters. The significance of this form of interaction based on narrative discourse is given in their own words:

> It's something that encourages us.... At least once a week we have a group where they can go and talk in our own language and remember things and share things.

> I feel there is a lot of understanding within the group and we share things.

> Some of the ladies have problems with their children and they go and talk about it. I've never had those problems, but I share with them, I understand it.

There are people who have shared their stories. Like there are people who have told about their problems with their children, their problems with their grand-children, or how life was in Chile.

What I like about the group is that it's very united, and from the door, when they come in, when they pass the door, ... all politics, religion, ideologies, they're out, they're in ... their main interest is to have a good time and to share and to speak their language.

Those are the kinds of stories that people share there, for example when their children ask them to babysit the grandchildren then they have to tell them if you want me to babysit you have to ask your children to speak Spanish to me.... They share those stories, they share those stories in the group.

We share sad things too.... We would talk about these sad things within the group ... and yes, each couple or person, would talk about things they had seen or they had experienced.

The more people there are, the more they talk because there are more stories to talk about. If you're sitting there and ... well maybe I start telling you just like this ... start telling you my daughter-in-law is really mean with me or my son is not be-having or he's mistreating me and everybody listens and that's the way it goes. People talk about their lives a lot.

As can be seen in these statements, the discourse of group self-description is to some extent organized around the notion of sharing. Members would often interchangeably refer to sharing experiences and sharing stories. It is useful to consider the kinds of stories that members would share with one another, and with the researcher. The stories ranged from being celebrations of personal agency to documentations of suffer-ing. For example:

Something that happened is that my daughters asked me to take care of their children. But then what happens? They didn't teach them Spanish so then I cannot understand my own grandchildren so I suffer and they suffer because we don't understand each other and I love them very dearly. My family is the most important thing to me but we do not understand each other. Sometimes they cry for maybe something really insignificant but I cannot do anything because I don't know what they want. I'm a loving grandmother with them but we just don't understand each other.

In these words we can grasp the distinction between the *taxonomic* and *narrative* discourses on self-identity. We have an autobiographic account of someone enduring the actions of another. If we focus on the role categories and the extent to which these are respectively incorpo-rated into identities, we are merely drawing on the *relative-to* logic of social taxonomy. This parent, like any other parent, is located in a differ-ent social category relative to this child, and any other child. If, how-ever, we want to focus on the question of identity and power implicated in the account, then we need to draw on an *in-relation-to* logic. This particular child is an agent in his/her relation to this particular parent, and, at the same time, this particular parent is a sufferer in his/her relation to this particular child.

Ricoeur extends the sociological concept of action by reminding us that the other side of action is suffering.[13] The asymmetry of action requires us to theorize suffering in the same moment that we theorize agency. We are capable of action, yet our own agency may be suppressed or denied by the action of others. We re-cognize ourselves in terms of our suffering as well as our agency in the stories we tell, and in the stories we follow. Narrative provides identity to one as an actor, and as a sufferer in these terms. Narrative discourse thus provides the communicative basis for connecting agency with identity. In this sense, narrative discourse counters the categorical bias of taxonomic discourse. It enables one to interpret oneself as an agent and sufferer in relation to social others and conditions of existence. This form of self-interpretation is made possible thanks to the way life narratives – such as accounts remembered or constructed in social interaction – serve to direct the interpretation of self.

This same principle also creates the space in which two or more individuals, having their separate experiences, can construct a sense of commonality – a sense of belonging to one another – by virtue of the way their life narratives converge. In other words, the transition from personal identity ("I") to collective identity ("we") is a narrative accomplishment. Ricoeur has claimed that the identity of a community is constituted in a manner similar to that of an individual.[14] Nonetheless, he does not elaborate further on narrative identity at the collective level; nor does he explore the relation between individual and collective identity. Yet we can still move toward understanding Ricoeur on this point by returning to his insight that we recognize our selves in the stories we tell about ourselves. Now we might extend this to the collective level by saying that in social interaction we recognize our selves in the stories that others tell about themselves. It would be more adequate, however, to say that we recognize our *stories* in the stories of others. Intersubjectivity, like subjectivity, is always mediated by discourse. We find in the narrative accounts of others formal parallels with our own accounts – patterns of action and suffering bearing some similarity to the patterns contained in our own history.

It is in this way I think that different (although not necessarily all) members of Primavera come to acknowledge that they share something fundamental with one another. This sense of belonging is accomplished through a very common activity in the everyday social world – the exchange of diverse experience through comparable narratives. Again, this is not to say that they share their experiences as such, but rather that they are to some extent able to bridge the gulf that isolates individual experience, thanks to the properties of narrative discourse.

Thus, we can comprehend the notion of collective identity by building upon the concept of "belonging." I subjectively belong to a collective or a social group to the extent that I am able to interweave my interpretation of self with their own reflexive interpretations through narrative discourse. I belong to community in the strong sense to the extent that I can coordinate my life narrative with those of other community members. The discussion above leads us here to recognize that belonging means more than to merely have attributes in common, or even to have common designations. In belonging, *my* identity as actor and sufferer becomes *our* identity as in relation to particular social others or given social conditions. Belonging, in this sense, is something more than the multiplication of personal identities – it gives us the authority to speak of we, us, and ourselves.

The reciprocal interpretation of life stories in everyday life constitutes a common, but nonetheless important form of interaction ritual. Entry to contexts of interaction – for example, establishing new relationships or rekindling old relationships – might well turn on my ability to demonstrate to you that we have stories in common. It may be hypothesized that this narrative mechanism provides the foundation for the subsequent accomplishment of community histories and other forms of social interaction. Once we construct the commonality of our separate accounts – and therefore the commonality of our identities – we become better positioned to construct narratives of our group as a whole, and to coordinate our actions.

Narrative interaction needs to be mastered as a competency through developmental participation in such social rituals.[15] Such socialization is possible because, as Ricoeur points out, narrative discourse is a form of thinking and speaking that is pre-given through cultural tradition.[16] According to Bruner, there is an underlying commonality within the narrative field. In other words, the capacity to self-interpret by way of telling and following (hi)stories is given to the subject through canonical narratives.[17] These provide the basis for a conventionalization of discourse such that stories and histories are fundamentally communicable.

The presence of a culture of narration was evident in the accounts of the group members, especially when they discussed their theater production. Primavera meets every Saturday at 2:00 p.m. This became the basis for a play the group produced. The play recreates on stage the social interaction of the group meetings. It was performed by the group members themselves to audiences drawn from the local Latin American community (about 300 people overall attended three performances). The following dialogue from the play captures the sense in which the play was a narrative text about suffering as well as efficacy, and about the negotiation of collective narrative identity. (Note the reference to the comparable story.)

> *Carlos:* When we arrived in Canada it was during the economic boom.... They sent
> me to work at the slaughterhouse for animals. (He smiles with sadness
> moving his head.) ... I didn't have the slightest idea what the work was
> going to be like. After only a few days in my new country. (Getting angry.)
> Stuck in the shit and the blood! Well, that only lasted until they closed the
> slaughterhouse. Almost without warning and there no compensation.
> There was nothing to do if one was an immigrant and on top of that, old....
> So then, we went to unemployment. We were in it for almost one year and
> from there we went to welfare. As you can see, Don Pedro, our story is not
> that different, is it?
>
> *Pedro:* (defensively) Yes, but at least we here one can live better, right?
>
> *Carlos:* Shit, Pedrito! But, that is not the point. What I am saying is that why in hell
> one is not allowed to work here. I worked for over 30 years in my country,
> almost 10 years here and all of a sudden I'm not good any more. Just when
> I think I am good for something.

The play, in which the denial of agency is represented, became itself the basis for a narrative for the celebration of agency.

> When we have the play ready, we will let people know all these good things that
> we can do. We're not good only for taking care of children, or doing housework,
> we're also good at acting and singing, at reciting or doing other things.

While the play was a means to present their claims of capability, the production and performance of the play served in turn to validate these claims of being more than just "old people." The play was constructed – through the efforts of a community worker – from the stories that members told each other during their gatherings. The reflexive character of the play is not lost in the accounts of the members.

> The play talks about real life. It takes stories that have happened to all of us.... All
> those little things are reflected there in the play.

> Through theater the people show their feelings, they channel their feelings, they
> channel their disagreement with the system. The people they can laugh at them-
> selves. This is good to take this with humor. They see themselves in the play and
> laugh at it.

Moreover, the play born out of stories in turn becomes the subject of narration within the group. Once the group had performed the play, I conducted an interview with the group as a whole. I wanted to know how they felt about the experience and themselves. Each member that spoke addressed the whole group and not merely myself.

> In this group there are people with different capabilities. And, here the group gives an opportunity for them to show those skills, to use them because this has been like being asleep and the group triggers those things in them and they wake up. And that's what happened in the play. The play was an opportunity to trigger those things in them.

> I myself feel very good about this because it has proven that on the outside we may be wrinkled, we may be old people but in the inside there's still a lot to give and this is why the play was an opportunity to show because we didn't have any theatrical experience but we could show all those things we have inside.

> For me it was a very important personal experience to participate in the play, and also to participate in the group because we created a bond in the group that is in the play itself. We shared many things among the participants in the play and I felt like they were a family to me.

> In some of our children this triggered some emotion, some very deep emotion. Some of them cried because they could see in us, they could see what getting old means.... So this triggered some deep emotions in our children. We didn't have to be actors or actresses to do this because it was very natural, we did it from our hearts.

> I think that all of the members of this group should feel that their heart is really big because we have proven that this is a very strong group and I want to ask you, the group, to be always united, to be always the way we are, to put our name high, really high, not for pride or vanity, but because we have proved that we are a group of older people who are really worthwhile, to value ourselves. This group helps us value ourselves as people.

Closing Thoughts

This case study suggests quite strongly that there is more to collective identity than common or even shared categories. The sense of "I" or "we" turns to a large degree on the conceptualization of self or selves in terms of human agency, and this occurs primarily through narrative modes of discourse. This does not, however, justify giving undue priority to narrative in our efforts to understand the process of identification. As Ricoeur reminds us, the narrative mode weaves together categorical and ethical modes for representing the subject. In his words,

> [the] successive stages of our inquiry should not be dealt with in a serial way but in a cumulative way; the ethical dimensions are grafted onto the practical ones in the same way as the practical ones are grafted onto the linguistic dimensions. We must be capable of describing persons as basic particulars and selves as self-designating subjects of discourse in order to be able to characterize actions as intentionally-brought-forth events, and agents as the owners and authors of their actions; and we must understand what agency means in order to apply to actions a moral judgement of imputation and to call persons responsible selves.[18]

The narrative representation of action and suffering in everyday inter-action does appear to hold promise for understanding how personal identity becomes collective identity. In this case study, the emergence of collective identity is intertwined with negotiated accounts of selves and actors and sufferers. This implies that to adequately contend with questions of political subjects, and their realization of self as dominated and resistant, we must understand the fundamental narrative processes in everyday social life. Yet this does not mean that collective identities are static phenomena. Identity is mutable as well as cohesive.[19] The tension between given and potential meanings of the self ensures that the process of self-interpretation remains open. In Primavera, social relations have been refigured through collective narration, these narratives have in turn served to refigure identities and those same social relations. The play has told stories and has become the subject of stories, as have the tellers along with it.

Notes

1 David D. Brown, "Discursive Moments of Identification," *Current Perspectives in Social Theory* 14 (1994): 269-92.

2 For exceptions to this pattern, see V. Gecas and M. Schwalbe, "Beyond the Looking-Glass Self: Social Structure and Efficacy-Based Self-Esteem." *Social Psychology Quarterly* 46 (1983): 77-88 and P. Wexler, *Critical Social Psychology* (London: Routledge & Kegan Paul, 1983).

3 Paul Ricoeur, "Humans as the Subject Matter of Philosophy," in *The Narrative Path*, ed. T.P. Kemp and D. Rasmussen (Cambridge, MA: MIT Press, 1989), 89-101, and Paul Ricoeur, "The Human Actor: Describing, Narrating and Prescribing," paper presented to the Ninth International Human Science Research Conference, Université Laval, Québec, 1990.

4 M. Freeman, "Paul Ricoeur in Interpretation: The Model of the Text and the Idea of Development." *Human Development* 28 (1985):295-312.

5 See, for example, Hayden White, "The Value of Narrativity in the Representation of Reality," *Critical Inquiry* 7 (1980):5-27; Victor Turner, "Social Dramas and Stories about Them," *Critical Inquiry* 7 (1980):141-68; Mary M. Gergen and Kenneth J. Gergen, *Historical Social Psychology* (Hillsdale, N. J.: Lawrence Erlbaum Associates, 1984); David E. Polkinghorne, *Narrative Knowing and the Human Sciences* (Albany: State University of New York, 1988); K. Nelson (ed.), *Narratives from the Crib* (Cambridge, MA: Harvard University Press, 1989); and David R. Maines, "Narrative's Moment and Sociology's Phenomena: Toward a Narrative Sociology," *The Sociological Quarterly* 34(1) (1993): 17-38.

6 For sociology, see M. Kohli, "Biography: account, text, method," in Daniel Bertaux (ed.), *Biography and Society* (London: Sage, 1981), 61-76, and Daniel Bertaux and M. Kohli, "The Life Story Approach: A Continental View," *Annual Review of Sociology* 10 (1984): 215-37; Franco Ferrarotti, "On the autonomy of the biographical method," in D. Bertaux (ed.), *Biography and Society*, 19-28, and F. Ferrarotti,

"Postscript," *Current Sociology* 37(2) (1989): 92-111. For anthropology, see Vincent Crapanzano, "Life Histories," *American Anthropologist* 86 (1984): 953-60. For psychology, see Jerome Bruner, *Actual Minds, Possible Worlds* (Cambridge: Harvard University Press, 1986), J. Bruner, "Life as Narrative," *Social Research* 54(1) (1987): 1-32, and J. Bruner, "The Narrative Construction of Reality," *Critical Inquiry* 18 (1991): 1-21.

7 See Margaret Wetherell and Jonathan Potter, *Discourse and Social Psychology* (Sage, 1987) and Wetherell and Potter, "Discourse analysis and the identification of interpretive repertoires," in C. Antaki (ed.), *Analysing Everyday Explanation* (Sage, 1988), 168-83.

8 Paul Ricoeur, *Hermeneutics and the Human Sciences: Essays on Language, Action and Interpretation*, ed. and trans. J. B. Thompson (Cambridge: Cambridge University Press, 1981) and Paul Ricoeur, *Time and Narrative*, III, trans. K. Blamey and D. Pellauer (Chicago: Chicago University Press, 1988 [1985]).

9 Hannah Arendt, *The Human Condition* (Chicago: University of Chicago Press, 1958), 161-7.

10 For a useful discussion on the pragmatics of presence and absence, see Arthur W. Frank, "The Self at the Funeral: An Ethnography on the Limits of Postmodernism," *Studies in Symbolic Interactionism* 11 (1990): 191-206, and Jürgen Habermas, *The Philosophical Discourse of Modernity* (Cambridge, MA: MIT Press, 1987).

11 Ricoeur, *Time and Narrative*, III, 247.

12 Ricoeur, *Hermeneutics and Social Sciences*, 279.

13 Ricoeur, "Humans as the Subject Matter," 96-7.

14 Ricoeur, *Time and Narrative*, III, 247.

15 David Sudnow, *Talk's Body: A Meditation between Two Keyboards* (New York: Knopf, 1979), and Nelson, *Narratives from the Crib*.

16 Ricoeur, *Hermeneutics and Social Sciences*, 287.

17 Bruner, "Life as Narrative," 1987.

18 Ricoeur, "Humans as the Subject Matter," 100-1.

19 Ricoeur, *Time and Narrative*, III, 246.

Québec Narratives:
The Process of Refiguration

DOMINIQUE PERRON

In 1991, Ricoeur published an article entitled "L'identité narrative" in *La Revue des sciences humaines*.[1] This paper dealt with some concepts already examined by the theoretician in previous works, such as *Time and Narrative*. However, in the last part of his reflections, Ricoeur put the emphasis more specifically on the identity of a character – *identité du personnage* – and what he calls the appropriation of this character: the refigured "I." For someone like me, who is more interested in sociocriticism, these two specific concepts appear to be operative and accurate in order to point out more closely the meaning of identity, and, therefore, the sphere of what we call in French "*l'identitaire*." If the term "*identity*" is somewhat problematic, as Ricoeur has stressed, the word "*identitaire*" (for which I have no English translation) is far more complicated to convey properly. But the notion of "*identitaire*" is essential for one who wants a better understanding of the link between fiction and society in Québec's contemporary narrative. Moreover, to relate a bit more clearly this notion of a character's identity to that of *identitaire*, I am conscious of the obligation to twist slightly Ricoeur's ideas in a direction which would be more fruitful for my purpose. Therefore, I will leave the fields of temporality and narratology, which, though important for Ricoeur, are not considered to be of real use here, in order to remain closer to the area of reception theory, or refiguration, as Ricoeur understands it. But before continuing, I would like to try to say a word about the ambiguous definition of "*identitaire*" and how this notion can be related to Ricoeur's approach.

Sherry Simons, in her essay "Espaces incertains de la culture," links *identitaire* immediately to culture, but to a conception of culture which has "as a primordial function to be used as a sign of acknowledgement, and thus, of division. Thus the culture (in a large sense) gives the keys allowing the drawing of the horizon of identity. But how does one define the limits which can aid the constitution of individual, social, and national identity?"[2] It can easily be realized that identity is seen here as a basic question of difference (of gender, language, religion) and that the motivation of these differences comes from political confrontation.

Another interesting point raised by Simons is the paradox that "the power of naming and defining one's cultural difference would come precisely at the moment when the evidence of this difference would be weakening."[3] Hence, it is possible, at another level of Ricoeur, to consider the *identitaire* as a sum of fluid differences and moving affirmations, sometimes contradictory, coming from different sources as origins, such as gender, ethnicity, language or religion. The idea of identity, however, especially according to Ricoeur, is far narrower because it is of course related to fiction, but it demonstrates nonetheless a relation which could be placed parallel to the concept of "*identitaire*." Two more quotations from "L'identité narrative" seem crucial here:

> If one can consider every story as a chain of transformation – going from an initial situation to a final situation – then the narrative identity of the hero cannot be other than the homogeneous style of a subjective transformation in agreement with some objective transformations which obey the rule of the totality [*complétude*] and unity of the intrigue.... That is why in what we called the apprenticeship novel as well as in the novel of "stream of consciousness," the transformation of the character constitutes the central point of the narrative.[4]

And "the self never knows himself in an immediate way, but only in an indirect way, by a detour through different cultural codes."[5] Thus, identity, as it is related to narrative by Ricoeur, as a subjective and objective narratological transformation, is approximately the same concept as *l'identitaire* related to the literary in general. That is, both are constituted as a sum of transhistorical subjective and objective transformations of which the traces are always legible in a given literary corpus but not immediately evident as a narratological perspective. Moreover, since Ricoeur regards identity as a "detour through different cultural codes," it can be taken as a supplementary dimension closer to *identitaire*, inasmuch as *identitaire* is precisely related to a notion of culture defined itself as difference. Thus, a comparison can be made: identity is composed of transformations, but of transformations that take their meaning from those cultural codes in which we are all caught. *Identitaire* is the sum of the process of these transformations which lead the subject from one cultural code, or a series of codes, to another.

It then becomes a question as to how some aspects of Ricoeur's theory could help point out the most tangible manifestations and paradoxes of narrative identity as it relates to *identitaire*. At this point, it is necessary to include another theoretical tool offered by Ricoeur. This is the notion of "refiguration," undertaken by Ricoeur as the third level of articulation in the work of narrative. This final step, refiguration, is narrowly associated with reading and, as Micheline Cambron insisted in her works on "cultural discourses in Québec," absolutely necessary to the process of reception. Cambron comments on Ricoeur in this way: "The *récit* is placed in a communicative situation and the activity of deciphering done by the reader should be seen as an intrinsic component of the actual or effective signification of the text."[6] She then forcefully points out another datum, which can be seen as the key of the refiguration – the reference. Again quoting Ricoeur, she says that if the reading is the "intersection between the world of the work and the world of the reader, we cannot maintain the work in its immanence. The reference, as traces, is rebuilt by the reading imagination, in such a way that the fiction as the narrative could constitute itself as a work."[7]

Having combined these various concepts of identity and their relation to the act of reading as postulated by Ricoeur, it now becomes a question of application – specifically to see if it is possible to reach a better comprehension of the functioning and the manifestation of narrative identity and of *identitaire* in a given Québec narrative. I would like to focus on the work of Jacques Poulin, specifically his novel, *Le Vieux Chagrin*, which, when published in 1989, was considered to be quite remarkable within the Québec literary landscape.[8]

First, a few words of introduction concerning Poulin. A well-known writer for twenty years, he has created for himself a singular place in the Québec literary institution by writing short and intimate novels that deal with the daily life of misfit children, teenagers or adults in a frame where very few actions occur. His style is very simple, sometimes simplistic, which curiously has a resemblance to Salinger in French translation. Overall, the rhythm of his narratives is generally very slow, which has led some critics to entitle their review of him as: "*L'éloge de la lenteur*" ("In praise of slowness").

Despite the lack of dramatic activity in his work, his reputation in Québec is built on his capacity to spellbind the reader with this very absence of incident. His narrative concentrates on realistic representations which serve, by their opacity, to express a general doubt about the nature of fiction. However, Poulin's work is more than simply vague generalities regarding the lack of form in life and fiction, as is evident in his most well-known novel, *Volkswagen Blues*.[9] This novel deals with a specific aspect of the Québec *identitaire*, which we call "*americanité*." In recent Québec literary tradition, "*americanité*" means the discovery or reflection about being French-speaking in a North American culture, with the ghost of Jack Kerouac featuring as the most appropriate emblem.

The principal interest in *Le Vieux Chagrin* – the story of a solitary writer and his lukewarm relationship with a teenage girl – arises from the reading of what appears to be a work in progress, a work blocked by hesitations, gaps and uncertainty. In so doing, the reader comes to share the author's doubts concerning the existence of the necessary conditions for telling a story. Some critics also qualified *Le Vieux Chagrin* as a reflection about "the evanescence of the literary project." But, in this novel, it is not only the literary project which is evanescent, but also the identity itself of the writer, who tends to be dismantled as an immanent entity. This does not mean that he has had no identity, but instead, that this authorial "I," as it is represented, is strongly marked by indecision, so that the author is forced to defer to a double and relies on this other to represent him.

As an example, in the chapter entitled "Papa Hemingway," it is this legendary American writer's specific way of approaching and seducing a woman to which the hero refers in a long phantasmagorical scene. What he describes is in fact what Hemingway would do, and not he himself. In the same breath, in order to depict himself physically, he borrows the face of another famous character: "And what's he like physically? He's a skinny man with a sunken face. With a red wool cap on his head, he could pass for the brother of Captain Cousteau."[10] The author thus presents himself through the guise of multiple characters and their qualities – never his own specific identity.

Even the writer's own brother is delegated to meeting a possibly imaginary woman, because the hero is too intimidated by her. Moreover, he constantly relies on the cat, Chagrin, to upset the teenage girl who wants to stay with him. Almost everywhere in the novel, in the moments of action as well as in the elements of passion, the hero is not really there, he is always somewhere else – in the past, as in both his imaginary scenarios, and in his hesitations. Curiously, he turns to English expressions in order to define himself, even in a negative way: "I was ashamed of myself for having run like a coward. Despite the appearances, I was neither a coward nor a loser nor even a beautiful loser. I was only a Libra, a damned Libra, that is to say, a torn man, balancing contradictory desires."[11]

In this case of reconfiguration, what the narrator gives to the reader is more a composite *identitaire*, rather than an actual identity. Of course, it is still an identity, since as Ricoeur said, the "je," who is submitted to subjective and objective transformation in the frame of the narrative action, is always the same, from the beginning to the end of the novel. But what grows in him is the feeling and the capability of being another, of being able to contemplate different parts of himself. In this view, the hero concludes about the imaginary woman of whom he dreamed: "Marika didn't really exist, she was but the projection of a desire, a part of myself, my feminine side, my better half."[12] Thus, what is he telling us about *identitaire*, specifically concerning his internal split which, after so much deliberation, is solved by this final entity, which reflects his own feminine aspect? Basically, not much, except that the narrator permits the reader to see in this text a reflection of whatever ambivalences she shares with the narrator.

In fact, the problematic identification of the hero with the figures of Hemingway and Cousteau is a manifestation of a dilemma, both historical and ahistorical, that is contained in the concept of "identity." In the novel, the narrator constantly remembers his stay in Europe, and his travels in America in such detail as: "Places as varied as Key West, San Francisco, the Magdelen Islands, the 11th arrondissement in Paris, the suburbs of Prague, a hillside in the Rhone Valley, a village near Heidelberg in Germany...."[13] But the actual setting of this long summer of hesitations related in the novel is on the shore of the Saint Lawrence River, near Québec City, and the action of the fiction that he hopelessly wants to write takes place in the Vieux-Québec.

Another interesting intertextual manifestation is the reference to Hemingway (as the hero's model writer), who is surprisingly associated with Colette (perhaps as an exotic connection with Paris and European exile). Then, there is a reference to the only Québec writer in the novel, Gabrielle Roy, author of *The Tin Flute*, one of the main writers of "exile," but also relevant for the notion of "wandering." And it is this notion of wandering in "errance" that, in the literary context of the eighties and the nineties in Québec, is perceived as the most important paradigm of *identitaire*, set within the perspective of *américanité*. Here, the ghost of Jack Kerouac continues to hover, particularly evocative of the instability in the definition of *identitaire*. In such a tenuous setting, it is Gabrielle Roy who provides the light and happy side of the sense of "exile," while Kerouac's is a darker one.

The Québécois readers of *Le Vieux Chagrin* were able to project onto this narrative their own feeling of "to be there or not to be there, to be there and not to be there," that is, to be that and not to be this, in an oxymoronic mood similar to that of the beautiful loser. There is another representation of this ambiguous state in *Le Vieux Chagrin*. Talking about his previous books, Poulin says:

> Certain pages set in Quebec City were written on a beach in Key West, or in San Francisco Bay, or even on a campground at the side of a hill in Florence, or near the airport in Venice, or in the suburbs of Vienna or Prague: I drew the curtains of the van, I put in earplugs and I wrote, well insulated from the outside world.[14]

Such a fluidity of location, of imagined destinations, yet stationary isolation, can account for the singular success of *Le Vieux Chagrin* in both Québec and France. In such a narrative, refiguration of reality is fully working to highlight a fundamental characterization of a collective *identitaire*: the association of an origin erased in everything but the language (an allusion to the exotic ambiance of Paris, which the hero inhabited at different times). It also illuminates the obsession of an idealized territory, which cannot be erased like the Saint Lawrence or the city of Québec and is the key to the constant fluid, fluctuating cultural codes, mostly American, which are seen through the opacity of another language. A beautiful loser cannot be *un beau perdant*. There is no exact translation. It is always something else, as is all the fluidity of the *identitaire*: always being different, in the sameness of difference. Between Colette and Hemingway, by way of Gabrielle Roy – it is a cultural intersection, which mirrors another intersection mentioned by Ricoeur. "The fundamental intentionality shown by the discourse: this intersection between the world of the reader and the world of the fiction."[15]

Le Vieux Chagrin is itself a world of intersections, where an uncertain identity closely allied to what Québec readers feel about themselves could be depicted. The consciousness of *identitaire* as a singular expression of the main process of reading and textual reception in a society like Québec is crucial for its being. As it is understood, non-identity is still an identity, and wandering, as everybody knows, is at its core. Québécois need to read of this non-identity and to build it as an *identitaire* by means of refiguration in the reception of a text. Of this fact the narrator, as a writer, is perfectly conscious: "In books, there is nothing important, or almost nothing: everything is in the mind of the one who reads."[16] I believe that Ricoeur would not disagree with this affirmation.

Notes

1 Paul Ricoeur, "L'identité narrative," *Revue des Sciences Humaines*, 221 (1991): 44.

2 Sherry Simons, "Espaces incertains de la culture," in *Fictions de l'Identitaire au Québec*, Editions XYZ, 1991, 19.

3 Simons, "Espaces incertains," 16.

4 Ricoeur, "L'identité narrative," 40.

5 Ricoeur, "L'identité narrative," 44.

6 Micheline Cambron, "Une société, un récit: Discours culturel au Québec, 1967-76, *Essais Littéraires*, Montreal: L'Hexagone, 1989, 28.

7 Cambron, "Discours littéraires," 31.

8 Jacques Poulin, *Le Vieux Chagrin*, Montreal, Editions Actes-Sud-Leméac, 1993.

9   Jacques Poulin, *Volkswagen Blues*, Québec: Editions Québec-Amérique, 1984.

10   Poulin, *Le Vieux Chagrin*, 28. (All translations are by the present author.)

11   Poulin, *Le Vieux Chagrin*, 30.

12   Poulin, *Le Vieux Chagrin*, 153.

13   Poulin, *Le Vieux Chagrin*, 38.

14   Poulin, *Le Vieux Chagrin*, 74.

15   Poulin, *Le Vieux Chagrin*, 27.

16   Poulin, *Le Vieux Chagrin*, 138.

Ricoeur
and
Political Identity*

BERNARD P. DAUENHAUER

The phenomenon of political identity is troublesome. To have a political identity, one must accept as normatively binding a set of claims and practices not wholly of his or her own determination. Among these claims are those that require the division of humanity into an included "us" and an excluded "them." Further, every political identity calls for its own perpetuation through inculcation in new members, principally children but also immigrants.

These features of political identity are troublesome because they appear to be at odds either with the autonomy that a person should exercise or with the common humanity that one should admit that he or she shares with every other person or with both. The history of the several versions of nationalism and ethnicity prominent since the nineteenth century certainly give one pause about accepting the normative claims regularly advanced on the basis of a group's political identity.

Nonetheless, at least for a large part of the human family, having a political identity is indispensable, or nearly so, for leading a full human life. Getting rid of the multiplicity of political identities in favor of a full-blown cosmopolitanism is, for the foreseeable future, simply not feasible. Apart from its feasibility, the very desirability of such a cosmopolitanism is highly dubious.

And so, we are apparently stuck with a world containing multiple political identities. One therefore has reason to ask whether we can find a firm basis for discriminating between defensible and indefensible political identities. If so, what are the distinguishing characteristics of the defensible ones?

---

* An earlier version of this paper appeared in *Philosophy Today* 39/1 (Spring 1995): 47-55.

In this paper, I propose to show how Paul Ricoeur's analyses of the constitution of *personal* identity provide us with resources applicable to the task of dealing with these two questions.[1] These resources help to make clear both (*a*) why no political identity can be immune to reasonable criticism, and (*b*) what at least some of the conditions are that a particular political identity has to satisfy if it is to be defensible.

To make this case, I will first outline Ricoeur's account of the constitution of personal identity. Then I will compare the constituents of personal identity with those of political identity. Third, on the assumption that maintaining a political identity can be defensible, I will propose a way to distinguish the defensible ones from those that are indefensible. Finally, to indicate the fruitfulness of my Ricoeurian proposal, I will apply it to two specific cases, the old case of the confrontation between the Athenians and the Melians and the current case of the Québécois.

Personal Identity

At the heart of Ricoeur's account of the constitution of personal identity is his distinction between two senses of the term "identity." With Heidegger, he distinguishes between the identity of sameness (*idem*-identity) that belongs to every entity, human or otherwise, and the identity of self (*ipse*-identity) that only human beings can have.[2] Each of these sorts of identity involves some sort of temporal continuity or permanence. To raise the question of personal identity is to ask how one understands the fit between these two kinds of identity in one and the same person. It is to ask what sort of permanence is distinctively characteristic of human beings.

In a person, the identity of sameness shows up not only in bodiliness but in an especially striking fashion in his or her character. The constituents of character are: (*a*) the particular perspective on the world that one receives at birth and retains throughout life, (*b*) acquired habits, and (*c*) the set of identifications he or she makes or accepts. By contrast with this *idem*-identity, identity of self (*ipse*-identity) consists in the permanent capacity to make and keep promises regardless of whether they support or undercut permanence of character. This is the sort of identity involved in keeping one's word or self-maintenance. These two sorts of permanence are in tension with one another. In Ricoeur's words:

> When we speak of ourselves, we in fact have available to us two models of permanence in time which can be summed up in two expressions that are at once descriptive and emblematic: *character* and *keeping one's word*. In both of these, we easily recognize a permanence which we say belongs to us. My hypothesis is that the polarity of these two models of permanence with respect to persons results from the fact that the permanence of character expresses the almost complete mutual overlapping

of the problem of *idem* and *ipse*, while faithfulness to oneself in keeping one's word marks the extreme gap between the permanence of the self and that of the same and so attests fully to the irreducibility of the two problematics one to the other.[3]

Ricoeur argues that the concept of narrative identity solves the aporias of personal identity that the irreducibility of these two sorts of identity generates.[4] Narrative identity intervenes in the conceptual constitution of personal identity as a "mediator between the pole of character, where *idem* and *ipse* tend to coincide, and the pole of self-maintenance, where selfhood frees itself from sameness."[5]

In and through narrative, on Ricoeur's account, we come to understand ourselves both as distinct individuals and as one person among others who all share a common humanity.[6] Narratives emplot actions that people perform and events that transpire into a temporal continuity. They show that people, their respective abiding characters notwithstanding, have a future that is nontrivially open to projects they can initiate and remain faithful to. Their characters of course are never irrelevant to the initiatives they take. Character predelineates the field of genuinely available initiatives. It also contributes to the intelligibility of the initiatives that are taken. But, as narratives of personal identity show, initiatives are not merely the products of what has previously come to be. They inaugurate something genuinely new.

Every narrative of personal identity, as Ricoeur makes plain, contains evaluations, for there can be no narrative without a plurality of persons, at least some of whom make assessments of what they or others think or do.[7] These narratives in turn are themselves subjects for evaluation. Ideally, this process of making and reflecting on evaluations should yield stable, "considered convictions."[8] These convictions should guide subsequent thought or action.

But the narratives relevant to the constitution of personal identity are always partial. They are partial in at least three ways. They are partial (*a*) because they exclude some items that they could include, (*b*) because they make contestable distributions of emphasis among the items they do include, and (*c*) because there are always alternatives with different inclusions and emphases that could be told. Hence the convictions they can yield can never be exhaustively considered. However well-considered they may be, they always remain subject to reform in the light of further reflection.

Steadfastly to admit the reformability of one's own most settled convictions amounts to preserving the gap between *idem*-identity and *ipse*-identity. Even more, it is to accord some primacy to *ipse*-identity. It is to acknowledge that the constitution of one's personal identity, though it is already underway and has already received a character of some sort, is a task that should have no *determinate* terminus. Rather, it is a task that should continue until death cuts it off. But it is just this primacy of *ipse*-identity that the phenomenon of political identity appears to deny.

Political Identity

Every political society demands that its members identify themselves with its constitutive practices and institutions even though it be costly to their own individual aspirations and objectives. The identifications that a citizen makes or accepts become part of his or her character or *idem*-identity. To make or accept these identifications is unavoidably to deny the unequivocal primacy of self-maintenance over character.

As I indicated at the outset, this denial has momentous normative consequences. These normative issues are perhaps most vividly evident in the way that a political society perpetuates itself. It always aims to have its present members instill in newcomers, their children or immigrants, an identification with it and its distinctive set of practices and institutions.

Like personal identity, a political identity is constituted by way of narratives. Its establishment and perpetuation takes place largely by way of the stories that people tell and hear about it and their membership in it. To be effective, these narratives have to mold how the members understand crucial parts of their lives.

To see in fuller detail the normative issues raised by political identities, consider more closely the features of the narratives that constitute them. In many respects, these narratives are quite like those that constitute personal identity. They too distinguish between and emplot both actions and events. They too find reinforcement in the very process of telling and hearing them. And they too predelineate their own extension and development through actions and events the tellers and hearers anticipate in their future.

Particularly noteworthy is the fact that both of these sorts of narratives are always partial in several ways. Both exclude some items and distribute emphases among the items they do include. Both also are narratives for which there are always possible, even plausible, alternatives. But political narratives are partial in at least two other important ways. First, they claim exclusive right to the territory they speak of as their homeland. And second, they accord to their own society a uniquely strong title to endure in perpetuity, a title stronger than they accord to other political societies. In fact, though, no actual political society can establish an incontestable "clear title" to its land.[9] And what evidence could prove that some particular society has a uniquely strong title to perdure?

Because narratives of political identity are partial in all of these ways, they always make stronger claims than can provide conclusive evidence for. Hence they are always, in Ricoeur's technical sense, either ideological or utopian or both.[10]

One gains an even fuller appreciation of the normative issues that narratives of political identity raise when one takes into account the crucial difference in which they, in contrast with narratives of personal identity, treat at least two pivotal moments in the citizen's life, namely his or her death and birth. Nowhere is it clearer just how strong are the demands that a political society makes on its members to identify with it and to contribute to its perpetuation.[11]

In terms of personal identity, death marks the end of a unique, unsubstitutable individual, with his or her convictions and self-selected projects. My death will bring to an end the commitments I have made to the woman who is my wife. It will bring to an end my ambition to master medieval logic. And it will bring to an end my enthusiasm for collecting Caribbean postage stamps. It will also terminate my efforts to avoid becoming compulsive or obsessive about the projects that I have selected. To put the matter in Ricoeurian terms, death brings to an end the giving and keeping of one's word and the project of self-maintenance. Or more generally, it terminates what Ricoeur calls the struggle to preserve a non-coincidence between one's poles of *idem*-identity and *ipse*-identity.

Thus, it makes some sense for a narrative of personal identity to assess the timeliness of a person's death in terms of this struggle. We can say without absurdity that some people die timely deaths, in fullness of years with their projects largely satisfied or sensibly abandoned. Others die too soon, not having had a chance to realize their projects. Still others perhaps die too late, living on despite their inability any longer to pursue a project of any significance.

From the standpoint of political identity, the death of a member has an importantly different meaning. It marks the line for passing a baton to a successor rather than the line at the end of the race. A person's political identity consists in membership in the joint pursuit of a common project. From its inception, this project is meant to outlast the lives of any of its individual members. Except perhaps in revolutionary times, members take their common project to be one that antedates them, one that they receive rather than establish.[12]

To assess a person's death in terms of political identity is not primarily to ask about the timeliness of the death. A youthful death in the service of one's political society is never untimely. Rather, to assess it politically is to ask about the deceased's fidelity to the society's common project. Civic monuments testify to this fact for some few of a society's members. But in principle this sort of assessment is appropriate for each member. A crucial part of this political fidelity consists in doing what one can to rear new members to replace those who die. No member is totally without responsibility for the perpetuation of his or her political society.

Just as narratives of political identity deal with a person's death differently than narratives of personal identity do, so too do they deal differently with a person's birth. A human birth, unlike births in other animal species, takes place in a particular cultural world. A preeminent part of this world is the particular political society into which one is born.

The child enters a human world as a newcomer, a stranger. Because it is capable of action, it can take up the task of preserving its political society. But it can also deploy this capacity in such a way that this society is undercut.

As a consequence, the child's elders have a twofold responsibility. They are responsible both for developing the child and for preserving their world. These responsibilities can and often do conflict. To protect and develop the child's capacity for action, for initiative, requires that in some respects one help the child resist the world's established, often routinized ways. But the child must also be restrained from ignorantly or negligently undercutting the world. As Hannah Arendt says:

> [T]he child requires special protection and care so that nothing destructive may happen to him from the world. But the world, too, needs protection to keep it from being overrun and destroyed by the onslaught of the new that bursts upon it with each new generation.[13]

This twofold task, however, poses a quandary, particularly in the matter of rearing children into political membership. To preserve a political society, its members must shape the character of the newcomers in their midst by instilling in them a particular set of identifications.[14] A crucial part of this set is the conviction that one is obligated to perpetuate the society. It is not enough that newcomers adopt this conviction for themselves. They are expected to pass this set of identifications on to successor generations. Only loyalty to this sort of commitment counts as patriotism.[15]

Defensible Political Identities

At first blush, it would appear that the requirements of a responsible personal identity, namely that one should preserve the non-coincidence between the poles of *idem*-identity and *ipse*-identity would forbid one from committing himself or herself to such political identifications. But if, as I said at the outset, a political identity is for many people practically indispensable for leading a full human life, then there is strong reason to hold that at least some political identities can be defensible. And if this is so, what distinguishes defensible political identities from indefensible ones? How one answers this question bears heavily on such matters as under what conditions one could rightfully go to war or sue for peace and for what reasons one could rightfully support federation or secession.

On the assumption that some political identities can be defensible, I will now propose a way to determine what conditions a political identity must satisfy if it is to be defensible. Though my proposal is modest, its modesty is appropriate to the subject matter. Stronger proposals would risk setting unfeasibly demanding standards.

My proposal does not present a set of principles from which one could deduce conclusions about the defensibility of a particular political identity. Indeed, my proposal amounts to a denial that such a set of principles is achievable. Rather, I propose that there are a set of questions that one should always ask about a given political identity before accepting its claims. This set of questions amounts to a test that no actual political identity ever definitively passes. If it passes the test at one time, it always remains subject to retesting when circumstances have changed.

On my proposal, one should insist that a political identity, and its constitutive narratives, should meet at least the following two related conditions, namely (*a*) that it admit that it is always both in need of improvement and in danger of degeneration, and (*b*) that there can be a plurality of defensible political identities. Only a political identity that satisfies both of these conditions encourages the members of its society to engage in the sort of critical reflection that can reach considered convictions. Only such a political identity properly respects its members' *ipse*-identity.

Let me briefly clarify this proposal. Its two conditions in effect call for narratives that acknowledge the historicality and finitude of the society whose identity they seek to promote. There are at least four aspects of this historicality and finitude that are relevant here.

First, because of the several ways in which these narratives are partial, they and the societies they help to constitute are always open to reformation, which reformation can be either for the better or the worse. Second, the narratives must admit that every political society, by reason of the actions that it promotes and coordinates regularly impinges both in foreseeable and unforeseeable ways upon other political societies. Hence no defensible narrative can claim that its society is entitled to be wholly unimpinged upon. To do so would be to deny that there can be a plurality of genuinely defensible political societies. Nor of course can a narrative deny that its society impinges upon others. Third, a defensible narrative cannot deny that its society can become not merely obsolete but even dangerously so. No narrative can rightfully claim that the continued existence of its political society is indispensable for either the survival or the flourishing of humanity. Finally, no society's constitutive narratives can rightfully claim to possess the definitive word about their own defensibility. Each society must face the judgment of subsequent generations, both of its own members and of foreigners. That is, to paraphrase Merleau-Ponty, a defensible society is one that shows itself to later generations as having been worthy for its times.[16] It is the task of narratives of political identity to help, either explicitly or implicitly, its society's members recognize these aspects of its historicality and finitude.

Narratives of political identity that satisfy these requirements in effect encourage the society's members to admit that they cannot give *wholly* unqualified allegiance to any concrete state of their political society. They must always be open to its reformation and even to the possibility that it should cease to be. In Ricoeur's terminology, they cannot rightfully so identify with it that they effectively deny the *ipse*-identity that is part of their essential make-up. To make this admission is not to preclude committing oneself to one's political society. But it is to admit that one should do so, as Arendt has noted, with a spirit of asking and giving forgiveness for the inevitable impingements of political societies upon one another. These commitments should be made with clear-headed hope rather than blind faith. Commitments made with forgiveness and hope can be strong enough to bring about loyalty unto death. But they resist fanaticism of all sorts.[17]

Examples of Political Identity

To illustrate what my proposal amounts to and to indicate something of its fruitfulness, let me briefly point out how it could be used to assess actual instances of efforts to sustain a political identity. Two useful cases for this purpose are those of the ancient Melians and the contemporary Québécois. To my sketch of these cases, the reader should add his or her own imaginary alternative stories. Considering not only the actual narratives that do support a particular political identity but also plausible alternatives that might support it is the only fair way to assess it.

Thucydides relates the story of the confrontation between the Melians and the Athenians during the Peloponnesian War. The powerful Athenians called upon the Melian leaders, who had refused to let the Athenians address all the Melian people for fear of panic, to surrender themselves, their people, and their island. In support of their demand the Athenians cited the prevailing conventional wisdom according to which it was for the strong to rule and for the weak to obey as well as the folly of trusting allies to intervene contrary to their own interests. The Melian leaders, after protestations to the Athenians of their determination to remain neutral and after discussions among themselves, decided to resist, even though the odds were heavily against them. They insisted that they had given the Athenians no cause to deprive them of their independence.[18]

Let me now turn to the Québécois. Consider Charles Taylor's expression of their political objectives. Québec governments, Taylor says, take it as "axiomatic" that the survival and flourishing of Québec-French language and culture is a good whose preservation it is their task to ensure. They aspire to ensure it through indefinitely many future generations. Accordingly, they refuse to be neutral between those who want to remain true to and to perpetuate their ancestral culture and those who might want instead to pursue some individual goal of self-fulfilment regardless of its effects upon the future of this culture. Hence these governments adopt policies that "actively seek to *create* members of the community, for instance, in assuring that future generations continue to identify as French-speakers."[19]

In Taylor's view, there is nothing idiosyncratic about the Québécois' efforts. Canadian Indian tribes have similar aspirations and work to satisfy them. So too do many other ethnic, tribal, or cultural groups throughout the world.[20] And I would add that there are also prominent liberal democratic theorists who hold a somewhat similar position about inculcating liberalism in newcomers and thereby preserving liberal democratic political societies.[21]

Obviously there are stories that articulate and promote these and comparable efforts to promote the members' identification with their political society. Which narratives do so defensibly and which do not? On my proposal one should ask whether a narrative in effect admits (*a*) its multifaceted partiality and reformability, (*b*) the ineliminable threat that its society poses to others, (*c*) the fact that its society can become dangerously obsolete, and (*d*) that the defensibility of its society cannot be determined exclusively by its own members, but rather always needs corroboration from other sources. If a society's constitutive narratives embody these four admissions, and if its practices match the narratives, then it and its narratives are defensible.

Note that if Taylor's remarks about the Québécois are taken literally and are accurate, then the Québécois position is indefensible. On my proposal, there can be no political *axioms*, no unchallengeable premises from which conclusions for conduct can be deduced. Nor can one rightfully seek to *create* members of a certain sort. Members must always have room to reflect upon their political society and to call for its reshaping.

Note also that my proposal provides no sure bulwark against tragic outcomes from adhering to a political identity. Even if the Melian narratives fully satisfied the conditions I propose (Thucydides' report is too sketchy to tell whether they did), that would not have protected them from the Athenian reaction. For the Athenians, after a siege, conquered them and "put to death all the men of military age whom they took, and sold the women and children as slaves. Melos they took over for themselves...."[22]

But no test of the defensibility of a political identity can guarantee against tragedy. And history yields no unequivocal answers. Who could say that the Melians should certainly have acted otherwise? It is by no means inconceivable that the Athenians might have decided that it was not worth their trouble either to lay the siege or to persist in it or to suffer the losses necessary to overcome the resistance. And so they might have simply abandoned their demand. But neither is it inconceivable that if the Melians had yielded at the outset, the Athenians might have ruled them benignly. The Melians had to make their decision without foreknowledge of its consequences.

But even if history yields no unequivocal answers to issues of this sort, it does give us leads about the sorts of questions we should address to political societies and their constitutive narratives. My Ricoeurian proposal, even if it is neither complete nor foolproof, provides considerable insurance against adopting or countenancing political identities that are tyrannical. And it does so without requiring one to deny that a political identity, troublesome as it inevitably is, can be defensible. Hence this proposal in effect makes the case that the only appropriate way in which to accept a political identity is with an attitude of asking for and offering pardon from holders of other political identities. So to hold a political identity is to hold it in hope and not blindly.

Notes

1 For present purposes, I will not go into ontological questions about personal identity, questions that Ricoeur has addressed in interesting ways in many of his works. Here, with Charles Taylor, I take the notion of "identity," when applied to human beings, to refer to something like a person's understanding of his or her fundamental make-up. See Taylor, *Multiculturalism and the "Politics of Recognition"* (Princeton: Princeton University Press, 1992), 25. See also Maurice Merleau-Ponty, *Phenomenology of Perception*, trans. Colin Smith (London: Routledge and Kegan Paul, 1962), 346-8.

2 Nonhuman entities, caught up as they are in causal processes that in principle permit the exhaustive explanation of their present states by antecedents, are the paradigm cases of *idem*-identity. Analogously, the states of some constituents or some aspects can also receive exhaustive, or near exhaustive, explanation from antecedent states

of these constituents and their context. Thus human entities too have a kind of *idem*-identity. But Ricoeur, following Heidegger, recognizes that there is a difference between the *idem*-identity of human entities and that of nonhuman ones.

3   Paul Ricoeur, *Oneself as Another*, trans. by Kathleen Blamey (Chicago: University of Chicago Press, 1992), 118. See also his "Narrative Identity," in David Wood (ed.), *On Paul Ricoeur: Narrative and Interpretation* (London: Routledge, 1991), 188-92.

4   Wood, *On Paul Ricoeur*, 192.

5   Ricoeur, *Oneself as Another*, 119.

6   Ricoeur, *Oneself as Another*, 180-1.

7   See Ricoeur, *Oneself as Another*, 250-2, 262-8, and passim.

8   Ricoeur, *Oneself as Another*, 288.

9   Even Iceland, I would argue, is no exception. But this is not the place to make such a case.

10   For Ricoeur's technical sense of "ideology" and "utopia," see his *Lectures on Ideology and Utopia*, ed. George H. Taylor (New York: Columbia University Press, 1986), esp. 10 and 250.

11   So far as I can tell, the phenomenon of political identity requires that its members adopt what Ronald Dworkin calls an impact model for assessing the worth of their lives instead of the challenge model that he espouses. Whereas the impact model takes the ethical value of a human life to be wholly dependent on and measured by the value its consequences have for others, the challenge model holds that "living a life is itself a performance that demands skill, that it is the most comprehensive and important challenge we face, and that our critical interests consist in the achievements, events, and experiences that mean that we have met the challenge well." See Dworkin's "Foundations of Liberal Equality," in *The Tanner Lectures on Human Value*, XI (Salt Lake City: University of Utah Press, 1990), 57.

12   This view of political societies as long-lived, even perpetual, is not peculiar to communitarian thought. Rawls develops his political conception of justice for a stable society, one "conceived as existing in perpetuity: it produces and reproduces itself and its institutions and culture over generations and there is no time at which it is expected to wind up its affairs," *Political Liberalism* (New York: Columbia University Press, 1993), 18.

13   Hannah Arendt, *Between Past and Future* (New York: Penguin, 1983), 186.

14   *Mutatis mutandis*, immigrants are political newcomers no less than children are.

15   It is worth mentioning in this context Alasdair MacIntyre's "Is Patriotism a Virtue?" The Lindley Lecture, University of Kansas, March 26, 1984. Though I do not fully subscribe to his position, he is right to ascribe heavy normative weight to patriotism.

16   See Maurice Merleau-Ponty, *Adventures of the Dialectic*, trans. Joseph Bien (Evanston: Northwestern University Press, 1973), 29.

17   On at least one occasion, Ricoeur says that a sort of fideism is necessary if there is to be politics at all. See his *Lectures*, 312. He does not repeat this fideism in *Oneself as Another*. I have argued that, on Ricoeur's own grounds, he has no need to resort to fideism of any sort. See my "Ideology, Utopia, and Responsible Politics," *Man and World* 22 (1989): 38-41.

18 See Thucydides, *History of the Peloponnesian War*, trans. Rex Warner (Baltimore: Penguin Books, 1954), 363-6.

19 Taylor, *Multiculturalism*, 58-9.

20 Taylor, *Multiculturalism*, 40-1.

21 See, for example, Dworkin, "Foundations," 117, and Amy Gutmann, *Democratic Education* (Princeton: Princeton University Press, 1987), 14 and passim.

22 Thucydides, *History*, 366.

Essay/ing Ricoeur:
A Challenge to Ricoeur's Construction
of Historical and Fictional
(and Metaphorical) Truth

C. BRYN PINCHIN

Can Paul Ricoeur's phenomenological theory of narrative and metaphor provide a satisfactory framework from which one may explore highly metaphoric, contemporary texts written by women or people of color? Can it be relevant to texts written from a post-colonial context whose very purpose it is to challenge or at least to destabilize the essentialist constructs which Ricoeur's theory of metaphor seems to privilege? The answer is no. However, an analysis of Ricoeur's theory of metaphor can provide an opening for a more fruitful exploration of metaphor within a feminist context.

This "essay" is exactly what its title (the real part, that is, the part before the colon) says it is. It is an "essay/ing" of Ricoeur, a trying, even a trying on, within the feminist critical frame of reference which informs my work. In what follows, I offer a diacritical reading of two essays by Paul Ricoeur.[1] In "Can Fictional Narratives Be True?",[2] he engages the paradoxical relationship between fiction and truth by postulating a structural unity between history and fiction as narrative discourses. In "The Function of Fiction in Shaping Reality,"[3] Ricoeur views metaphor as a site of linguistic innovation. The papers are similar in argument and even phraseology. The former links history and fiction and a concept of truth by means of a theory of reference; the latter links fiction and truth to language through a theory of metaphor. It is notable that Ricoeur does not link his constructs of fictional and metaphorical truth to concerns of ideology and power. Indeed, voices, and bodies, behind, beyond and within texts are largely absent from his essays.

My reading of Ricoeur's theories as a key to an ideological position stems from Terry Eagleton's observation that "whole social ideologies may be implicit in an apparently neutral critical method."[4] From this perspective, my essay/ing raises two further theoretical problems for me. First, Ricoeur's construct of "*epoché*" or the bracketing of fiction from the "ordinary world of human action and of the descriptions of this ordinary world in ordinary discourse"[5] seems effectively to remove its referent from any genuine interchange with the world outside the text, etherealizing fiction into what Ricoeur himself calls a place of "non-engagement."[6] Second, Ricoeur's unease with the possibilities of destabilization offered by a reading of fiction outside these brackets is evident in the language in which he couches his analysis of the metaphoric process. In my view, the semiotic tension that he identifies at the heart of metaphor may also be seen as an ideological tension when the value or truth of past positions is challenged by new readings inserted into language by means of metaphoric innovation. In these terms, the power of fiction to shape and then, by implication, to reshape reality may be read as the power of fiction to destabilize entrenched, even unconscious, ideological positions.

Ricoeur's argument links the narrative genres of history and fiction in terms of their referential dimension.[7] In order to establish reference as the nexus between them, Ricoeur questions the accepted distinctions between history and fiction, in such a way that "history appear[s] to be more *fictional* ... and narrative fictions ... appear to be more *mimetic*,"[8] despite what he calls "our tendency to deny any role to fiction in history and to *mimesis* in tales, dramas and novels."[9] In his view, it is the convergence of the different but complementary referential claims of history and fiction that bring fundamental historicity to language. But, since in the end, this "fundamental historicity" seems to involve only the repatterning and reaffirmation in the present of those values which are the "common treasure of mankind"[10] as "history opens us to the possible, [and] fiction by opening us to the unreal, brings us back to the essential,"[11] it is here that I want to intervene in Ricoeur's argument.

In "Can Fictional Narratives Be True?", Ricoeur does not establish a link between history and fiction in order to underscore the "constructed" nature of history as it would be viewed from a postmodern position, for example, wherein the distinction between event and story implies a critical awareness of ideological complicity. Rather, his view of history writing as something that the "great historian"[12] does when constructing a fictive representation of reality seems limited to concerns of emplotment and the structuring of story. It is not a concern about the fictions that *may be* history. Such an approach to historical fictions would, in turn, bring into question the influence of gender, race and/or class in the shaping of his/story. Indeed, Ricoeur seems to regard the processes of emplotment and representation in the writing of history as "natural," at most, categorizeable in a way similar to Frye's structures, limited only by the rules of evidence that history shares with the other empirical sciences. I do not. I am acutely and ironically aware that Ricoeur's "great historian" is a "he."[13]

In his argument, history shares the referential claims of fiction because history writing produces a literary artefact, whose world, "'the work's world' – is assumed to *stand for* some actual occurrences in the 'real' world."[14] Such a text acquires the status of a "self-contained system of symbols."[15] The phrase, "self-contained," is important here. Elsewhere, Ricoeur has defined text as a "work"[16] and a "work," variously, as "a closed sequence of discourse," and "a closed chain of meaning."[17] It would seem that the fiction inherent in history may "stand for" actual events in the world outside or beyond the text, but it may not engage, contest, or be contested by the social context of that world since the self-contained system of symbols is closed. Ricoeur does not explain how a system of symbols that is language may be closed from the context from which it arose, or, perhaps more accurately, from the context which the system of symbols, that is language, shaped in the first place. But, with this argument Ricoeur seems to cut the historical text, and its reader, off from the materiality of the world surrounding it, and, as a result, the premises which underpin its patterning of historical narrative remain unchallengeable.

For Ricoeur, the work of history is the preservation of that which, as a society, we mark as "memorable." Accordingly, what "is most worthy of being kept in our memories are the *values* which ruled the individual actions, the life of the institutions, and the social struggles of the past."[18] "Thanks to the objective work of the historian," whose willingness to suspend his [sic] own condition provides the means by which the alterity of the past is preserved intact in the present, these values are added to "the common treasure of mankind [sic]."[19] It is impossible for me to be anything but ironic here. Where does Ricoeur's faith in the uncontested truth of historical reference come from? And why can't I share it? The answer that is obvious to me is that Ricoeur's assumptions about historical truth are grounded in the unconscious or unproblematized power position from which he writes. Consider the presumptions which underlie his use of pronouns, for example. Generally we find the first person in these essays, singular and plural. For example, in "Can Fictional Narratives Be True?", he introduces himself as "I" in the first paragraph and then continues ... "the time has come to remind "*our*selves," ... of "*our* language," ... of "*our* historical condition," ... of "*our* tendenc[ies]." Or, "what do *we* mean by being historical?" Ultimately he is able to conclude that history opens "*us*" to the possible. While on the surface this language seems inclusive, I note that his references are invariably European, and invariably male. He refers throughout to "*mankind*." Remember that the "great historian" is a he.

It seems to me that Ricoeur's complacency about the truth claims of history stem from his inclusion in the closed club which is marked by the subjectivity of a white European male. Ricoeur is always at home in history because his view of the truth of history re-invents "him," or, at least the centrality of "his" own transcendent subjectivity. He writes, "historical imagination refers to a broader temporal field within which *my* personal history is related in a three-fold way to the temporalities of *my* contemporaries, *my* predecessors, and *my* successors."[20] There is no vision here of historical tradition as oppressive, imperialist or patriarchal, and no sense of struggle, discontinuity or exclusion. It is in these terms that we may read the absence of critical concern for stories of oppression in this essay, and his celebration of the stable and recurrent patterns of historical and fictional narrative as a reflection of a position of power associated firmly with a Western modernist tradition of thought.

This tradition is marked by a faith in the neutrality of reasoned judgment, in scientific objectivity and most importantly, to quote Nancy Hartsock, "by a denial of the centrality of power to knowledge and concomitantly by a denial of the centrality of systematic domination in human societies."[21] Ricoeur's schematics of historicity celebrates what he calls a "ruled creativity," which is "the spontaneous submission to recurrent patterns"[22] of the infinite variety of stories told by mankind. The unproblematized use of the word "submission" is instructive here in that it suggests that Ricoeur does not acknowledge the role of power in shaping historical narratives, the fact that this "submission" is not always benign. Terry Eagleton points out that "the unending dialogue of human history is as often as not a monologue by the powerful to the powerless, or that if it is indeed a dialogue, then the partners – men and women, for example – hardly occupy equal positions."[23] By privileging historical patterning over multiplicity, by using the word "submission" in this context, it can be said that a discourse in which Ricoeur most signally fails to recognize the play of power is his own.

In order to establish a similar truth claim for fictional narratives, Ricoeur links fiction and reference by means of a practised reading of the Aristotelian concept of "mimesis," which, he posits, re-enacts reality (which is human action) "according to its essential and magnified traits."[24] In these terms, mimesis provides a kind of metaphorizing of reality which Ricoeur associates with iconic augmentation. The work of fiction is also augmentation in that, in this argument, fiction adds to reality. The reference of fiction is not the "nothingness of absence" but rather the "nothingness of unreality."[25] The lack of a primary reference for fiction opens new ways of referring to the paradox of fictional reality because, while "fictions do not refer in a reproductive manner to reality as already given, they [may] refer in a productive manner to reality as prescribed by them."[26] Note the authority given to fiction by the word "prescribe." Within the world of the work, which is the world of the text, what Ricoeur calls the "productive reference of fiction" changes reality in that it both re-invents and re-discovers it. If the truth of history lies in its power to add the values of the past to the "common treasure of mankind," the truth of fiction lies in its power to reshape these essential values in the present.

Such a concept of fictional truth seems, at first glance, a utopian one, offering the possibility of innovation and destabilization. In a significant way, the "saying, making, and emplotting"[27] of fictional texts "opens the real to the possible."[28] Ricoeur maintains that fictions "re-organize the world in terms of the works and works in terms of the world."[29] But when he approaches the level of interpretation of the work, the level of discourse wherein the reader of fiction must operate with two worlds, that is her own and that provided by the symbolic system of the text, I sense that Ricoeur pulls away from fully embracing the destabilizing potential of his position. Instead, the re-descriptive capacity of fiction is limited strictly to the terms of the work, and the work is effectively cut off from any contestatory interchange with the world outside it. The work and the world of the work are rigorously connected. The world outside the work is as rigorously excluded. This is made grammatically clear when he writes: "Imagination at work – in a work – produces itself as a world."[30]

He accomplishes this feat of separation by means of the phenomenological *epoché*, the bracketing of the world of the text from the ordinary world of human action and discourse. Ricoeur links this movement of the *epoché* to Roman Jacobson's notion of split reference, which is here reduced to the assertion that

> the suppression of [that] which we have called conventionally the "description" of the world – is the condition of the possibility of a second order reference which we are here calling the re-description of the world. A literary work ... is ... a work whose ultimate reference has as its condition a suspension of the referential claim of conventional language.[31]

It would seem that the re-descriptive, re-making power of fiction, which at first reading seemed to offer a means of destabilizing conservative truth claims, is only possible if the contestatory interaction of the text and the reader's world is surrendered. Ricoeur advocates a kind of wise passivity when approaching the text.

> The ultimate role of the image ... is to suspend our attention to the real, to place us in a state of non-engagement with regard to perception, or action, in short to suspend meaning in the neutralized atmosphere to which one could give the name of the dimension of fiction.[32]

Dominick LaCapra notes that the implications for the understanding of the literary work in these terms are conservative and contemplative. He writes,

> what is lost is the heuristic power of fiction that Ricoeur himself notes, for the redescription of reality which he presents as the achievement of literature amounts to little more than a purely aesthetic way of seeing things differently, with no implications for understanding or action in the ordinary world.[33]

I would go further. The passivity that Ricoeur advocates as an approach to the reference of fiction is desirable at all only if the reader's position in the face of the world created by the text is an empowered one. What is missing (again) is any sense of the need to contest the text in terms of the world it constructs and offers, its subjectivity, or its politics of gender, race, or class. If the reader is to be passively engaged within the text, it follows that s/he must be at home within it. Quite obviously this is not always the case. Ricoeur's presumption that the world of fiction is a comfortable one may be paralleled to the impression that he also, seemingly, is always "at home" within the traditional constructs of history. I linked that complacency to his position within patriarchy. I think that position is also evident here.

Ricoeur identifies metaphor as the site where the productive reference of fiction intersects with the productive aspects of language. It follows, then, that within language metaphor is at the same time the site of a semantic power struggle where conservative instincts meet utopian ones, where the urge to hold on to past meaning intersects with the power to redefine or reshape it. Metaphor is, in these terms, the locus of a conflicted semantic agenda. Metaphoric innovation is as much a matter of power as of language. The possibility of destabilization that lies at the heart of language seems at odds with Ricoeur's conservative vision of historical and fictional truth, however bracketed it might be from ordinary life and language. This unease is evident in the language he uses to theorize the metaphoric process. His theory of metaphor which at one level attempts to define a shift in predication within the metaphoric copula, also encodes a clash of power positions using images of struggle, defiance, and, ultimately, rape.

In "The Function of Fiction in Shaping Reality," Ricoeur defines metaphor as a "deviating use of predicates"[34] within the framework of an entire phrase. His theory of metaphor is noteworthy for the fact that he has recast the rhetorical perspective on metaphor away from a theory of substitution with the word as its unit of reference toward the sentence as the carrier of meaning. In this view, the sentence becomes the text of the metaphor; it is "necessary to speak of a metaphorical statement rather than of nouns used metaphorically."[35] Within the sentence, the metaphor is a case of "bizarre predication." He calls the "deviating" predication, which produces the clash between semantic fields at the heart of the metaphoric copula "predicative impertinence." In order to respond to the challenge issued by the semantic clash produced by the impertinent predication which "shatters" prior categorizations, we produce new predicative pertinence. This new pertinence, or "appropriateness," at the level of the entire sentence, creates the extension of meaning which identifies the metaphor. Metaphorical innovation is thus a clash of "pertinence" and "impertinence." The metaphor is "impertinent" or "deviating" or "bizarre" predication in light of previous linguistic categorizations. However, pertinent and impertinent are not, as would first appear, opposites. They are not even semantically parallel.[36]

"Pertinent" means "referring centrally to" matter being discussed while "impertinent" means "speaking disrespectfully or showing an offensive lack of respect." While I do not quarrel with Ricoeur's analysis of the metaphoric process, I find this language revealing. The semantic "clash," which causes tension within the metaphoric copula is the "impertinent" challenge to which we respond by producing a new pertinence, which in turn becomes a new "appropriateness." New meaning emerges from the "ruins" of literal predication. In his words,

> ... one could speak here of *predicative assimilation*, in order to underline by the word "assimilation" ... that it is not a question of a passively recorded similitude, but of an active operation, co-extensive with the *rapprochement* performed by the metaphorical statement.[37]

It would seem that the moment when we are not passive before a text is that moment within metaphor when pertinence resists impertinence, when past categorizations resist new ones. Predicative impertinence becomes pertinence by means of assimilation, or absorption. Assimilation is a "rapprochement." This word suggests a renewal of friendly relations after a war. In fact, in his paper "The Metaphorical Process as Cognition, Imagination and Feeling,"[38] Ricoeur describes assimilation as a level of "Conceptual peace and rest" after the "war" between distance and proximity within metaphoric predication.[39] In these terms, "deviant," "impertinent," "clash," "shatter" and "assimilate," the struggle within metaphor is a violent one indeed.

Ricoeur notes that when we speak of figurative language it is as if "metaphor gives a body, a contour, a face to discourse."[40] Thus we can metaphorize the trope in human terms and move away from the connotations of battle evoked above. But that construction evokes another metaphor of metaphor, originally coined by Nelson Goodman in *Languages of Art*. Metaphor is "an affair between a predicate with a past and an object that yields while protesting."[41] Ricoeur cites Goodman in both of the essays considered here, and, in his *Rule of Metaphor*, cites and amplifies Goodman's definition of metaphor uncritically in terms that emphasize the struggle for power around or within the body and enlarges on this singularly offensive definition as follows:

> To yield while protesting is ... our paradox. To protest is what remains from the former marriage, the literal assignation, destroyed by contradiction: the yielding is what finally happens to the new rapprochement.[42]

In *The Rule of Metaphor*, Ricoeur calls Goodman's metaphor "droll." We may infer from his uncharacteristic exclamation mark that he is delighted when he notes that "this time [the] screen filter, grill, and lens [of this metaphor of metaphor] gives way to carnal union!"[43] The rapprochement which marks the new semantic pertinence constructed by means of metaphoric innovation is either rapprochement or rape. Either way, new meaning invoked metaphorically clearly marks a significant defeat for the previous semantic categorizations.

Interactive metaphors shatter prior categorizations. But, as history restores us to tradition, and fiction restores us to "essentials,"[44] Ricoeur holds on to the past even within metaphoric innovation. By isolating the tension resonating within the binary "is like and is not like" contained in the metaphoric copula, which defines the tension between belief and unbelief in metaphoric predication, he is able to say that the new concept is always informed by a residue of the old.

> The idea of semantic impertinence preserves this: an order, logically antecedent, resists, and is not completely abolished by the new pertinence.... I continue to perceive the previous incompatibility through the new compatibility. Remoteness persists in closeness. This is why to see similarity is to see the likeness in spite of the difference.[45]

It is noteworthy to me that Ricoeur uses almost the same phraseology, and the same dialectic, in "Can Fictional Narratives Be True?", to bring history and fiction back to what is "essential." He writes, "a dialectic between what is foreign and what is familiar, between what is remote and what is near ... is precisely what brings history close to fiction."[46] Metaphor seems reduced to a kind of linguistic palimpsest wherein old constructs, resistant to change, are apt to linger.

However, the continuing resonance of the "is not like" pole of the metaphor that Ricoeur identifies, but whose subversive potential he avoids, challenges the frequent reading of metaphor as limited to the tension between the polarities of a binary. Given the overtly gendered nature of the binary structure, which Elizabeth Grosz describes as "implicitly *sexualized*, pervaded with sexual-political values, and related to the patriarchal differentiation of the sexes," this challenge would seem a more fruitful approach to the trope, since, as Grosz points out, it is not adequate simply to refuse the oppositional structure of the binary, pretending it does not exist.

> It pervades all our conceptual systems and criteria for their assessment. It [shapes] the terms by which we are able to think or articulate.... Nor ... can this structure simply be accepted without question. It must be continually challenged and displaced, pushed to its limits.[47]

The same can be said of metaphor. The interception of literal belief embodied in the "is not like" pole of the metaphoric binary may usefully be read as a liminal space that challenges metaphoric closure, imposing doubts, variants and shifts in image formation, fostering play and subversion.

Such a reading of metaphor is marked by continuing resistance to past constructs and a naming of the interstice within the poles of the binary as a place, not of reassurance, but rather one of resistance and destabilization. The subversive potential inherent in this reading of the metaphoric binary becomes more tangible if the trope itself is read in ideological rather than purely linguistic or epistemological terms. Steve McCaffrey provides an example by metaphorizing metaphor as an economy rather than a structure. He notes that the reduction of difference to identity is never an absolute moment in metaphor.[48] Rather, the operation of metaphor is a

> locus for the contestation of difference. In effect, there is always the threat of substitution going astray in the substitutional passage, of the movement elsewhere towards the appropriation of the otherness collapsing and actually engendering a heterogeneity.[49]

Metaphor is "seditious" because it replaces "the unequivocal relation of the word to truth with skew, breach and uncertainty."[50] Rather than the power play of substitution, which is imposition and certainty, this reading of the resonating pole of the metaphoric copula holds the possibility of spinning off into linguistic sedition displacing ideological (patriarchal, racist, colonizing, orthodox) certitudes.

Nicole Brossard identifies "movements in the gestation of thought" from which transgressive or subversive content emerges.[51] These movements are strikingly similar to the centrifugal view of metaphor outlined above. She identifies "oscillating movement, which manifests a certain ambivalence; ... repetitive movement, as if to exorcise the patriarchal voice; ... spiraling movement, which serves to gradually conquer the territory concerned; and ... floating movement, where thought is suspended over the void."[52] Brossard's spirals spinning toward "new perspectives, new configurations of woman-as-being-in-the-world, of what's real, of reality, and of fiction"[53] prevent the borderlines of sense and non-sense, of pertinence and impertinence, of essential and non-essential from closing in. Without such possibilities, Paul Ricoeur's theory of metaphor makes an uncomfortable fit.

Notes

1   I am aware that these essays are translations from the original French – and I face the critical conundrum that the questions I pose in the following pages may well be rooted in problems of translation. I must consider the issues incurred by translation more carefully as my research progresses. For now, my position is that Ricoeur's work is widely available and used in English and so must face critical attention in that language.

2   Paul Ricoeur, "Can Fictional Narratives Be True?", *Analecta Husserliana*, 14, ed. A.T. Tymieniecka (Dordrecht: Reidel, 1983), 3-19.

3   Paul Ricoeur, "The Function of Fiction in Shaping Reality," *A Ricoeur Reader: Reflection and Imagination*, ed. Mario J. Valdés (Toronto: University of Toronto Press, 1991), 117-37.

4   Terry Eagleton, *Literary Theory: An Introduction* (Minneapolis: University of Minnesota Press, 1983), 124.

5   Ricoeur, "Fictional Narratives," 10.

6   Ricoeur, "The Function of Fiction," 128.

7   Ricoeur, "Fictional Narratives," 5.

8   Ricoeur, "Fictional Narratives," 4.

9   Ricoeur, "Fictional Narratives," 4.

10   Ricoeur, "Fictional Narratives," 16.

11   Ricoeur, "Fictional Narratives," 16.

12   Ricoeur, "Fictional Narratives," 7.

13   Ricoeur, "Fictional Narratives," 7.

14   Ricoeur, "Fictional Narratives," 7.

15   Ricoeur, "Fictional Narratives," 7.

16   Paul Ricoeur, "Metaphor and the Main Problem of Hermeneutics," *New Literary History* 6/1 (1974): 95-109.

17   Ricoeur, "Metaphor and the Main Problem," 104.

18   Ricoeur, "Fictional Narratives," 16.

19   Ricoeur, "Fictional Narratives," 16.

20   Ricoeur, "Fictional Narratives," 13. Italics added.

21   Nancy Hartsock, "Postmodernism and Political Change: Issues for Feminist Theory," *Cultural Critique* (Winter 1989-90): 17.

22   Ricoeur, "Fictional Narratives," 13.

23   Eagleton, *Literary Theory*, 73.

24   Ricoeur, "Function of Fiction," 20.

25   Ricoeur, "Function of Fiction," 20.

26   Ricoeur, "Fictional Narratives," 9.

27   Ricoeur, "Fictional Narratives," 10.

28 Ricoeur, "Fictional Narratives," 16.

29 Ricoeur, "Fictional Narratives," 10.

30 Ricoeur, "Function of Fiction," 123.

31 Ricoeur, "Fictional Narratives, 11. In his gloss of Jacobson's theory of split refer-ence, in *The Rule of Metaphor*, trans. Robert Czerny (Toronto: University of Toronto Press, 1977), 222, Ricoeur provides a reductive treatment of the relationship of the poetic to the non-poetic. Jacobson notes that "the supremacy of poetic function over referential function does not obliterate the reference but makes it ambiguous" (quoted by Ricoeur, ibid., 224). To illustrate this split reference, Jacobson quotes Majorcan storytellers: "It was and it was not" (ibid.).

32 Ricoeur, "Function of Fiction," 128.

33 Dominick LaCapra, *Rethinking Intellectual History* (Ithaca: Cornell University Press, 1983), 127.

34 Ricoeur, "Function of Fiction," 125.

35 Ricoeur, "Function of Fiction," 124.

36 I am grateful to Dr. Susan Rudy Dorscht for her insight here, and to the comments of my colleagues, Nicole Markotic and Jeff Derksen, who made me look again.

37 Ricoeur, "Function of Fiction," 125.

38 Ricoeur, "The Metaphorical Process as Cognition, Imagination and Feeling," in *On Metaphor*, ed. Sheldon Sacks (Chicago: University of Chicago Press, 1979), 141-57.

39 Ricoeur, "The Metaphorical Process," 146.

40 Ricoeur, "Function of Fiction," 125.

41 Nelson Goodman, *Languages of Art* (Indianapolis: Hackett, 1976), 69.

42 Ricoeur, *The Rule of Metaphor*, 196.

43 Ricoeur, *The Rule of Metaphor*, 235.

44 Ricoeur, "Fictional Narratives," 16.

45 Ricoeur, "Function of Fiction," 125.

46 Ricoeur, "Fictional Narratives," 16.

47 Elizabeth Grosz, "Introduction," in *A Reader in Feminist Knowledge*, ed. Sneja Gunew (London: Routledge, 1991), 87.

48 Steve McCaffrey, "Writing as a General Economy," *North of Intention* (Toronto: Nightwood Editions, 1986), 205.

49 Steve McCaffrey, "Writing as a General Economy," 205.

50 Steve McCaffrey, "Writing as a General Economy," 206.

51 I am taking liberties here. In the quotation that follows, Brossard is speaking of "feminine content." It is my position that such self-conscious "feminine content" is inherently subversive, transgressive and/or resistant, content.

52 Nicole Brossard, *The Aerial Letter*, trans. Marlene Wildeman (Toronto: Woman's Press, 1988), 92.

53 Brossard, *The Aerial Letter*, 117.

The Tragic Face
of Narrative Judgment:
Christian Reflections on
Paul Ricoeur's Theory of Narrative

JAMES FODOR

Introduction

Allow me to say a few words about the intention and strategy of this paper. My aim, first of all, is to engage Ricoeur's narrative project at one particular point; namely, his retrieval and rehabilitation of the notion of *muthos* (emplotment) from Aristotle's *Poetics*. While I want to register general agreement with Ricoeur's enterprise of giving *muthos* a broader extension and a more fundamental understanding than that conveyed by Aristotle's *Poetics* – the latter being too closely tied to a conceptuality patterned after Greek tragedy – I nevertheless want to enter some reservations concerning Ricoeur's proposed extrapolation.[1] Quite simply, my fear is that whatever Ricoeur's account of narrative gains in theoretical clarity and rigor, it loses in concrete versatility and practical usefulness.[2] In other words, although Ricoeur is right to insist that Aristotle's model of tragic emplotment requires further development and expansion – accomplished in part by redescribing *muthos* under the category of a "synthesis of the heterogeneous,"[3] but also by engrafting onto this narrative function a rather sophisticated analysis of human temporality[4] – what tends to get neglected in the process is any sustained attention to what might be called "narrative judgment."[5]

The charge that Ricoeur's account neglects or at least underdevelops narrative judgment requires clarification and defense. After all, Ricoeur certainly does recognize and appreciate the inherently evaluative aspects of narrative emplotment. Poetics, he concedes, never stops borrowing from ethics just as ethical judgment never ceases to be informed and refined by poetics.[6] Indeed, Ricoeur does go some way toward addressing the normative dimensions of emplotment when he articulates the mimetic process according to its threefold movement of prefiguration, configuration, and refiguration. Moreover, in his most recent work on narrative identity and the ethical dimensions of selfhood, Ricoeur begins to specify a number of important relations between narrativity and ethics.[7] Despite these overtures, his notion of narrative judgment proves deficient exactly because its level of accuracy remains indeterminate. Judgment, after all, is narrative specific and insofar as Ricoeur attempts to provide a universal theory of narrative, the result is a conception of judgment at once too abstract, too formal and thus too empty to be of any practical value when it comes to discriminating among the various practices inherent in any one particular tradition. Indeed, the strength of Ricoeur's narrative theory remains precarious precisely to the extent that it continues to trade upon an ambiguity in his use of tragic emplotment.[8] On the one hand, "tragedy" (*muthos*) names for Ricoeur practices, virtues and dispositions peculiar to and distinctive of ancient Greek society. On the other hand, *muthos* serves as a technical term characterizing "literary" compositions in general.[9] By exploiting this ambiguity, Ricoeur is able to make his case for a general theory of narrative without fully acknowledging the extent to which his account remains parasitic on the practices and content (both moral and religious) of specific narrative traditions.[10]

A useful way to illustrate this unacknowledged dependency is through a concrete example. Stories of courage are befitting for at least two reasons. First of all, courage is a virtue highly prized not only among the ancient Greeks but also among Christians of all ages, and thus it provides an invaluable means by which to compare critically profoundly different narrative traditions.[11] Secondly, narrative displays of courage elucidate the intimate connections between religious and ethical dimensions of life. Courage exposes the gap between tragic wisdom and practical reason, showing how the religious constantly encroaches upon the ethical, exposing its limits and challenging its pretensions.[12]

What I propose to do, then, is to draw Ricoeur's discussion back closer to Aristotle's *Poetics* with a view to suggesting how his rehabilitation of *muthos* might be made more productive for Christian reflection, particularly regarding its ethical and religious possibilities. At the same time, I wish to underscore, by articulating the differences between Christian courage and courage as understood in ancient Greek culture, the limitations of any *theory* of narrative. I want to argue that narrative understanding[13] or narrative judgment is not so much an intellectual process in need of explanation (read: theoretical elucidation) as an acquired skill in need of training and refinement.[14]

Ricoeur on Narrative Emplotment

Let me begin, then, by sketching very briefly Ricoeur's proposed agenda for giving Aristotle's notion of emplotment a broader extension.[15] Although Aristotle's *Poetics* affords a useful starting point for Ricoeur, it cannot serve as a model, let alone an exclusive norm.[16] For one thing, Aristotle's account of *muthos* was "conceived during an age when only tragedy, comedy, and epic were recognized as genres worthy of philosophical reflection."[17] Ricoeur wants to expand this notion to include every composition to which the name narrative might be ascribed.[18] Thus Ricoeur's project in *Time and Narrative* represents in large part a broadening, radicalizing, enriching, and opening up to the outside the notion of emplotment as handed down by the Aristotelian tradition.[19]

Beginning with Aristotle's definition of tragedy as the imitation of an action (*mimesis praxeos*),[20] Ricoeur observes how imitation (*mimesis*) and emplotment (*muthos*) find mutual definition within the realm of human action.[21] *Muthos* signifies an integrative configuring process, an act of bringing together and arranging incidents into a unique and complete action. *Mimesis*, likewise, is a creative activity, a particular type of "making" (*poiêsis*) that is not the production of a copy – a weakened image of some preexisting reality – but an augmentation of meaning in the field of action.[22]

The complexities of Aristotle's philosophy of action will not detain us here except to say that Aristotle conceives of the mimetic activity of emplotment in relationship to two particular kinds of action: *poiêsis* and *praxis*, "making" and "doing."[23] The former, *poiêsis*, is an action whose end is extrinsic to itself (*Nicomachean Ethics*, 1140b6). In other words, "making" is an action which changes the external world; its end is therefore in the things made rather than in the agent who makes them. For example, the activity of the builder building is occurring, not in the builder, but in the house being built. *Praxis*, on the other hand, is an action whose end is intrinsic to itself. "Doing" is no longer directed to the transformation of anything in the external world but consists in changing the agent himself.[24] For example, one engages in charitable acts for their own sake and not in order to attain some further end (happiness, for instance).[25] As Aristotle says, "good action itself is its end" (*Nicomachean Ethics*, 1140b7). In *praxis*, therefore, the source, end, and activity of "doing" are fully immanent to each other.[26]

Now it sounds rather odd – at least to modern ears – that tragedy should be defined as the imitation of something "done" rather than something "made." After all, the artistic product appears to be a "manufactured" good, much like a house is the creation of its builder.[27] Moreover, if the plot imitates a *praxis* – a fully self-sufficient action whose origin and end are intrinsic to the processes of its self-unfolding – then it seems that tragedy can have no purpose apart from its performance.[28] Tragedy, in short, seems to have no didactic value, pedagogical benefit or ethical import.[29] However, Ricoeur is quick to point out that objects produced by the poet are not tangible entities (like houses) but mimetic constructs in the sphere of the imaginary. That is to say, "artisans who work with words produce not things but quasi-things; they invent the as-if."[30] Poetry, therefore, is clearly a *praxis*, a "doing," albeit a fictive and poetical doing and not an actual, ethical doing.[31]

By virtue of its double allegiance to the realm of the real and the domain of the imaginary, *praxis* establishes a certain continuity between ethics and poetics.[32] Yet at the same time – insofar as the activity of emplotment metaphorically transposes the practical field into an imaginary realm – a break is also made with the domain of the real.[33] The fact that mimesis can function both as a rupture and a connection indicates to Ricoeur the presence of certain polysemic features which he articulates as $mimesis_1$, $mimesis_2$, and $mimesis_3$. Although capable of being inflected in terms of a threefold set of operations, each with its own distinctive function, Ricoeur insists that the whole mimetic process must be seen as one continuous movement.[34] The implications of this redescription for the relation between life and narrative are nothing short of profound.[35] For one thing, any opposition between the inside of fiction and the outside of life is dissolved. As Ricoeur puts it, "we must stop seeing the text as its own interior and life as exterior to it. Instead we must accompany that structuring operation that begins in life, is invested in the text, then returns to life."[36] The work of figuration, in other words, describes one uninterrupted, concrete process by which practical experience is transformed into works, authors, and readers.[37]

Two important corollaries ensue. First, the reception of a work is an integral part of the constitution of its meaning.[38] Meaning is always the joint product of the text and its reader or recipient; the two emerge together synergetically.[39] Second, narrative configuration and ethical evaluation are not only inseparable but mutually enriching.[40] That is, every work of emplotment represents a synthetic act of comprehension – a "grasping together" the details of action into the unity of the plot – but also a reflective act of judgment of which that configuring action is an instance.[41] Indeed, any action, whether real or imaginary, necessarily gives rise to reprobation or approbation; it is never ethically neutral. Telling a story, according to Ricoeur, means "deploying an imaginary space for thought experiments in which moral judgment operates in a hypothetical mode."[42] Indeed, one of the oldest functions of literary and dramatic art is to provide a certain imaginary space – an ethical laboratory if you will – where one can pursue through the mode of fiction experimentation with values.[43]

Of course, exploring a virtually endless number of imaginative variations between action and agent presented in the fictional narrative calls for an interruption of our everyday ethical judgments.[44] However, far from abolishing moral judgment altogether, the imaginary world of the text engages our evaluative capacities at a deeper and more fundamental level. In a move reminiscent of the one he makes in *The Rule of Metaphor*, where a suspension of first-order reference is a condition for the emergence of a second-order reference,[45] Ricoeur argues for an analogous doubling in the realm of ethics, where a break in life and in discourse is a necessary prerequisite for the creation of a second-order continuity.[46] To be sure, engaging the imaginary world of the text means that "we suspend all real moral judgment at the same time that we suspend action itself. But in the unreal sphere of fiction we never tire of exploring new ways of evaluating actions and characters. The thought experiments we conduct in the great laboratory of the imaginary are also explorations in the realm of good and evil." As Ricoeur puts it, "transvaluing, even devaluing, is still evaluating."[47]

The confrontation between the world of the text and the world of the reader, therefore, "constitutes both an interruption in the course of action and a new impetus to action."[48] Indeed, any encounter with the text's imaginary world disrupts in some sense the reader's everyday moral actions; but in so doing it challenges the reader to find ever new and interesting ways of ordering the actual world, thereby enhancing her powers of moral discernment and extending her ethical vision over a greater portion of the practical domain.[49] In short, it is through the act of narrating that we learn how to negotiate our world, acquiring – as we tell and retell our most determinative stories – a certain ethical dexterity, a particular finesse in our moral judgments.[50] The act of narrating, therefore, exhibits a distinctive type of intelligence akin to what Aristotle calls *phronesis*, a form of rationality "closer to practical wisdom and moral judgment than it is to science and, more generally, to the theoretical use of reason."[51] However, if tragic drama is to inform our moral judgments, educate our powers of deliberation, and realign our ethical vision, it must do so "indirectly," so to speak, through our emotions.[52]

The Inseparability of Tragic Form and Tragic Content

The indispensable role of emotion in shaping moral judgment is clearly a theme common to Ricoeur and Aristotle. Ironically, however, the point at which they are in closest agreement is also the point at which differences between their respective approaches begin to appear. Recall Aristotle's canonical definition of tragic *muthos*. According to the *Poetics*, tragedy is the imitation, not merely of an action, but of an action that is "serious" and "complete" with the express purpose of effecting, through pity and fear, a certain *catharsis* of those emotions. (*Poetics* 1449b23-27). Although Ricoeur picks up on the first part of this definition – that tragedy is an imitation of action – he omits any extended discussion of the elements of "seriousness" and "completeness" and only briefly touches on the question of pity and fear. This is not altogether surprising, given the fact that Ricoeur considers the Aristotelian concept of emplotment as a seed for a considerable development and expansion.[53] However, the fact that Ricoeur is compelled to discuss the connections between ethical judgment and emotional formation with specific reference to Greek tragedy is revealing. For one thing, it suggests that Aristotle's definition is so indissociably tied to a particular literary genre, to distinct practices and traditions, that any appropriation of its formal characteristics cannot be had without some reference to its actual content.[54] This may not be so obvious when Ricoeur discusses the "completeness" of an emplotted action, but it is clearly apparent when questions of an action's "seriousness" are raised, and it is inescapable when considerations of fear and pity are broached.

"Completeness" refers to the teleological ordering of the plot's episodes in order that the action might be brought to its proper conclusion. The episodes, in other words, cannot simply follow one another by chance but must be ordered according to a certain *telos*. "Seriousness," on the other hand, refers to ethically significant actions and events. In ancient Greek culture, "serious" actions mainly described the feats of outstanding men,[55] the most central of which had to do with valiant acts of war.[56] Courageous exploits on the battlefield, where issues of honor and shame were predominant, are common themes in Greek literature, tragedy included.[57] (The integral connections between war, fear, and shame in the tragic drama will be important when we take up the example of courage.) Indeed, the emotional content of fear and pity can only be understood against the wider social and religious contexts in which tragic drama was performed. The *catharsis* of these emotions – and hence their role is shaping one's ethical and political judgments – remains indeterminate apart from this background.

The meaning of *catharsis* in Aristotle's *Poetics* is notoriously difficult to ascertain, but whatever its exact force – whether religious cleansing, medical "purging" and purification, or intellectual clarification – *catharsis* is intimately linked to the emotions.[58] For Aristotle, learning how to feel emotion correctly is inseparable from learning how to form sound ethical judgments; indeed, any display of emotion is already an incipient moral discrimination.[59] Tragedy thus directly effects the emotions through which the audience's capacities for deliberation are augmented and refined.[60] The sad and terrible events of the tragic drama, the complications, the irreparable error committed in ignorance, the reversal of fortune, all evoke pity from the audience for the undeserved suffering of the tragic hero. Yet in sympathizing with the downfall of the protagonist – a person not wholly unlike themselves – the audience is also moved to fear for their own real possibilities.[61] The disaster which befell the protagonist, after all, might just as well have happened to them.[62] Therefore, to the extent that tragedy cultivates fellow-feeling through the display of fearful and pitiful events, thereby informing the audience's personal and political judgment, it is possible to see how tragedy constitutes an integral part of the ethical formation of the average citizen in ancient Greece.[63]

This "moral" view of tragedy is reinforced and supported by what is generally known of the broader social, political and religious contexts of Greek antiquity. For one thing, "tragedies were performed at the most solemn civic religious festivals of the year." Indeed, the whole occasion was a time of "communal experience, in which the city explored together some of the deepest problems it was facing in its efforts to live well. Dramas were regularly assessed on the basis of their ethical content; and political debate frequently appealed to tragic examples as a source of serious ethical insight."[64] "In the days preceding the performances, children of those who died for the city were presented, honors to outstanding citizens were proclaimed, ambassadors were publicly received and prisoners released from jail, as the city reconsecrated, remembered and re-dedicated itself to sustaining its traditions of collective life."[65] Insofar as tragedy represents one of the chief means of inculcating civic virtue,[66] its contribution to the formation and preservation of a healthy political order cannot be overestimated.[67]

Notwithstanding its indisputable ethical/political value, tragedy also serves as a reminder of human vulnerability.[68] That good people are susceptible to ethically significant reversals in spite of – indeed, precisely *because of* – their virtuous actions, is one of Greek tragedy's central themes.[69] The conflicts most often portrayed concern virtuous characters who are unable to avoid their own destruction, not because they have failed to carry out their moral obligations, but exactly because they are so rigorously and faithfully committed to exercising those virtues.[70] Their tragic downfall, in other words, seems "to grow out of their very striving for moral virtue."[71] Hence, tragedy poignantly displays how the virtues can make claims upon us that are, at times, incompatible. In certain situations, we find that we can neither default on any one of them nor successfully perform what each demands.[72]

Ethical dilemmas, however, represent only one level of conflict that threatens the narrative unity of life.[73] A discordance of a much more radical kind also appears in the gap opened up by the dramatic narrative between practical reason and tragic wisdom. Tragic wisdom challenges practical reason's illusory pretensions of providing the moral agent with a complete guide to a life of happiness.[74] It throws into question the belief "that ethical success, acting and living well, are things that depend [entirely] on human effort, are things that human beings can always control."[75] By stirring up spiritual powers, archaic and mythical energies, tragic wisdom reveals the extent to which humans are not fully in command of their own destiny.[76] To be sure, tragedy exhorts the audience "to deliberate well" and to "think correctly," but this "instruction" does not come in the form of a moral teaching or set of principles.[77] What tragic wisdom occasions, rather, is something akin to a revelation, an experience of disclosure; it precipitates a conversion in one's manner of looking, a re-orientation in how one sees the world. Indeed, the power of tragedy is precisely its ability to "touch" what Ricoeur calls, after George Steiner, "the agonistic ground of human experience."[78]

A Critical Engagement with Ricoeur

Notice, however, that in giving the Aristotelian notion of emplotment a broader extension, Ricoeur tends to oscillate between a formal and a substantive use of the term "tragedy." On the one hand, *muthos* functions as a designation specifying formal features of narrative emplotment[79] and, on the other, as the name of a common literary genre of ancient Greece. There is, of course, nothing that commits Ricoeur to employing *muthos* in only one sense of the term. After all, the semantic range of "tragic emplotment" (*muthos*) is sufficiently wide to include reference not only to a distinctive literary genre, or the activity of narrative emplotment itself, but also the particular type of experience that accompanies, or is elicited by, that activity.[80] However, because these various uses of tragic *muthos* are not always clearly distinguished, the misleading impression is given that Ricoeur's account of narrative is truly universal in scope while in fact it remains parasitic on the practices and content (both moral and religious) of a particular narrative tradition.

One reason why this subtle shift between various senses of *muthos* largely goes undetected, is because Ricoeur's level of analysis remains so formal and abstract. Bent on developing a truly general theory of narrative that privileges no one particular tradition, but is open to and inclusive of all, Ricoeur ends up never quite doing justice to any of them precisely because he fails to sufficiently attend to the individual "discordant concordances" displayed in the respective narrative traditions.[81] Insofar as these important differences are overlooked, Ricoeur's analysis tends to obscure rather than clarify the actual relationship between practical reason and tragic wisdom. Tragedy, you recall, functions as a reminder of human vulnerability in bringing to light the deep ontological tensions intrinsic to the human condition.[82] But it does so only by working through particular ethical conflicts generated by individual narrative traditions and not by circumventing them. What constitutes fear and pity, let alone what constitutes virtue and sound ethical judgment, cannot be known independent of the particular narrative in which those terms are embedded and within which they are deployed. Ricoeur, however, gives very little indication of the significant differences in ethical conflicts across narrative traditions. Rather, he assumes that there is just one universal experience of "the tragic" to which all these ethical conflicts point, and that the emotions of pity and fear which each of these dilemmas cathartically provoke and "purify," carry essentially the same cognitive content.[83] But this is simply not true, as is evident from even a cursory comparison between Greek and Christian traditions.[84]

Courage: Narrative Specific Examples

While a citizen of ancient Greece would probably find the expression "the agonistic ground of human experience" unintelligible, he would have no trouble understanding courage or the unavoidable nature of conflict in the moral life. He would know, for example, that situations may arise in which he will be asked to act virtuously and courageously, even though it may cost him his life. Given the fact that tragic dilemmas are inescapable in a life well lived, courage becomes indispensable. For of all the virtues courage is most "especially concerned with facing, and controlling, one's fear of death."[85] Indeed, being educated and trained into the moral life is, for the ancient Greeks, to be schooled in the art of dying well. Part of this ethical formation, of course, included tragic drama which, through repeated exposure and regular participation, disciplined, shaped and refined the audience's sense of pity and fear. Witnessing on the tragic stage brave men steadily facing their fated death helped prepare the audience to confront the hard and tragic choices they would most likely confront in their own lives. This training was especially important for the citizen soldier, for whom the highest exemplification of courage was his willingness to face death in battle on behalf of the city.[86]

To live virtuously and courageously in the face of life's tragic dilemmas is, for the Christian, an altogether different matter. For one thing, the highest exemplification of courage is not a willingness to face death in battle, but to give one's life in martyrdom.[87] For what is ultimately at stake for the Christian is not the survival of the city, but the furtherance of the Kingdom. Unlike the Greeks, the Christian's greatest fear was not physical death but the destruction of their souls by not possessing fully the spiritual goods pertaining to a life lived in obedience to God. This is not to say that Christians no longer fear physical death, but the meaning of that fear was fundamentally altered when its object acquired, in the death and resurrection of Jesus, an entirely new significance. The Christian's purpose, in other words, is not to survive indefinitely, but to pursue a rich but finite life.[88] Indeed, inherent to the practice of Christian faith is a commitment to sustain life under less than happy conditions, and in order to do that one must have recourse, not to a set of principles, but to a substantive narrative that will train one in making moral judgments that will sustain life in a finite, limited and fallen world.[89] Courage, of course, will also be an indispensable virtue in this venture. However, insofar as Christians are being made part of God's economy of salvation, their sense of fear and pity – and, concomitantly, the very character of their courage – is also being transformed.

Indeed, one of the most distinguishing marks of Christian courage is the manner in which it accepts, as its guide, suffering, patience and endurance rather than coercion, attack and violence. Christians, in other words, are not enjoined to slaughter courageously their enemies in the heat of battle, but to persevere patiently in the face of persecution, even allowing themselves to be killed rather than to kill. While Christians are forbidden to despair in the face of the dividedness of the world, they are not prevented from living in the hope that God will overcome those differences non-violently. That is why, for the Christian, tragedy lies not so much in the limited good accomplished through coercive means, but in the fact that the peace to which they are called to bear witness may well make the world more violent.[90] If anything, "Christians are committed to the kind of life that makes tragic outcomes unavoidable."[91] This may sound despairing rather than hopeful, but only if tragedy is mistaken for a sign of our helplessness rather than as a reminder of our finitude.[92] Alas, a truly moral life cannot be lived without risking our own and other's lives for the goods and values we find necessary to maintain our life together.[93]

If Christians cannot lead lives free from tragic dilemmas, they can at least hope for the gift of patience.[94] At first glance, patience seems so impotent in the face of tragedy. Indeed, for the ancient Greeks, whose ethical judgments were formed according to a radically different set of emotions and practices and virtues, patience would certainly appear to be the height of folly. But because the Christian's ethical judgments are formed within a narrative tradition that rules out violence as one of its options, patience and perseverance are necessarily intrinsic to Christian courage.[95] It may very well be the case, as Ricoeur reminds us, that the "lesson" we receive from tragedy is one that cannot cure anything, or even alleviate suffering.[96] But for all that it is a "lesson" that nonetheless helps us live faithfully as finite and fallen creatures in the light of God's grace. Indeed, it is only within the Christian tradition that the category of "the tragic" becomes transposed into the language of gift and grace. The Christian, after all, is not under the power of indifferent fate but is subject to the power of Providence.[97]

Conclusion

Part of Ricoeur's theory of narrative incorporates the project of giving theoretical expression to the activity of emplotment (the structuration)[98] that characterizes all narrative displays. He is convinced that this activity of "synthesizing the heterogeneous" is intrinsically conflictual and exhibits aporia-producing limit experiences not restricted to the level of the ethical, but which extends to a deeper, more primordial level of conflict which, in Steiner's words, touches "the agonistic ground of human experience." I have argued that Ricoeur's project remains too formal and too abstract and thus fails to do justice to the individual differences that narrative judgment makes across various narrative traditions. By using the concrete example of courage as understood by the ancient Greeks and by Christian tradition, I have argued that even though there may seem to be structural similarities between the two, the type of ethical judgments and tragic dilemmas produced within each are vastly different – one might even say, "worlds apart." This raises questions about the value of narrative theories as a whole.

While I agree with Ricoeur that the disclosive or revelatory possibilities of narrative judgment extend beyond certain overly determined literary genres – namely, ancient Greek tragedy – I seriously doubt whether there is something like a universal experience of "the tragic."[99] To be sure, "the religious" continually encroaches on and challenges our accumulated moral wisdom, confounding our practical reason, exposing our vulnerability. But the naming of those powers that effectively put our lives "out of control" is always narrative specific. Indeed, it makes all the difference to the content and shape of narrative judgment if those powers are known as Father, Son and Holy Spirit or, like the gods of ancient Greece, they are known as deities indifferent to and pitiless in the face of human suffering.[100] Ricoeur's theory of narrative is rather powerless to discriminate between these important differences, thereby undermining its own universal claims.

Notes

1   Paul Ricoeur, *Time and Narrative*, II, trans. Kathleen McLaughlin and David Pellauer (Chicago: University of Chicago Press, 1985), 157.

2   This is rather ironic, given Ricoeur's (rightful) insistence that the "logic" of the plot displays "an intelligibility appropriate to the field of praxis, not that of theoria, and therefore one neighboring on phronesis, which is the intelligent use of action." *Time and Narrative*, I, 40.

3   *Time and Narrative*, I, 229.

4   Two great texts of the Western world provide the impetus for Ricoeur's *Time and Narrative*: Augustine's *Confessions* and Aristotle's *Poetics*. These texts, though interesting in their own right, are relevant to Ricoeur only insofar as they offer two independent sources, two distinct analyses or points of access, to one circular problematic; namely, how the work of emplotment correlates with, is complicated and deepened by, our existential experience of time. The crucial insight that emerges from Ricoeur's analysis of time and narrative is not so much that the *Confessions* and the *Poetics* represent inverted images of one another, or even that both are animated by the same dialectical interplay between concordance and discordance. The key discovery, rather, concerns the aporetic character of both forms of analysis. There can be, in short, no speculative resolution either to the problems of time or to the problems of narrative. To be sure, Ricoeur contends that narrative activity constitutes the most appropriate response to the paradoxes generated by reflections on time (*Time and Narrative*, I, 6). But responding to, and providing a speculative solution for, an aporia are not the same thing. Indeed, the perplexities generated by speculations on time are most appropriately met by constructing plots which, though not capable of *resolving* the aporia theoretically, are nonetheless capable of *clarifying* those aporias poetically or practically. Here the issue of narrative judgment comes to the fore.

5   Perhaps it might be more accurate to say that Ricoeur's understanding of narrative judgment lacks the appropriate level of precision rather than sustained attention *per se*. After all, Ricoeur does give considerable space to developing the ethical dimensions of the self and to showing how one moves from moral norms (general maxims of action) to moral judgment in situation. But again, Ricoeur's analysis of this movement or dialectic remains too abstract.

6   *Time and Narrative*, I, 59.

7   Cf. *Oneself as Another*, trans. Kathleen Blamey (Chicago: University of Chicago Press, 1992); and "The Human Being as the Subject Matter of Philosophy," *Philosophy and Social Criticism* 14/2 (1988): 203-15. In these works, Ricoeur begins to articulate the ethical bearing implicit in the categories of action, the narrative unity of life, identity, personhood, etc. Ricoeur is quite explicit about the limited parameters of his task. For one thing, he is not about to sketch a typology of values or an ethics of virtues. Rather, his aim is "to show the potential contribution of such processes of evaluation to the constitution of the person as self." "The Human Being as the Subject Matter of Philosophy," 213.

8   In his earlier reflections, Ricoeur appears skeptical about any approach to tragedy which proceeds by a "process of induction and amplification." *The Symbolism of Evil* (Boston: Beacon Press, 1967), 211. In other words, the philosopher's task is not to approach Greek tragedy with "a category of the tragic already in mind" or with

"a working definition broad enough to include all tragic works." Rather, one must start with Greek tragedy itself, inasmuch as the originary and authentic expression of the tragic begins there. Greek tragedy, in short, represents "the sudden and complete manifestation of the essence of the tragic" and "it is by grasping the essence in its Greek phenomenon that we can understand all other tragedy as analogous to Greek tragedy," 211.

9   The term "literary" is in ironic quotes to indicate that "literature" remains a contestable notion. Nothing hinges on the term except the idea that the configurations Ricoeur is primarily interested in are those of a written, textual sort.

10   This ambivalence – this subtle interchange between *muthos* as a description of the dramatic performances of the ancient Greeks and *muthos* as a technical term for the activity of emplotment common to all narrative traditions – gives Ricoeur's narrative theory a certain aura of universality that is belied as soon as one begins to apply it to specific traditions.

11   Moreover, examples of courage also highlight a tension in Ricoeur's own philosophy between his long-standing fascination with Greek tragedy and his equally abiding interest in biblical narrative. Ricoeur's fascination with Greek tragedy is clearly seen in his early work on *The Symbolism of Evil*, and it continues to play a central role in his most recent reflections on *Time and Narrative* and in *Oneself as Another*. Indeed, according to an interview given with Charles Reagan, the tragic constitutes a major item in Ricoeur's projected agenda. Cf. "Interview avec Paul Ricoeur, le 8 juillet, 1991," *Bulletin de la société américaine de philosophie de langue française* 3/3 (Winter 1991): 155-172, 172.

12   The notion of "challenge" is viewed by Ricoeur, at least in regard to the question of evil, as "turn by turn a failure for syntheses which are always premature and a provocation to think more and differently." "Evil, A Challenge to Philosophy and Theology," in *Gottes Zukunft-Zukunft der Welt: Festschrift für Jürgen Moltmann zum 60. Gerburtstag*, ed. Herman Dueser, Gerhard M. Martin, Konrad Stock and Michael Welker (München: Chr. Kaiser Verlag, 1986), 358. In this regard, evil or the tragic (the voice of non-philosophy) awakens us "not only to the illusions of the heart but also to the illusions born of the hubris of practical reason itself." *Oneself as Another*, 241.

13   What I will call "narrative understanding," Ricoeur calls "narrative intelligibility" (as opposed to "narratological rationality"). See *Oneself as Another*, 143, note 5, for an account of this important distinction.

14   Following Ludwig Wittgenstein, *Philosophical Investigations*, trans. G.E.M. Anscombe (Oxford: Basil Blackwell, 1953), § 154.

15   Space does not permit even a summary of this project, which consists, for the most part, of *Time and Narrative*, II. Suffice it to say that Ricoeur adopts two broad notions in order to broaden and deepen the Aristotelian conception of emplotment: "concordant discordance" and "the synthesis of the heterogeneous." See *Time and Narrative*, I, 66.

16   As Ricoeur puts it in the second volume of *Time and Narrative*, "I adopted as my guideline ... the ... notions of 'the temporal synthesis of the heterogeneous' and 'discordant concordance' that carry the formal principle of Aristotelian *muthos* beyond its particular instantiation in overly determined genres and literary types." *Time and Narrative*, II, 157.

17   *Time and Narrative*, II, 7.

18   For Ricoeur, the question is "whether the paradigm of order, characteristic of tragedy,

is capable of extension and transformation to the point where it can be applied to the whole narrative field." *Time and Narrative*, I, 38. Ricoeur's wager is that Aristotle's concept of emplotment can be the seed for a considerable development and expansion.

19 *Time and Narrative*, II, 4. Although Ricoeur's generalization of emplotment requires the removal of a number of restrictions and prohibitions set forth in Aristotle's *Poetics*, he is in essential agreement with Aristotle on a number of key points.

20 Aristotle states his definition of tragedy at the beginning of the sixth chapter of the *Poetics*: "A tragedy ... is the imitation of an action that is serious and complete, having magnitude, expressed in seasoned language, each of the kinds appearing separately in its parts, in a dramatic and not a narrative form, accomplishing through pity and fear the catharsis of such affections." (1449b24-28). Cited in Jacob Bernays, "Aristotle on the Effect of Tragedy," in *Articles on Aristotle: Vol. 4, Psychology and Aesthetics*, edited by Jonathan Barnes, Malcolm Schofield and Richard Sorabji (London: Duckworth, 1979), 154.

21 The framework in which one places a study of the *Poetics* is therefore crucial. The sense in which the *Poetics* continues – and thus constitutes a sequel to – the philosophical interests central to Aristotle's *Ethics* and the *Politics* cannot be underestimated. See Aryeh Kosman, "Acting: Drama as the Mimesis of Praxis," in *Essays on Aristotle's Poetics*, ed. Amélie Oksenberg Rorty (Princeton: Princeton University Press, 1992), 68.

22 Ricoeur considers Aristotle's *Poetics* as a treatise primarily concerned with composition and not, as is the *Rhetoric*, with the reception of the work. This is not to say that the *Poetics'* principal interest concerns simply the internal structures of the text to the exclusion of the effects it has on its audience. Indeed, such a division would be inconceivable for Aristotle. In this regard, it might be better to speak of structuration rather than structure as the principal concern of the *Poetics*. For "structuration is an oriented activity that is only completed in the spectator or the reader." *Time and Narrative*, I, 48.

23 For a more extended discussion of Aristotle's theory of action, see David Charles, *Aristotle's Philosophy of Action* (Ithaca: Cornell University Press, 1984). On the *poiêsis/ praxis* distinction, see especially pp. 65-6 and 153-5. The categories of *poiêsis* and *praxis* must of course be seen in relation to two modes of knowledge or reasoning which Aristotle distinguishes, in book 6 of the *Nicomachean Ethics*, by the terms *technê* and *phronesis*. For a truly masterful treatment of these two modes of practical (as distinct from theoretical) knowledge, not only in Aristotle but as they are retrieved in modern philosophy, see Joseph Dunne, *Back to the Rough Ground: 'Phronesis' and 'Techne' in Modern Philosophy and in Aristotle* (Notre Dame: University of Notre Dame Press, 1993).

24 As Ricoeur describes it, *praxis*, like power, "exhausts its meaning in its own exercise." *Oneself as Another*, 196. A.O. Rorty likewise remarks, in distinguishing processes from activities, that "an action [*praxis*] takes the form of an activity when it is self-contained, whole and complete, fully performed, its ends achieved in the very performance." "The Psychology of Aristotelian Tragedy," in *Essays on Aristotle's Poetics* (Princeton: Princeton University Press, 1992), 6.

25 Indeed, happiness is not a good over and above the charitable deed done but is intrinsic to, and thus coterminus with, the performance of the charitable action as such.

26 Although Ricoeur generally accepts this broad Aristotelian distinction, he is not wholly satisfied with the way in which Aristotle deploys his *poiêsis/praxis* distinc-

tion. For Ricoeur, "no action is only *poiêsis* or only *praxis*." See *Oneself as Another*, 176, note 6. Cf. also 172, note 1. In this regard, Ricoeur is more Hegelian than Aristotelian. Hegel, of course, found the Aristotelian notion of *poiêsis* inadequate precisely because, according to Hegel, all action is dialectical: all action produces a reaction and thus no action can be merely transitive. "Aristotle thought that 'making' was only a transitive action whose end consisted in an external thing. Certainly, to work is still to produce something. But what is new is that, besides the thing that is made, work is the act of a subject and this act is acting on the agent himself. If Ricoeur's reading of *praxis* is indebted to Hegel, it is also modified and expanded through Heidegger's philosophy. Ricoeur's project of extending the notion of tragic *muthos* beyond the overly determined genres of Greek tragedy to encompass all forms of narrative emplotment is part of his larger project of reappropriating Aristotle through Heidegger. Indeed, Ricoeur believes that a comparison of Heidegger's *Sorge* (care) and Aristotle's *praxis* can occasion a deeper understanding of both concepts. The former, for example, gives to Aristotelian *praxis* an ontological weight that does not seem to have been a major intention of Aristotle in his *Ethics* (*Oneself as Another*, 311). Through this Heideggerian re-reading of Aristotle, Ricoeur believes that *praxis* assumes a revelatory function (*Oneself as Another*, 312, note 15).

27   According to Aristotle, *mimesis* occurs only within the sphere of human production. Ricoeur echoes this when he says, "there is *mimesis* only where there is *poiêsis*," *A Ricoeur Reader: Reflection and Imagination*, ed. Mario J. Valdés (Toronto: University of Toronto Press, 1991), 138. See also 317.

28   The description of an action whose origin and end are intrinsic to the processes of its self-unfolding is perhaps best seen by comparing the *praxis* of poetry with the *praxis* of nature. In *Physics* 194a22, Aristotle claims that "art imitates nature." The English rendering of *hê technê mimeitai tên phusin*, however, is somewhat ambiguous. It does not mean, as it might initially suggest, that "art imitates natural objects" in the same way a copy may be said to mirror its original. Rather, the point Aristotle is making exactly parallels his distinction between *praxis* and *poiêsis*. That is to say, natural beings (or better, natural processes), like *praxis*, have within themselves the very principle and reason of their motion, growth and self-unfolding.

29   Aristotle's definition of tragedy has precipitated a great deal of controversy among interpreters and is cause for a major division between those who would view Aristotle's understanding of mimesis along strictly "formalist" lines and those who would argue for a more "holistic" reading of mimesis. That plot is more fundamental than character to Aristotle's understanding of tragedy does explain, at least partially, why his use of *praxis* in the *Poetics* primarily refers to the "single action" of the plot rather than the individual actions, morally praiseworthy or otherwise, of its characters. Of course, the plot's "single action" is not something which any one person does, but is a product of interaction. Nevertheless, this interaction is largely constituted by the actions of many agents, and these actions are as such appropriate candidates for moral evaluation. A purely formalist understanding of mimesis, therefore, seems hardly sustainable.

30   *Time and Narrative*, I, 45. Cf. also *Ricoeur Reader*, 139.

31   *Time and Narrative*, I, 40. As Ricoeur remarks elsewhere, "*mimesis* is an action about action." *Ricoeur Reader*, 150.

32   *Time and Narrative*, I, 47.

33   The realm of ethics and the realm of poetics, though intimately related, are finally

incommensurate with one another. There is, in other words, no direct equation between "the imitation of action" (mimesis) and "the organization of events" (*muthos*). Because there is no exact "fit" or complete coincidence between them, a certain gap appears which, far from constituting a flaw, actually proves productive. It allows for a mimetic displacement from ethics to poetics. Tragic *muthos*, in other words, serves as a counterpoint to ethics by showing how virtuous actions performed by good people lead to unhappiness. The world opened up by the poetic text is thus an experimental world "in which novel types of life are explored in the mode of fiction." *Oneself as Another*, 288.

34 *Ricoeur Reader*, 140, 151.

35 *Ricoeur Reader*, 426.

36 *Ricoeur Reader*, 151; Cf. also *Time and Narrative*, I, 76.

37 At most, Ricoeur is willing to concede the inside/outside distinction as "a methodological artefact" of textual semiotics.

38 As Ricoeur puts it, "without the reader who accompanies it, there is no configuring act at work in the text; and without a reader to appropriate it, there is no world unfolded before the text," *Ricoeur Reader*, 395.

39 *Ricoeur Reader*, 412.

40 One might say that the level of the imaginary presupposes the work of the ethical just as the ethical level requires the aid of the imaginary. This symbiotic relationship is described by Ricoeur under the rubric of the symbolic mediation of all action – whether real, ethical action or imaginary, poetical action.

41 *Ricoeur Reader*, 151; Cf. also *Time and Narrative*, I, 76, 156.

42 *Oneself as Another*, 170.

43 *Time and Narrative*, I, 59.

44 "Interruption" is perhaps too strong or too misleading a word here. It does, however, point to one of the deep problems with Ricoeur's hermeneutics; namely, a tendency to split language into different orders or levels, where first-order discourse is assumed to be "standard" or "ordinary" and operates almost by default until it produces a paradox or aporia. Only then does the second-order level of discourse come into play. A good example of Ricoeur's residual positivism can be seen in his understanding of metaphor where first-order, literal interpretation must founder or shatter before a second-order meaning can emerge. But why describe this as an "interruption"? Why not just describe this as another among many different language games? The same holds true of understanding fictional texts or narrative dramas. There is no need to assume that these literary forms somehow "interrupt" or "suspend" our so-called "normal," everyday ethical judgments. They are simply different ways our everyday judgments are shaped and made. One suspects that Ricoeur's residual positivism is symptomatic of a tendency to privilege "natural scientific" explanatory modes over forms of "human understanding" that were so characteristic of the *Erklären/Verstehen* debate. For an incisive critique, see John Milbank, *Theology & Social Theory: Beyond Secular Reason* (Oxford: Basil Blackwell, 1990), 263-8.

45 "The effacement of the ostensive and descriptive reference liberates a power of reference to aspects of our being in the world that cannot be said in a direct descriptive way, but only alluded to, thanks to the referential values of metaphoric and, in general, symbolic expressions." This second-order reference, of course, "no longer

touches the world at the level of manipulable objects, but at a deeper level which Husserl designated by the term 'life-world' (*Lebenswelt*) and Heidegger by that of being-in-the-world (*in-der-Welt-Sein*)." Paul Ricoeur, *Interpretation Theory* (Fort Worth: Texas Christian University Press, 1976), 37 and "Philosophical Hermeneutics and Theology," *Theology Digest*, 24(22) (Summer 1976): 160.

46   *Oneself as Another*, 180. This notion of the continuance of a certain continuity in spite of a significant break is particularly important for Ricoeur when he tries to mediate between a teleological approach to moral philosophy, as exemplified by Aristotle's ethics of virtue, and a deontological approach, as heralded by Kant's ethics of duty.

47   *Oneself as Another*, 164. Clearly Ricoeur denies the possibility that there can be a mode of reading that would be entirely free from ethical evaluation. As he puts it, "poetics does not stop borrowing from ethics, even when it advocates the suspension of all ethical judgment or its ironic inversion. The very project of ethical neutrality presupposes the original ethical quality of action on the prior side of fiction." *Time and Narrative*, I, 59.

48   In describing the dialectical structure between the text and its readers, Ricoeur remarks on two divergent, albeit complementary, moments: interruption (*stasis*) and impetus. "These two perspectives on reading result directly from its functions of confrontation and connection between the imaginary world of the text and the actual world of readers. To the extent that readers subordinate their expectations to those developed by the text, they themselves become unreal to a degree comparable to the unreality of the fictive world towards which they emigrate. Reading then becomes a place, itself unreal, where reflection takes a pause. On the other hand, inasmuch as readers incorporate – little matter whether consciously or unconsciously – into their vision of the world the lessons of their readings, in order to increase the prior readability of this vision, then reading is for them something other than a place where they come to rest; it is a medium they cross through." The act of reading, therefore, constitutes at once a *stasis* and an impetus (*Ricoeur Reader*, 414).

49   Contrasting "the world of the text" with "the world of the reader" is fraught with all kinds of difficulties. It is open to misunderstanding on every side. Perhaps the commonest temptation is to accord primacy to the actual world of everyday, as if that were simply a given.

50   Cf. Alasdair MacIntyre, *After Virtue: A Study in Moral Theory* (Notre Dame: University of Notre Dame Press, 1984), 121.

51   *Ricoeur Reader*, p. 428. Ricoeur's understanding of narrative intelligence applies equally to the act of configuring a narrative plot and to the act of following, appropriating or actualizing the plot through reading. According to Ricoeur, the act of reading belongs to the same dynamism as the configuring act, prolonging it and bringing it to its end (*Time and Narrative*, I, 71). Reading, in other words, means to follow the plot and thus actualize the configurational process. Another way to put it would be to say that the reader, by following the sketch outlined by the plot, "completes" or "finishes" the text.

52   To speak of an "indirect" influence presupposes that a more direct and straightforward route is available and, given other circumstances, that would be the more preferable path. However, this would be misleading in two ways. First, it inappropriately privileges a rationalist outlook that subordinates emotion to reason. Second, it promotes the false view that our evaluative abilities engage only certain aspects our being; namely, our intellectual or cognitive capacities separate from our emotional and affective sensibilities.

53 *Time and Narrative*, I, 32. Indeed, Ricoeur describes his overall enterprise in *Time and Narrative* as one of giving "the notion of emplotment a broader extension and a more fundamental understanding than that conveyed by Aristotle's *muthos*, dependent as it is on his interpretation of Greek tragedy." *Time and Narrative*, II, 157.

54 Although Ricoeur is clearly under no obligation to provide a commentary on the *Poetics* or use it as an exclusive norm for his own project, and although he is free to appropriate only those formal features deemed useful in developing his own poetics, still it is hard to envision how one can borrow so deeply and fundamentally from Aristotle's definition of tragic *muthos* without also buying into some of Aristotle's wider presuppositions.

55 Stephen Halliwell, *The* Poetics *of Aristotle* (Chapel Hill: University of North Carolina Press, 1987), 89.

56 "Serious" is a term with complex overtones, a full discussion of which goes beyond the concerns of this paper. For a fuller treatment see Leon Golden, "Is Tragedy the 'Imitation of a *Serious* Action'?" *Greek, Roman and Byzantine Studies* 6/4 (Winter 1965): 283-9. What is important to note for present purposes is that, although there was much debate among philosophers over what constituted "serious" matters, it was probably a commonly held view among the ancient Greeks, given their warrior ethos, that war figured highly among them.

57 The way in which fear serves as the underside of shame is clearly articulated by Bernard Williams. See, *Shame and Necessity* (Berkeley: University of California Press, 1986), 78ff.

58 See Stephen R. Leighton, "Aristotle and the Emotions," *Phronesis* 27/2 (1982): 144-74. Part of the difficulty of determining Aristotle's understanding of *catharsis* is that he employs the term in various contexts without ever explicitly discussing its meaning.

59 Ricoeur is insistent – and rightly so – on the reciprocal and circular relation between the emotions and ethical discernment: "even the discernment of the tragic fault is brought about by the emotional quality of pity, fear, and our sense for what is human. The relation is therefore a circular one. It is the composition of the plot that purges the emotions, by bringing to representation the pitiable and fearful incidents, and it is these purged emotions that govern our discernment of the tragic" (*Time and Narrative*, I, 45). Thus, the emotions cannot be seen as something "added onto" or separable from the tragic drama, but as part of the dramatic texture itself.

60 Although tragedy can only be of indirect value to the formation of a virtuous life – in the sense that it primarily addresses the audience's emotions – it is nevertheless indispensable. Tragedy, in other words, has its didactic value by enhancing our perceptions, which is precisely to improve our capacities for moral judgment.

61 As Aristotle puts it, "pity may be defined as a feeling of pain caused by the sight of some evil ... which befalls one who does not deserve it, and which we might expect to befall ourselves" (*Rhetoric* 1385b13 ff.) The importance Greek society attached to pity as a characteristic of the virtuous person (who is thus also the good citizen) should not be underestimated.

62 As Martha Nussbaum aptly puts it, "in pity the human characters draw close to the one who suffers [in the tragic drama], acknowledging that their own possibilities are similar, and that both together live in a world of terrible reversals, in which the difference between pitier and pitied is a matter far more of luck than of deliberate action." "Tragedy and Self-Sufficiency: Plato and Aristotle on Fear and Pity," *Oxford Studies in Ancient Philosophy*, X, ed. Julia Annas (Oxford: Clarendon Press, 1992), 120.

63   Although the *cathartic* effects of tragedy may not be directly equated with *paideia* – a term signifying the education of young children in ancient Greece – this does not exclude the possibility of seeing tragic poetry as a form of education for adults.

64   Martha Nussbaum, "Tragedy and Self-Sufficiency," 115-6.

65   J. Peter Euben, "Introduction," in *Greek Tragedy and Political Theory*, ed. J. Peter Euben (Berkeley: University of California Press, 1986), 1-42.

66   "In sum, tragedy was a form of public discourse that inculcated civic virtue and enhanced the citizen audience's capacity to act with foresight and judge with insight." J. Peter Euben, "Introduction" to *Greek Tragedy and Political Theory*, 23.

67   J. Peter Euben contends that "tragedy's importance in sustaining the quality of public life is indicated by the fact that it was a liturgy equal to the maintenance of a trireme, as if to suggest that the cultural survival of the Athenians depended on the courage of its people in confronting the risks of tragedy in the same way as its physical survival depended on its sailors' courageously meeting the risks of battle." "Introduction" to *Greek Tragedy and Political Theory*, 22-3.

68   The power of misfortune to impair, obstruct or otherwise dislodge a good person from living a truly happy life, constitutes an important theme in Aristotle's *Ethics*. Although Aristotle does not give a univocal response to this question, one thing is clear: tragedy exposes the gap between being good and living well.

69   What Aristotle means by *hamartia* is subject to much debate. A number of useful articles outline the relevant issues at stake in the discussion. Cf., for example, Nancy Sherman, "*Hamartia* and Virtue," in *Essays on Aristotle's Poetics*, 1992, 177-96.

70   As Stanley Hauerwas puts it, "tragedy is not the result of a 'flaw' of character, but the result of living faithful to what is best about our character. Moralistic judgments about weakness of character or the flaw in an otherwise strong person's character result finally in a failure to appreciate how character is at once necessary and the cause of tragedy.... Our character is therefore the source of our strength, as it provides us with a history of commitment, but in doing so it also sets the stage for the possibility of tragedy." *A Community of Character: Toward a Constructive Christian Social Ethic* (Notre Dame: University of Notre Dame Press, 1981), 106.

71   John D. Barbour, *Tragedy as a Critique of Virtue: The Novel and Ethical Reflection*, (Chico, CA: Scholars Press, 1984), 7.

72   As J. Peter Euben puts it, "Choosing one [virtue] does not exempt us from the authority of the claim we choose against." "Introduction" to *Greek Tragedy and Political Theory*, 17.

73   Stanley Hauerwas captures this well: "tragedy often involves the conflict of right with right," which is but "a form of a more profound sense of tragedy inherent in living in a divided world." *A Community of Character*, 106.

74   *Oneself as Another*, 241.

75   Martha Nussbaum, "Tragedy and Self-Sufficiency," 110.

76   *Oneself as Another*, 241.

77   *Oneself as Another*, 247. In other words, tragic wisdom is a "showing" which is not a "telling." Ricoeur puts it well when he remarks: "poetry does not proceed conceptually." *Oneself as Another*, 245.

78   *Oneself as Another*, 243. Ricoeur contends that the work of tragedy is comparable to the aporia-producing limit experiences that have already been encountered on the

level of the narrative identity. Tragedy, in other words, "repeats" the aporias of the quest for the narrative unity of life, thereby re-doubling the conflict already present at the level of the ethical. In short, tragedy produces "an ethicopractical aporia" that is "added onto" those that have appeared throughout Ricoeur's quest for selfhood. Cf. *Oneself as Another*, 247.

79   After all, Ricoeur's central concern throughout *Time and Narrative* is "whether the paradigm of order, characteristic of tragedy, is capable of extension and transformation to the point where it can be applied to the whole narrative field." *Time and Narrative*, I, 38.

80   *Oneself as Another*, 243. Although Ricoeur shares with Aristotle the desire to rehabilitate tragedy within the philosopher's field of vision (Aristotle by broaching the question of whether or not good character might be overthrown by great reversals of fortune and Ricoeur by analyzing the religious/ontological disclosive possibilities of tragedy in a critically reflective life), Ricoeur's analysis of tragic *muthos* goes beyond Aristotle, who does not, for the most part, attend to the religious aspects of tragedy or distinguish practical wisdom from tragic wisdom. Aristotle does not explicitly address the social, political or religious context of tragedy in the *Poetics*.

81   This is not altogether true. In his early studies on myth and symbol, Ricoeur gives a much more detailed attention to different narrative traditions.

82   For Ricoeur, tragedy is comparable to the aporia-producing limit experiences. *Oneself as Another*, 243.

83   A Christian's fear is not the same as the fear of the tragic hero of ancient Greece or the citizen soldier who witnessed those tragic dramas, nor is their pity the same.

84   For the general contours of the argument that follows, I am indebted to Stanley Hauerwas's article, "The Difference of Virtue and the Difference it Makes: Courage Exemplified," *Modern Theology* 9/3 (July 1993): 253-4.

85   John Casey, *Pagan Virtue: An Essay in Ethics* (Oxford: Clarendon Press, 1990), 100. Casey provides a purely formal account of courage as "a disposition to aim at an end, using deliberation, confronting the difficulties and dangers." Ibid., 64.

86   According to Aristotle, the noblest deaths occur on the battlefield, "for these take place in the greatest and noblest danger." *Nicomachean Ethics*, 1115a30-35.

87   In this regard, John Casey is simply wrong in stating that both Aquinas and Aristotle "think that courage is above all shown in facing death in warfare." *Pagan Virtue*, 100. Casey has not read Aquinas carefully. Cf. Hauerwas, "The Difference of Virtue and the Difference it Makes": 258ff.

88   Stanley Hauerwas, *Truthfulness and Tragedy* (Notre Dame: University of Notre Dame Press, 1977), 109.

89   Hauerwas, *Truthfulness and Tragedy*, 202.

90   Stanley Hauerwas, *The Peaceable Kingdom: A Primer in Christian Ethics* (Notre Dame: University of Notre Dame Press, 1983), 145.

91   Hauerwas, *The Peaceable Kingdom*, 172, note 17.

92   Hauerwas, *Truthfulness and Tragedy*, 190.

93   Hauerwas, *Truthfulness and Tragedy*, 69-70.

94   As Stanley Hauerwas puts it, "a spirituality that acknowledges the tragic, and thus enables the Christian to remain faithful, is one that is schooled in patience." Hauerwas, *The Peaceable Kingdom*, 1983, 145.

95   Patience may not sound like much, but that is all we have if we refuse – as Ricoeur rightly advises that we must – the alternative of violence that would force premature syntheses on the world. (See note 12 above.)

96   *Oneself as Another*, 244, note 7.

97   Hauerwas, *Truthfulness and Tragedy*, 200.

98   Compare note 22 above.

99   A remark made in the Interlude on Tragic Action, which begins the Ninth Study in *Oneself as Another*, captures well the extent to which Ricoeur shows himself to be a student of Hegel as much as he is a student of Aristotle. "If the tragedy of *Antigone* can teach us something," Ricoeur says, "it is because the very content of the conflict – despite the lost and unrepeatable character of the mythical ground from which it emerges and of the festive environment surrounding the celebration of the spectacle – has maintained an ineffaceable permanence," 243. For purposes of this paper, Ricoeur's remark about the tragedy of *Antigone* is important for a slightly different, but related, reason. It reveals the extent to which Ricoeur's account of narrative judgment remains deficient and undeveloped. Ricoeur's comment concerning tragedy's "ineffaceable permanence," of course, is not so much wrong as it is empty. For just as the content of one's moral judgments are relative to the ethical content of the particular virtues which inform them – virtues which are in turn dependent on the specific narrative in which they are embedded – so too one's understanding of "the tragic" is always relative to the narrative in question. In other words, to say that "the very content of the [tragic] conflict" maintains "an ineffaceable permanence" separate from its particular social, political, moral and religious contexts is precisely to obscure important differences the ignoring of which makes the invocation of "the tragic" little more than an unintelligible gesture.

100 Martha Nussbaum speaks of the pitiless, always smiling countenance of Dionysus – a reminder that because the gods lacked an understanding of suffering as a possibility for themselves, they necessarily lacked pity also. Indeed, it was commonly assumed that the gods often acted in cruel and heartless ways. This only reinforces the vast differences between Greek and Christian conceptions of deity. "Tragedy and Self-Sufficiency," 120, 158.

Narrative Theology *Post Mortem Dei*?
Paul Ricoeur's *Time and Narrative*, III, and Postmodern Theologies

TERRENCE W. TILLEY

What could stamp a theology for a post-age? Is theology after the death of God like biology after the end of life: a discipline without a subject? Have our sacred canopies been so rotted out by the acid rains of modernity that only a useless skeleton of bare rigging remains? Are theologians homeless wanderers blindly trekking in a barren wilderness? Hardly.

Numerous patterns of theological thought have emerged for making religious thinking a real possibility in a post-age. It is far beyond the scope of the present paper to survey all the theological options. Instead, I will investigate aspects of Ricoeur's work on narrative and their implications for theology. First, I comment somewhat critically on Ricoeur's notions of action and narration. I argue that some significant modifications will need to be made to sustain his insights, especially with regard to his understanding of mimesis$_3$. I believe that these modifications do not undermine the insight or thrust of his work.

Second, I investigate the implications of Ricoeur's work on narrative for contemporary religious thought. To evaluate Ricoeur's contribution, I examine two representatives of some of the trends – the postliberal theology of George Lindbeck (especially his influential *The Nature of Doctrine*) and the postmodern explorations of Edith Wyschogrod (especially her provocative *Saints and Postmodernism*). Using the analysis and argument developed in the first section, I show how the identity narratives created by these thinkers are unstable. The identity Lindbeck creates for Christianity is an identity which, finally, is not coherent. Wyschogrod's work attempts to use saintly narratives to resolve aporias in contemporary moral and social theory. While she attempts valiantly to create a space for the new to emerge, her work finally deconstructs itself and leaves us with the problem of constructing a postmodern ethic unresolved.

Finally, I address the question of whether there can be "narrative theologies *post mortem dei*." I do not propose to answer this fully here. How-

175

ever, I sketch the identity of the god who has died and argue that He [sic] had his identity narrated in the discourse of modernity. I suggest that insofar as there are communities where mimesis$_3$ (to use Ricoeur's concept) is valued, narrative theologies are the most reasonable theologies after the death of God.

Ricoeur on Action and Narration

It seems to me that, especially with regard to the concepts of action, narration, and mimesis, Ricoeur's insights are generally plausible. Nonetheless, they also seem to require some modification by attending to the audience for which the narration is undertaken, the purposes for which it is performed, the results of performing the action (for which the agent is responsible), as well as the effects of performing the action (for all of which the agent cannot be responsible). A philosophical understanding of the conditions for performing actions is clearly central to Ricoeur's work.[1] In an introductory discussion of the power of history and fiction, Ricoeur writes:

> But fictions also have their effects that we shall have to pursue in our inquiry. We covered half this path when ... we introduced the notion of a world of the text, in the sense of a world we might inhabit and wherein we can unfold our ownmost potentialities. But this world of the text still constitutes just a form of transcendence in immanence. In this regard, it remains part of the text. The second half of our path lies in the mediation that reading brings about between the fictive world of the text and the actual world of the reader. *The effects of fictions, effects of revelation and transformation are essentially effects of reading.* It is by way of reading that literature returns to life, that is, to the practical and affective field of existence. Therefore it is along the pathway of a theory of reading that we shall seek to determine the relation of application that constitutes the equivalent of the relation of standing-for in the domain of fiction.[2]

There are some potential confusions in this passage (into which Ricoeur may fall and into which many theologians seem to fall). These possible problems have to do with the relationships between agent, action, product of action, and effects. Let me spell this out.

In writing a text, an author is performing an act. Intentionally, at least, it is a communicative act, for one of the author's purposes is to communicate with a subsequent reader – perhaps only herself, or perhaps a huge audience.[3] The results of that act are (among others) the production of a text. The effects or consequences of that act, however, are rather broader. *It is imperative to distinguish acts, their results, and their effects to have a theory of action.* Unfortunately, Ricoeur does not generally do so.

Let me illustrate my point: Let us say I perform the act of baking a cake. If I bake the cake, the directly intended results of my act will be, of course, a light and fluffy angel's food cake. My act will have other concomitant results such as a dirty cake pan, an increase in my electric bill, etc. Clearly I am responsible for the acts I perform, the directly intended results of the act, and the concomitant results of my act: I accept congratulations on the cake and responsibility for cleaning the pan and paying the electric bill. However, let's assume that you are allergic to egg whites and that you eat a large piece of my beautiful cake and get a horrendous belly ache. Am I responsible for your belly ache? No – at least in normal circumstances – I am not responsible for your illness; I am responsible for making the cake. You are responsible for your act of eating it. Your belly ache is a result of your act even though it is an effect of my cake (but *not* a result [or an effect] of my act).[4]

Now let's return from culinary to communicative actions. If I write a text, a directly intended result is the text written. And if it is a fictional or history text, either a directly intended or concomitant result will be its reproduction and distribution (and, one hopes, good reviews, royalties and *tenure!*). But now what action brings about the "revelation" or the "transformation" that Ricoeur has in mind? Obviously, the act of reading. He says so. But that is the *reader's* act. It is not the author's act. Just as your belly ache is a result of your act of eating, but an effect of my cake (and *not* a result or an effect of my act of baking), so the revelation that occurs is a result of your act of reading, and an effect of my text (but *not* a result or an effect of my act of authoring).

Once we sort out these points on actions, some significant problems arise for anyone who thinks that God reveals Godself through texts. Presuming Ricoeur right in saying that revelation is an effect of reading, then the author is not responsible for effective revelatory effects of texts. This does not mean that readers are *fully* responsible, either. But the upshot of this clarification of Ricoeur's work is that the human act of reading is at the center of the analysis of divine revelation. But this gets us ahead of ourselves.

Ricoeur apparently wants to get around this issue by "describing reading as an actualization of the text considered as a score to be performed."[5] However, a musical score is not a narrative; the composer is not an author of a narrative; the performer is a "reader" of the score, but not of any story. The analogy fails: for performing a symphony is neither an effect nor a result of reading the score, it *is* reading the score. The performing is the act, the performance is the product or result of that act, and the response to the beautiful or the banal must be "in the ear of the hearer" (on Ricoeur's account). Moreover, every time the score is read by musicians coming together to perform, the symphony is performed. However, not every time a text is read does the revelation occur. Revelation is an *effect* of reading the text, not the action of reading it. The analogy

fails, and so does the veiled attempt to allot some responsibility for revelation to the author of a text. The "responsibility" must be attributed to
the hearer's action of refiguring the text.

Is there a problem here? On one reading, we have uncovered here an
instability in Ricoeur's account, which has a profound effect on theology. The text can no longer carry revelation. Revelation cannot be a directly intended effect of the author/speaker. This is the loss of the sacredness
of the text and the sufficiency of the book to construct history and render
God and self. Mark C. Taylor puts it thus:

> God, self, history, and book are, thus, bound in an intricate relationship in which
> each mirrors the other. No single concept can be changed without altering all of the
> others. As a result of this thorough interdependence, the news of the death of God
> cannot really reach our ears until its reverberations are traced in the notions of self,
> history and book. The echoes of the death of God can be heard in the disappear-
> ance of the self, the end of history, and the closure of the book.[6]

If "revelation" is disconnected from the book, is this not another way
that leads to the "death of God"? Does the significance of each of these
connected concepts not shift and become unstable? Does Ricoeur's work
provide hidden support to deconstructionists like Taylor who says that
we need "a critical lever with which the entire inherited order can become creatively disorganized"?[7]

I think another reading is available. I will sketch here a view I would
not dare to call a Ricoeurian response, but perhaps it is not incompatible
with Ricoeur's work. It begins by denying the claim that a text is either
revealed or revelatory. It continues by denying the claim that the god
who is dead is God. Then it affirms that the necessary connections between God-self-history-book that Taylor finds are characteristic of modernity are not present in all religions – much less in Christianity. As
much as anyone, Walter J. Ong shows that even if the modern discourse
system is deconstructed, there is another way to construe the epiphany
of divinity without the intermediary of the book.[8] The basic approach is
to construe revelation as recognition, not interpretation.

The pattern for this is set by the Christian gospel of Mark. In the passion narrative incorporated into that gospel (and taken over by Matthew
and Luke), the key line is given to a "bit player" in the drama. Jesus is
hanging on the cross. The male disciples are notorious by their absence.
Some female disciples look on from afar. Some enemies come by to taunt
him. Some bystanders misunderstand his final words. One wants to offer him vinegar, while another says to wait to see if Elijah comes. In this
wretched tableau of death, desertion, distanciation, and disorientation,
a Roman centurion gets one line, his only line in the entire script. Not
even a Jew, not a member of the main cast, not even a significant sup-

porting role, but a man whose role would be played in a school drama by the well-meaning, but talentless, football lineman. His is the key line in the script, the line of real recognition: "And when the centurion, who stood facing him, saw that he thus breathed his last, he said, "Truly this man was the Son of God!" (Mk 15:40 RSV).

The centurion's speech act is a refiguration, a literary example of a form of mimesis$_3$. But here the centurion in the text does not respond to a text, but to an event. Of all people, he finally discloses the ill-kept secret: the crucified one is the Son of God. According to Ricoeur, mimesis$_3$

> marks the intersection between the world of the text and the world of the listener or the reader, the intersection, therefore, between the world configured by the poem and the world within which effective action is unfolded and itself unfolds its specific temporality (III:159).

I would expand Ricoeur's notion here: mimesis$_3$ must also be construed as a response occurring not only where the world of the text and the world of the reader intersect, but where events are the occasion for the world of the respondent to be reconfigured. Mimesis$_3$ is occasioned not only by texts, then, but can be occasioned by events as well; it is a response which is paradoxically the work of the respondent and the inspiration which the respondent cannot resist.[9] Revelation then is a *refigurative effect* of responding to a text or event. This may not settle well with those who find that revelation must somehow be *in* the text rather than *in* the reader (whatever those *in*'s might mean), yet I think it is consistent with Ricoeur's basic thrust and provides a clarification of this problem in his action theory in general and its theological importance in particular.

There is a second technical problem in the philosophy of action, i.e., Ricoeur's acceptance of A.C. Danto's distinction between basic and non-basic ("derived" is Ricoeur's word, and it is not quite accurate) actions. Ricoeur writes:

> Recall that, following Arthur Danto, I distinguished between basic actions, which we know how to do on the basis of mere familiarity with our powers, and derived actions, which require that we do something so that we bring about some event, which is not the result of our basic actions but the consequence of a strategy of action including calculations and practical syllogisms. This adding of strategic actions to basic actions is of the greatest importance for a theory of initiative.... This assertion is of the greatest importance for the quarrel about determinism, and it allows us to reformulate the Kantian antinomy of the free act, considered as the beginning of a causal chain (III: 231).

Unfortunately, the crucial distinction between "basic act" and "non-basic act" won't hold water. And that is not merely my view. It is the view of the same Arthur Danto who formulated the distinction! I will not replay the argument here,[10] but, in short, it is not really possible to distinguish basic actions from non-basic actions in a way that can make room for freedom and initiative while still accepting a form of causality. In fact, it may not be possible to identify a set of actions as "basic" for any purpose. Hence, the link of greatest importance on which Ricoeur hangs his theory of freedom and initiative not only will not support the weight Ricoeur puts on it, but is that weakest of all possible links, a broken one. In sum, Ricoeur's action theory, on which hinges his whole view of reading and hermeneutics and the closing of the hermeneutical circle by a poetics of narrative based on actions, needs some reworking. How might it be reworked?

Ricoeur's account does not need the basic/non-basic action duality. The reason for this is twofold. First, what we consider a human action is determined not so much by what the agent does, but by the context in which she does it. An insight of G.E.M. Anscombe's work[11] seems to me decisive on this point. When we ask what the intention of an action is or was, we place that event in a narrative of action and responsibility. "Why are you waving your arm?" "Oh, to greet Harry, who's coming through the gate" places the waving in a context as an action. "Why are you waving your arm?" "Huh??? I didn't know I was waving it" does not "illustrate" a putative difference between basic and non-basic actions, but takes the waving out of a context in which construing it as an action would make sense. It is saying "that wasn't an *action*" at all.[12] As with simple and complex things (Wittgenstein), so with "basic" and "non-basic" acts: their difference is contextual.

Second, Ricoeur's claim about non-totalization, which is the other major point that the basic/non-basic action dichotomy seems to support, does not need it. Ricoeur writes, "if the world is the totality of what is the case, doing cannot be included in this totality. Better, doing means [*fait*] that reality is not totalizable" (III: 231). A seemingly crucial step is the basic/non-basic action distinction: basic actions may be "what is the case"; but non-basic actions seem not to be. Ricoeur at this point also distinguishes the agent's from the narrator's perspective; they cannot be the same, on his account. But consider the problem John Milbank raises for virtue ethicists who make similar points:

> [M]any current proponents of an "ethics of virtue" began by insisting on "the agent's perspective," to distinguish intentionally informed action ... from mere natural causation which can be fully comprehended from "outside." However, they have quickly realized that post-Wittgensteinian considerations force one to see that if an intention is situated with an action, then it is also constituted through language, and so is in principle as comprehensible to an outside observer as to the agent herself.[13]

The solution is simply to bite the bullet and to accept the teleology of actions by refusing to reduce such actions "to a mere seamless, directionless continuum."[14] The point is that the solution cannot be found either by distinguishing basic from non-basic actions or by distinguishing agent's and narrator's perspectives. Instead, what needs to be affirmed is that narratives that ignore the goals of actions or that construe no agent as able to perform goal-oriented actions are either themselves the product of agents seeking goals which make the theories self-referentially incoherent or are nothing but noisy exercises of nonsense. Embracing such nonsensical narrative accounts is, of course, in some sense, possible; but at what price? How could one even account for such a preference, since they seem to deny that any narrative can in any non-Pickwickian sense be true? What has to be sacrificed is the possibility of anything like what any culture has construed, or apparently could construe, as the human social realm. Ricoeur does not have, I think, a knock-down argument against the modern masters of suspicion, the grandsons and granddaughters of Nietzsche, spawned by Derrida, Foucault, Lacan *et al.*, but in the face of their proclamations of instability and indeterminacy, he provides a practical, poetic way to account for the stability and instability of narratively created worlds. To put it another way, Ricoeur's account of mimesis remains a viable account of figuring, configuring, disfiguring, and reconfiguring our worlds which does not require that we pay the high – and perplexing – price of commitment to nihilism. Nor does it mean that we pay the high – and paradoxical – price of accepting yet another narrative (for that is what they offer us, just another story) that denies the importance of narrative.

In sum, slight revisions of Ricoeur's account of mimesis$_3$ in particular and his action theory in general strengthen his theory, especially its usefulness for theology.

Two Theological Approaches

Although I discern at least five patterns in "postmodern" theology,[15] at least two of them seem to me more to extend modern approaches than to reconfigure them. For instance, the theologians whose accounts are based on or are structured by Jürgen Habermas's theory of communicative action, or by Alfred North Whitehead's process cosmology, have appropriated the term "postmodern." But they use the term without accepting the relevance of the critiques of modernity and the analyses of postmodernity found in Lyotard, Foucault, Mark C. Taylor *et al.*[16] I will not consider these approaches here. However, the "postliberal" approach of George Lindbeck and the postmodernism of Edith Wyschogrod both seem to present important patterns in contemporary theology which take the postmodernist critiques of modernity seriously and use narrative and action theory in constructing their theological approaches.

George Lindbeck's methodological essay *The Nature of Doctrine* is the central text establishing postliberal theology. Lindbeck's work is clearly intratextual. As he put it, "Intratextual theology redescribes reality within the scriptural framework rather than translating Scripture into extra-scriptural categories. It is the text, so to speak, which absorbs the world, rather than the world the text."[17] The question is whether this description makes sense.

The basic problem with such an account is that it ignores the context of reading in which truly revelatory reading involves mimesis$_3$ in Ricoeur's terms. If, as argued above, revelation is an effect of reading a text, then a pure intratextual theology does not clarify the relationship of intratextual to "extratextual" meanings.[18] Examining the steps of the path Lindbeck walks in displaying his notion of fidelity as intratextuality shows this:

1. He begins with a formal claim that concepts acquire their meaning not from the entities to which they refer or from some experiences they symbolize, but from how the concept operates in a semiotic system composed of interpretive and communicative signs, symbols and actions (114).

2. He then construes religions as instantiations of such semiotic systems (114-6).

3. Next he construes the canonical writings of religious communities as constituting a distinct semiotic system or world. "For those who are steeped in them, no world is more real than the ones they create. A scriptural world is thus able to absorb the universe" (117). The biblical text is next identified as constituting the world into which all others are absorbed (118). When "extrabiblical material inserted into the biblical universe ... becomes the basic framework of interpretation" (120), the mainline church rejected the result as heresy, as it did gnosticism.

4. Past interpretive practices are redescribed as intratextual interpretation (117).

5. Finally, the fact that material conditions in late capitalist society are such that it is increasingly difficult for intratextual interpretation to be practised is noticed. This become a veiled (or not so veiled) advocacy of reading religions and their scriptures "in terms of their intrinsic sense" rather than attempting to translate them into popular categories (124; cf. 134-5).

Lindbeck's first step is unexceptional. The second step on Lindbeck's path is not so easily dismissed. It is not clear that all religious traditions can always be *independent* semiotic systems. Clearly, "a religion can be viewed as a kind of cultural and/or linguistic framework or medium that shapes the entirety of life and thought" (33). Some persons *can* and do "speak of all life and reality in French, or from an American or Jewish perspective" (114). But do American and Israeli Jews have the *same* semiotic system? Will the entirety of their lives and thought be shaped in the same way, given their different social locations? Do St. Augustine, St. Thomas, Luther, and Lindbeck live in the *same* cultural-linguistic framework?[19] Besides denying any real internal pluralism in the Christian tradition, Lindbeck's view also presumes a normality, a stability, of a religious framework, independent of its actual instantiations in multiple cultural contexts and social locations. But this contradicts the basic insight of a cultural-linguistic model of religion, that the meanings of concepts are determined by their place in the semiotic system which the community uses (114). Lindbeck skilfully exploits this model to argue that Buddhist compassion, Christian love, and French revolutionary *fraternité* are not expressions of a single underlying experience, emotion or attitude. These are "radically (i.e., from the root) distinct ways of experiencing and being oriented toward self, neighbor, cosmos"(40). But what he neglects to note is that the "self, neighbor, cosmos," to which compassion, love, and *fraternité* orient us, also differ radically. Not only is the Buddhist cosmos different from the Christian cosmos, but the cosmoi of Jesus, Augustine, Aquinas, Luther and Lindbeck are radically different. Either the meaning of Christian concepts is determined by a single semiotic system, without regard to the social location in which those concepts are deployed, or it is not clear how they can have the same meanings in those various locations.

Lindbeck opts for a single semiotic system. He proposes a "normal" framework in claiming that the "same content can be expressed in different formulations"(93). His example is the equivalence of "12" in base four to "6" in base ten notation. But to show such equivalence requires that both base systems are commensurable in terms of more general mathematical conventions. He goes on to say that "the only way to show that the doctrines of Nicaea and Chalcedon are distinguishable from the concepts in which they are formulated is to state these doctrines in different terms that nevertheless have equivalent consequences"(93). But a judgment of equivalency of consequences requires a framework in which commensurating consequences of terms drawn from other frameworks was possible. Lindbeck assumes that while Buddhist compassion, Christian love, and French revolutionary *fraternité* are incommensurable, one framework can accommodate "hypostasis," "ousia," "prosopon," "persona," "nature," etc. This assumption begs the question. As Richard Rorty put it in another context, "Alternative geometries are irreconcilable because they have axiomatic structures, and contradictory axioms. They are *designed* to be irreconcilable. Cultures are not so designed, and do not have axiomatic structures."[20] Lindbeck improperly conflates the *necessary* incommensurability and irreconcilability of mathematical systems with the *contingent* incommensurability (and not necessary irreconcilability) of cultural "systems." The issue of reconcilability finally is an open question, even if it is one profoundly difficult to resolve.

The issue is whether the concepts and practices in a religious framework which does not constitute the semiotic system of its cultural location can be understood completely independently of the framework of that location. If those concepts and practices cannot be so understood, then non-religious contexts partially constitute those concepts. If those concepts and practices can be so understood, then the religious framework alone is sufficient to determine how religious concepts are to be understood. But then the religious framework must be independent of its cultural-linguistic instantiation.

Lindbeck's third step identifies this culturally independent framework as the "scriptural world."[21] It "absorbs" all the other worlds. It presumes that this one text constitutes a world of its own. It provides, finally, the commensurating paradigm for all Christian concepts. However, this simply won't do. A close examination of the presuppositions which must be true if the "scriptural world" is to be a semiotic system sufficient to determine Christian concepts reveals that those presuppositions are at best dubitable and at worst false.

First, it must be true that texts *alone* are sufficient to establish a "world of meaning." Lindbeck begins his argument as follows:

> Masterpieces such as *Oedipus Rex* and *War and Peace*, for example, evoke their own domains of meaning. They do so by what they themselves say about the events and personages of which they tell. In order to understand them in their own terms, there is no need for extraneous references to, for example, Freud's theories or historical treatments of the Napoleonic wars. Further, such works shape the imagination and perceptions of the attentive reader so that he or she forever views the world to some extent through the lenses they supply (116-7).

Although the metaphor of "lenses" is far too thin to support Lindbeck's points, he is surely correct to say that understanding a text "in its own terms" requires no reference to "extratextual," e.g., Freudian analyses of those texts – no matter how useful such "extratextual" analyses may be for disclosing unexpected meanings in the text. But for a reader to understand a text in any terms, those terms must be accessible in the reader's world. In short, getting the point of a strange text, of one that is other than one's own narrative, or learning of a world in which one does not already live, requires mimesis$_3$, which Lindbeck, in his opposition to extratextualists, denies. Without refiguring, it is impossible to appropriate a world configured in a different time and place (compare III: 160-2).

A second, more general, problem also plagues the postliberal approach. A semiotic system cannot be separated from the community which constitutes that system. Frei put the matter nicely in the following:

> The descriptive context, then, for the *sensus literalis* [of Scripture] is the religion of which it is part, understood at once as a determinate code in which beliefs, ritual, and behavior patterns, ethos as well as narrative, come together as a common semiotic system, and also as the community which is that system in use – apart from which the very term ("semiotic system") is in this case no more than a misplaced metaphor. Clifford Geertz calls culture an "acted document," and the term applies also to religion.[22]

A religious community may be an acted document. But it is confused to think that an acted document is the scripture alone. The scripture is a *part*, in terms Frei adopts, of the "determinate code," not the determinate code itself. Scripture alone is not a sufficient means of determining the meaning of all the parts of the system or of the semiotic system as a whole. On the cultural-linguistic model, the Bible or the gospel is not and cannot be the only text which determines the semiotic system of a Christian community.

Lindbeck's fourth move, the redescription of past interpretive practices as intratextual practices, doesn't fit the facts. First, classic Christian theologians *materially* did not work within the same text. The writers of the New Testament, the writers of the patristic period, and Protestants in general did not recognize the same canon of scripture. Nor did they interpret it in similar ways: the exercise of the medieval fourfold exegesis differs radically from Luther's work. Lindbeck's step (4) which functions logically to legitimate the claim in step (3), that there is *a* biblical universe which provides *the* semiotic system for Christian intratextual interpretation, fails.

This means that step (5) is misstated. It is not only contemporary, postliberal society in which the conditions are such that the scriptures can be construed as providing a self-sufficient context for interpretation. Rather, the Christian tradition as a whole has the same "problem." It is intrinsically plural in that it has always had a multiplicity of canons and texts in which textual interpretation takes place. It has always been not a single "acted document" but a set of enacted texts. Lindbeck's dichotomy of either reading religions and their scriptures "in terms of their intrinsic sense" or attempting to translate them into popular categories (124) is finally a false dichotomy. So is Frei's distinction of a reading of scripture that is privatized to the believing community versus readings through extra-communal interpretive lenses. Both presume that Christian discourse is *essentially* a normal, commensurable, discourse which requires only configuration. But effective reading demands refiguration as Ricoeur points out (III: 159). The very dichotomy necessary for the postliberal position to make sense is deeply mistaken.[23]

If postliberalism construes the Christian *muthos* as both normal and normative, postmodernism seems to make the edifying (to use the term Rorty borrows from Kierkegaard) and the revolutionary the norm. Few theologians have attempted to confront this state of affairs head-on. But in *Saints and Postmodernism*, Edith Wyschogrod seeks to use life narratives, "specifically those of saints, defined in terms that both overlap and overturn traditional normative stipulations and that defy the structure of moral theory" to overcome the inadequacies of contemporary moral theory – and, one might add, the inadequacies of "normal" theology.[24]

Central to her work is her redefinition of sanctity. She disconnects saintliness from theism and generalizes the concept much as James suggested in *The Varieties of Religious Experience*. The definition she gives, however, is rather tricky:

> I shall ... define the saint – the subject of hagiographic narrative – as *one whose adult life in its entirety is devoted to the alleviation of sorrow (the psychological suffering) and pain (the physical suffering) that afflicts other persons without distinction of rank or group or, alternatively, that afflicts the sentient beings, whatever the cost to the saint in pain or sorrow* (34; italics in original).

This definition is tricky because the *unitalicized* part is the crucial part of the definition! A saint cannot be a person whose life has an incomplete narrative shape, but must be a character in a narrative, a narrative whose ending is determined ("adult life in its entirety"). The significance of this is rather obvious: there are no living saints, no clearly saintly acts, no saintly actualities.[25]

Wyschogrod distinguishes between ordinary work (i.e., effort to achieve a goal), and labor, which "as opposed to both work and violence, entails the corporeal involvement of the laborer but minimizes the input of forces extraneous to the laborer" (84). Saintly labor is "the psychological, social, and corporeal investment of the self's total resources when they are committed to altruistic existence" (85). Saints are unconcerned with techniques and work, especially with efficiency. Saints' labor, like the labor of unprepared natural childbirth, is a giving of self without consideration of any cost.[26]

What makes a person a saint more than anything else is her "motivation." But such motivation empowers the saint not "internally," but "externally."

> The topographical markers of alterity can be read by anyone – the crumpled body as a signifier of pain, the expressionless face as a signifier of depression – but for saints the Other's destitution is a vortex, a centripetal force, as it were, into which saintly desire on the Other's behalf is drawn. The more fissured the life of the Other, the greater the other's lack, the weightier its claim upon the saintly self. Saints are person-differentiating, but it is lack and not proximity that is encrypted in the body or "group body" of the Other that decides who receives preference (242).

Saints' selves are *consumed* by the needs of the other. What emerges is a new "self" centered selflessly on the other. But since one can never be sure that such altruism was the driving force of a saint's life, the saint remains necessarily insecure, mysterious: "it can never be established that there was a saint or proved that the primacy of the Other is the source of action" (149).

One can find few (if any) saints outside of fiction, if one accepts Wyschogrod's theory. Almost all her examples of saints are drawn not from classic hagiography intended to narrate an edifying truth about an actual life in the real world, but from modern and postmodern texts which make no pretense to being about an actual embodied person. Even some of the saints she cites in passing, like Saint Mary of Egypt who had been a prostitute, cannot fit the definition. Saints, then, are fictions for Wyschogrod.

The purpose of Wyschogrod's writing is clearly conveyed in the first part of her final paragraph of *Saints and Postmodernism*:

> The postmodern saintly life as a new path in ethics is not a proposal to revert to an older hagiographic discourse, least of all to hide behind its metaphysical presuppositions. It is instead a plea for boldness and risk, for an effort to develop a new altruism in an age grown cynical and hardened to catastrophe: war, genocide, the threat of worldwide ecological collapse, sporadic and unpredictable eruptions of urban violence, the use of torture, the emergence of new diseases. In an epoch grown weary not only of its calamities but of its ecstasies, of its collective political fantasies that destroyed millions of lives, and of its chemically induced stupors and joys, the postmodern saint shows the traces of these disasters.... Borrowing the compassionate strands of the world's religious traditions, the absurdist gestures of recent modernist art and literature, and modern technologies, saints try to fashion lives of compassion and generosity (257).

In analyzing the moral theory of Nicholas Rescher, Wyschogrod finds that his theory subverts itself because it relies on altruism as displayed in unnamed saintliness to measure the legitimacy of social theories. "It is, to use postmodern language, the saint's response to the Other – not, as Lyotard puts it, the grand meta-narratives of theory – that addresses me and mandates benevolence in everyday life" (243).

But not only does saintliness measure theory, but moral theory cannot convey the practice or the power of saintliness to a "reader." Theory is not enough. Somewhat like Ricoeur's account of reading, Wyschogrod analogizes understanding saintly practice to understanding music: there is an appreciative part and a performative part. And appreciation does not necessarily lead to action: one can admire altruism without becoming altruistic. In terms developed in the previous section, I would say that becoming altruistic is one possible effect of reading a text of altruism; it is not the action of the reading of the text. Becoming altruistic must be attributed to the hearer's action of refiguring the text.

And here Wyschogrod's attempts come to a grinding halt. The saintly narrative is to be used to resolve an aporia in moral theory. But the saint is a character of complete extravagance. To appreciate a saint is not necessarily to emulate one. So how does this narrative of a life or a display of saintly practice resolve theoretical issues? Why would a person emulate a saint? How could one do so? Without answers to such questions, how a narrative might resolve such aporias in moral theory remains remarkably unclear. Because Wyschogrod's theory is exclusively textual, construes saints as fictional, and renders the reality of saints profoundly uncertain, she cannot, unlike Ricoeur, provide an account of the way narrative resolves theoretical problems.

From Wyschogrod's text, it is clear that the motivation for an action is never finally decidable until the story of over, the narrative ended, the text closed – if even then, for the motivation of a character in a narrative might well be not merely constructed, but counterfactual. But while we live we never can reach such closure, a necessary condition for being and recognizing a saint. Hence, we can never be sure that any agent's motive is saintly. Nor can we ever become living saints. It is only when our life is narrated that we are saints. But it can be narrated only when we are dead. One could copy a narrative, but how could one emulate a saint?

What is needed here is a theory which incorporates mimesis$_3$. The person must refigure the saintliness configured in the hagiographic narrative in one's own life. But if the argument made in the previous section suggesting that reconfiguration is not an effect of the text, but an effect of the act of reading the text, is right, then there is no reason to think that only narratives could convey a saintliness which could be emulated. Many who knew Dorothy Day, for instance, considered her a "living saint." Her long, lonely path from the fast life of literary New York in the 1920s to the Catholic Worker movement seems a refiguration of the paths of earlier saints (maybe even St. Mary of Egypt), an old path to traditional asceticism and altruism. The key for Day is that she was learning to transpose that old path so it could be walked by a citizen in the new world. But it was just her lively self, her lively reconfiguration that inspired others to join the movement and reconfigure their own lives. It was not a narrative of the dead or fictional, but the encounter with the living person that was crucial for many.

This is not to deny Wyschogrod's claims that motives may never be known and that a partial story can never be surely a saintly one. The saint always remains mysterious. It is entirely possible, I suppose, that a person could be dissembling about what moves her or him, could be confused, etc. In theory, these points are so true as to be truisms. However, theory must come, finally, to a halt; questioning comes to an end; we hit bedrock; we must turn from our speculations to the human company at the backgammon table. Our spade, as Wittgenstein put it, is turned. "If this person was not altruistic, then altruism is a hoax, a concept without meaning." We come finally to the question of embracing a narrative. And again, as in the last section dealing with Ricoeur's work directly, we may ask: "at what price?"

If saintliness is a total hoax then the following points from Wyschogrod and William James about the power of saints to change the world are delusions:

> The effort to relieve suffering that is constitutive of saintly existence may fulfill or fall short of its aim. But even when this effort does not entirely succeed, saintly power can still be effective and its results may go deeper: saintly effort, even when it misfires, can morally *transfigure* other lives.[27]

> Momentarily considered, then, the saint may waste his tenderness and be the dupe and victim of his charitable fever, but the general function of his charity in social evolution is vital and essential. If things are ever to move upward, some one must be ready to take the first step, and assume the risk of it. No one who is not willing to try charity, to try nonresistance as the saint is always willing, can tell whether these methods will or will not succeed. When they do succeed, they are far more powerfully successful than force or worldly prudence. Force destroys enemies; and the best that can be said of prudence is that it keeps what we already have in safety. But non-resistance, when successful, *turns enemies into friends*; and charity *regenerates* its objects. These saintly methods are, as I said, creative energies; and genuine saints find in the elevated excitement with which their faith endows them an authority and impressiveness which makes them *irresistible* in situations where men of shallower nature cannot get on at all without the use of worldly prudence. This practical proof that worldly wisdom may be safely transcended is the saint's magic gift to mankind.[28]

The question is how these transformations of lives highlighted in these two texts can occur. And, in general, Ricoeur's concept of mimesis$_3$ (extended beyond textual interpretation as above) provides a satisfactory practical solution to this very practical problem. Basically, transformation is refiguration as an effect of reading a narrative or responding to a person.

But even if the "how" question can be resolved by narrative, the "why" question remains. Why emulate this saintly practice, that saintly life? In

Wyschogrod's view, these are the norms of moral and social theory, so no theoretical answer is possible for such a question. It is a question beyond theory. It is a question external to the narration of lives. Yet saints can "transfigure" others. They are "regenerative." And perhaps there is no clearer answer to this question than to say that just as the question, "why be moral?" is a question beyond the boundaries of moral theory and unanswerable by any moral or social theory, so the question, "why be saintly?" is a question beyond the boundaries of saintly narrative. It is unanswerable, save in terms that are finally not real answers: saints have "intrinsic authority" and "impressiveness."

Adapting Ricoeur's discussion of narrative identity, we can perhaps go beyond this apparent dead end. This may be very hard ground, but it is possible that it is not yet the "hard rock" which turns our conceptual shovel and halts our digging. It is possible to say that the impressiveness of the saint displays one way of having character:

> The circular relation between what we may call a "character" – which may be that of an individual as well as that of a people – and the narratives that both express and shape this character, illustrates in a marvelous way the circle referred to at the beginning of our description of threefold mimesis. The third mimetic relation of narrative [refiguring] leads back to the first relation [prefiguring] by way of the second relation [configuring].... At the end of our inquiry into the refiguration of time by narrative we can affirm without hesitation that this circle is a wholesome one. The first mimetic relation refers, in the case of an individual, to the semantics of desire, which only includes those prenarrative features attached to the demand constitutive of human desire. The third mimetic relation is defined by the narrative identity of an individual or a people, stemming from the endless rectification of a previous narrative by a subsequent one, and from the chain of refigurations that results from this. In a word, narrative identity is the poetic resolution of the hermeneutic circle (III:248).

In the present context, Ricoeur's poetic resolution is a practical resolution. It involves a praxis which instantiates a character. That character is not necessarily a finished character, but an evolving one. Adapting the insights of James, then, we can say that for each tradition, the saint is the one who provides a model of rectification. Why be a saint? Why try to act as a saint *of that tradition* would? Why emulate her or his reconfiguration of the past with a new reconfiguration of our own? Why engage in a religious form of mimesis$_3$? The answer is: if we desire to keep the chain of refigurations going, we will have to learn to be saintly, to express in some way the best of the character of our tradition. The saint evokes our desire, not only in the exalted sense of total dedication to the Other and to others (the height of sanctity), but also in the less exalted way of instantiating, in our own ways, as well as possible, the ever-evolving character of the tradition we inhabit.

If this is on target, then Wyschogrod's disconnection of saintliness from concrete and actual traditions undermines the possibility of even understanding why one might ask or answer the question "why be a saint." For the answer to the "why" question is simple: "to carry on." If one does not desire to carry on, if one's response to another, or to a reading of a text, does not evoke the desire to embody the character of the tradition, then the "why" question receives the opposite answer. One does not continue the chain of refigurations because it is not a tradition worth carrying on. It is let to die. No attempt should be made to resuscitate it. In its place, there is ludic nihilism, the Godot for whom we wait, or the prefigured beginning of a new tradition in which to dwell, a new tradition in which to figure our desires.

Narrative Theologies *Post Mortem Dei*?

I have here the space and time only for a brief promissory note. I think Ricoeur's analysis of mimesis provides a key element in providing both a sadly neglected aspect of the modern condition and a positive answer to the question of the viability of theology in the postmodern world.

Why is our era, as Nietzsche so eloquently and correctly put it, the age of the death of God? It is because the traditions of saintliness have died out. Arguments abound about how the culture of modernity has powerfully replicated itself by shaping our desires into patterns which then became desirable themselves. Perhaps the traditions themselves became degenerate. Perhaps the love of self and power shone more brightly than the love of Other and others. Perhaps no explanation is finally possible. Only observation can be charted. After all, even Augustine could not explain the original will to evil, but could only describe it as a turning away from the proper and the subsequent loss of measure, form and order. Whatever the explanation, if we can get the description right, we have enough to understand what is needed about modernity and its postmodern intensification in nihilism.

The question is what is to be done about it, if anything. Obviously, there is no certainty as to the right path. There may, however, be room for a hope that is yet not optimistic. For the theologian, it is necessary not to retreat to the world of the text (Lindbeck) nor to abstract particular *Lebensformen* from the traditions within which they make sense (Wyschogrod) nor to identify the death of the god of the Book with the death of God (Taylor). All of these are, finally, dead ends.

The fact of the matter is that our present religious practices prefigure the future. If these are practices of peace and justice, of rooting out of self-deceptions, of solidarity with and resistance to injustice, of patience with stumblers, of forgiveness of sinners, of courage in the face of suffering, and of saintly devotion, perhaps they will prove to be attractive. Keeping a tradition alive requires that its participants shape together a path of creative fidelity, but not that they attack those who keep other traditions alive.

Our theological reflections must help configure these paths. But there will be a future only to the extent to which refiguration remains a possibility evoked by encounter with saintly practitioners and the narratives they embody. Theology *post mortem dei* is not a discipline without a subject; it is what it always has been, a discipline in search of the Subject which always remains both fully present and yet completely absent. It concerns the Other found in the deepest self and yet Totally Alien, of the gracious Plot which we can never understand but within which we live because we cannot find a life worth living in any other place.

The possibility of theologies *post mortem dei*, then, with apologies to René Girard, is a question of the possibility of telling, and together living, the stories of creative, not destructive, mimetic desire.

Notes

1 After all, his early focus was on the will and his remarkable and most influential text, *The Symbolism of Evil*, focused not only on the suffering of defilement and the ways of cleansing, but also on (in my terms) the actions of sin and the counteraction of confession, as developed in Terrence W. Tilley, *The Evils of Theodicy* (Washington: Georgetown University Press, 1991), especially chapters 8 and 9.

2 III: 101; emphasis added. Subsequent parenthetical references throughout the paper which include III in the reference are to Paul Ricoeur, *Time and Narrative*, III, trans. Kathleen Blamey and David Pellauer (Chicago: University of Chicago Press, 1988).

3 I leave aside texts an author does not intend to be read; I argue elsewhere that such solipsistic authoring is a derivative action which is possible only if the practices of communicative actions have been mastered. See *The Evils of Theodicy*, chapters 1-3, where I lay out a form of speech-act theory to make this point.

4 Of course, we could construct a story which made me responsible (I know you can't resist angel food cake; I know you're coming over; I bake the cake and leave it where you are sure to find it), but if this story is true, then I have manipulated you viciously and the act I performed was vicious. You would not be responsible for your act; I would be; I brought it about. Of course, there are grey cases where it is hard to distinguish either what act I perform or my responsibility for it, but the primary purpose of such narratives is either to perplex philosophers or fatten lawyers' wallets. The "weasel words" here are "normal circumstances." I concede that it may be that one can never sustain a claim that one has exhaustively surveyed all the circumstances and conditions which make a given act possible. This is the major sustainable point of Derrida's deconstructionist critique of Searle's speech-act theory. I have argued elsewhere (*The Evils of Theodicy*, *Horizons*) that this critique is generally avoidable.

5 III: 181. I am in sympathy with this – see chapter 6 of *The Evils of Theodicy*, where I analyze Boethius's *Consolation of Philosophy* as a (dramatic) script for enactment so as to reinscribe the self.

6 Mark C. Taylor, *Erring: A Postmodern A/theology* (Chicago: University of Chicago Press, 1984), 7-8.

7 Taylor, *Erring*, 10.

8 For a brief synopsis of Ong's work, see my "The Gift of Walter Ong," *Horizons* 21/1 (Spring 1994), 172-8.

9 I do not mean to suggest that this is a free, unlocated *individual's* response. Stanley Fish has noted the importance of the interpretive community, which gives another aspect of the context for interpretation, a point whose theological significance has been ably explored by Stanley Hauerwas, *Unleashing the Scriptures* (Nashville: Abingdon, 1993), especially 19-28.

10 See A.C. Danto, "Action, Knowledge and Representation" in *Action Theory*, ed. Myles Brand and Douglas Walton (Dordrecht: Reidel, 1976) and "Basic Actions and Basic Concepts," *The Review of Metaphysics* 32 (March 1979), as cited in Steven W. Holtzer, "The Possibility of Incorporeal Agency" in *The Rationality of Religious Belief: Essays in Honour of Basil Mitchell*, ed. Steven W. Holtzer and William J. Abraham (Oxford: Clarendon, 1987).

11 See her *Intention* (Ithaca: Cornell University Press, 1957).

12 Of course, this theory runs into criteriological problems, but I would argue that in most cases these could be practically resolved; admittedly, I can imagine that some could not be resolved, at least this side of the grave, but that seems better to me than any of the other approaches of which I am aware.

13 John Milbank, *Theology and Social Theory: Beyond Secular Reason* (Oxford: Blackwell, 1990), 358 with reference to Stanley Hauerwas, *Character and the Christian Life* (San Antonio: Trinity University Press, 1985), xiii-xxxiii.

14 Milbank, *Theology and Social Theory*, 359.

15 See Terrence W. Tilley *et al.*, *Postmodern Theologies and the Problem of Religious Diversity* (Maryknoll: Orbis, 1995) for these points and for an expanded discussion of the points made in this section.

16 Edith Wyschogrod, *Saints and Postmodernism: Revisioning Moral Philosophy* (Chicago: University of Chicago Press, 1990) suggests that postmodernism is a constellation with six key characteristics including "differentiality," a tactic which undercuts standard accounts; "double coding," placing and noticing ambiguity; "eclecticism"; "alterity," recognizing the otherness of the other; "empowerment," even of a Nietzschean type of will to power; and "materialism" (xvi-xxi). I would say that she has identified the central and distinctive elements of the narrative of eliminative postmodernism. A "practical approach," found in the works of people as diverse as James Wm. McClendon, Jr., Stanley Hauerwas (arguably), David Tracy (perhaps), some forms of liberation theology (especially the works of Cornel West, Rebecca Chopp, Sharon Welch, Gustavo Gutierrez *et al.*) is left to the side for the present. While this sort of grouping violates the typical distinctions between "intratextualists" and "intertextualists" in narrative theology, I think this distinction finally bogus, especially as illustrated by the works of Gary Comstock and William Placher. It is also my own "methodological home."

17 George Lindbeck, *The Nature of Doctrine* (Philadelphia: Westminster, 1984), 118. Parenthetical references in the text are to this book. The late Yale scripture scholar Hans W. Frei also accepted this approach; see his "The 'Literal Reading' of Biblical Narrative in the Christian Tradition: Does it Stretch or Will it Break?" *The Bible and the Narrative Tradition*, ed. Frank McConnell (New York: Oxford University, 1986), 72. Paul Holmer, retired from Yale, is also associated with this "New Yale Theology." See his *The Grammar of Faith* (San Francisco: Harper & Row, 1978). Some of what follows is developed in my "Incommensurability, Intratextuality, and Fideism," *Modern Theology* 5/2 (January, 1989): 87-111.

18 I place 'extratextual' in scare quotes because, although intratextualists identify "extratextualist" readings, e.g., Freudian ones, as the opposition, their real opponents are *inter*textualists. Cf. Lindbeck, *The Nature of Doctrine*, 136. Frei opposes a version of intertextualism in "The 'Literal Reading'," the revisionist and hermeneutical position associated with Ricoeur and David Tracy. There is good reason to think that the opposition between intra- and intertextual theologies is overdrawn. Even if intertextual theory is as problematical as Frei argues, diverse intratextual strategies can be discerned in practice. For instance, see the contrast between fundamentalism and another intratextual approach, that of Martin Luther King, Jr., as developed in J. W. McClendon, Jr., *Biography as Theology* (Nashville: Abingdon, 1974), 83-86, 169.

19 Kenneth Surin, "Many Religions and the One True Faith," *Modern Theology* 4/2 (January, 1988): 201 also suggests this point.

20 Richard Rorty, "Solidarity of Objectivity," *Post Analytic Philosophy*, edited by John Rajchman and Cornel West (New York: Columbia University, 1985), 9. Rorty also persuasively argues that in a post-positivist context the anthropologists' distinctions between the intracultural and the intercultural collapse. The same sort of argument could also be used to dismantle the distinction between the intratextual and the intertextual.

21 Frei, "The 'Literal Reading'," 63-75 makes similar claims and explicitly associates his work with Lindbeck's.

22 Frei, "The 'Literal Reading'," 70-1, citing Clifford Geertz, *The Interpretation of Cultures* (New York: Basic Books, 1973), 110.

23 Lindbeck also falls into confusions about action theory, narration, and speech acts much like those examined above. See my "Intratextuality, Incommensurability and Fideism," especially 99-101.

24 Wyschogrod, xiii. Subsequent parenthetical references in the text are to this book. I am indebted to H. Frederick Filice whose presentation of Wyschogrod's work in a seminar in postmodern religious thought in Fall, 1993, evoked considerable profitable discussion of Wyschogrod's text. His paper arising out of that discussion was adapted and included in my *Postmodern Theology and Religious Diversity* (Maryknoll: Orbis, 1995).

25 One might contend that Wyschogrod's estimation of the people of Chambon giving sanctuary to Jews during the Nazi invasion and occupation of France is a counter-example. However, the example, and the use she makes of it, are terribly problematical. The saint's labor is immediate and avoids "technique." That a whole community avoided technique (in her sense) in undertaking a complex project and remained saintly is, bluntly, too far-fetched to be credible. I don't mean to deny the

heroic saintliness of Chambon. I mean to doubt the adequacy of Wyschogrod's account, especially her complete separation of work and labor, when confronted with real people whose lives are messy and confused, rather than fictional characters.

26 Wyschogrod seems here to divide *praxis* finally from *poiesis*. In light of Milbank's critique that such a division is always a social construct, this division of work from labor seems unwarranted. Cf. Milbank, 351-9.

27 44; emphasis added. I think this point is correct, but is also inconsistent with Wyschogrod's account of saintliness. It is not necessarily the narrative which changes lives. It may be the very person we encounter who is (for all anyone can tell) a saint, which is the powerful catalyst of change.

28 William James, *The Varieties of Religious Experience* (New York: Collier, 1961), 284; emphasis added.

Ricoeur on Ethics
and Narrative

ROBERT D. SWEENEY

Ricoeur's work on narrrative, as has been amply documented and explicated elsewhere in this book, represents a consistent development within his hermeneutical turn that began with a theory of the symbol.[1] The key themes – reference to (and construction of) temporality, a new version of the classical theory of "mimesis," plot as the "synthesis of the heterogeneous," the intersection of history and fiction, even the narrative self – are more or less consistent with his basic commitment to metaphoricity. The metaphor, as described in the *Rule of Metaphor*[2] and elsewhere, is characterized by a double meaning – "split reference" – that results from the self-cancellation of first-order, literal reference and the liberation of second-order, analogous, reference to "deep structures." Metaphorical split reference is the specific product of the hermeneutic imagination that combines separate semantic fields by way of the creativity that enables us to "shatter and increase our sense of reality." Narrativity has a comparable figurative dynamic as it imposes concordance on the discordance of time, moving from prefiguration (mimesis$_1$) to the configuration of plotting (mimesis$_2$) and the refiguration of reading and consequent action (mimesis$_3$).[3]

Continuity is less evident when it comes to Ricoeur's theory of ethics. Of course, ethics was rarely a central theme in his writings – there has been no book on ethics as such – even though it has been a strong underlying current in almost all his works, starting with *History and Truth*. A sketch of the discontinuity might begin with a reference to the early commitment to personalism as articulated in the pages of *Esprit* under the tutelage of Emmanuel Mounier. Its influence on Ricoeur would be difficult to measure, but, in any case, in a fairly recent writing (1983), *"Meurt le personalisme, revient la personne,"* he gives reasons for rejecting personalism as a political, social and ethical doctrine, mainly its failure

197

to win the conceptual battle against existentialism, marxism, etc. – all of which were carried away by the new wave of structuralism in any case.[4]

Nevertheless, one major aspect of personalism perdured for quite a while as a major theme in Ricoeur's philosophical discussion of ethics, viz., value. This theme reached Ricoeur through his study of German phenomenology – as well as French influences such as Nabert, Marcel, Lavelle and Le Senne – but he never gave it the primacy it had in Scheler and, to a lesser extent, in Husserl. Value was not an object of intuition, either intellectual or affective, as it was for Scheler; rather, it was an intermediating concept that had innovative aspects. For example, in *Freedom and Nature*, values are described as "fixed stars," which turn out, under severe stress, not to be such. Or again, values are dealt with in terms, not of a hierarchy, as in Scheler (spiritual down to "sensible") but of novel categories such as "organic" values that are revealed in the "lived body."[5]

In a later article, "The Problem of the Foundation of Moral Philosophy," value is assigned a central, mediating role between the freedom of the positive "urge to be" and the negativities of obligation and moral or natural law. This role incorporates a subjective positing, an act of evaluation proceeding from my will to actualize my freedom, but also a substantive, based on my leap to the second person, the you, i.e., to intersubjective recognition. A value like justice, then, is not an essence in the sense of an entity, but the "institutional instrument by which several freedoms may coexist." That is, justice stands for the scheme of actions that must be done to make institutionally possible the community and the communication of freedom. Thus, the concept of value is a mixed concept which effects a compromise between the desire for freedom of individual consciences and the demands of ethical situations. Ricoeur calls value, then, a compromise among an exigency, a recognition, and a situation. Consequently, it can be termed, he tells us, a "quasi-object," and therefore a transcendence that tempts us to invent a "world of values" in "platonist form."[6] But, in actuality, values are simply "deposits of evaluation," sorts of resting places between processes of evaluation. These processes are hard to express except in terms of their "products," i.e., of a substantialization of value predicates. We go naturally from "this is just" to justice simpliciter. Such quasi-objectivity, however, does not prevent a bond with my freedom, thus a predicative character in value that matches the concept of preference, Aristotle's *proairesis*. Because the preferential "worth-more" of value encounters the opposition of the desirable, we experience the negativity of obligation, the scission of the norm. The imperative, in turn, follows from this scission of self-command found in the voice of conscience, a scission that is then reflected in institutions split apart by the voice of authority and that is manifested institutionally in the law. [7]

Now this "value-ethics," apparent in Ricoeur's middle period, stands in sharp contrast to the *"petite éthique"* (Ricoeur's phrase) of *Soi-même comme un autre* (*Oneself as Another*, in the English translation), the last work published by Ricoeur and one that follows the elaboration of his narrative theory in *Time and Narrative*.[8] In *Oneself as Another*, value as such is barely mentioned. Instead, the focus is on the two central historical traditions: teleological ethics, as in Aristotle, and deontological ethics (*morale*), which emphasizes the moral norm, as in Kant. Ethics (Ricoeur asserts he is using a terminological convention here) is defined as "aiming at the good life with others in just institutions." *Morale* (moral norm) is defined in terms of obligation based on the rule of universalization. The two traditions are epitomized by the complementary attitudes of self-esteem and self-respect. Self-esteem captures the individual aspirations and valuations, while self-respect represents the self-monitoring of the Golden Rule and the Categorical Imperative. The relation between the two traditions involves both nearness and distance and hence is aporetic as well as dialectical, that is, while there is interaction in their polarization, there is no final synthesis between them. One might attempt to summarize this relation in the following dictum (with apologies to Kant): "Self-respect without self-esteem is empty; self-esteem without self-respect is blind."[9]

We should notice that the pattern of emphasis here is similar to that of Ricoeur's earlier writings: the *positive* character of ethics (the teleological or *eudaimonic*) gives it a certain priority over the deontological with its negative character in the sense of constraint. And, to be sure, value is included in the positive, in the teleological, but now barely mentioned and only in an informal way – as one way of describing the components of the "good life, " of the individual's projection of ends and, in the form of "evaluating," of the anticipation of universalism.[10]

However, if we examine the role of narrative *vis-à-vis* ethics, we many also get an insight as to what has happened to value, that is, one might say, how it seems to have been swallowed up by temporality. The full narrative theory, of course, as found full-blown in the three-volume work *Time and Narrative*,[11] and in smaller writings, cannot be explicated here. Suffice it to say that it features the role of emplotment as a "synthesis of the heterogeneous" and the intersection of history and fiction. Now, the relation of narrative to the two traditions (teleological and deontological) taken together as one ethics is usefully described by Ricoeur in a recent article in terms of both a positive and a negative connection – *"liaison"* and "*déliaison*." He insists that we first underscore the gap between the imaginary component of narrative and moral judgment. Fictional stories, he says, are thought experiments, and this "laboratory" status requires that we refrain from all moral censure aimed at the invention of plots and characters [*personnages*]. "Creation demands a free imaginary."[12]

At the same time, the "liaisons" between narratives and morality are real even if more subtle than the "*déliaisons*." For one thing, the wager behind a thought experiment is to test out, presumably, in terms of plausibility and applicability, original combinations of life and death, love and hate, pleasure and suffering, innocence and culpability, good and evil. Thus, ethics and morality are already implied in the imaginary mode in fictional stories; and literary fictions, as distinguished from science fiction, mysteries, etc., can be considered imaginative variations on the theme of the good life, which, Ricoeur avers, constitutes the first "ethico-moral cornerstone." In addition, fictional configuration on the imaginary level "cannot fail to contribute to the refiguration of the world of the reader"; even though conducted in the "kingdom of the possible," the thought experiments of the dramatist or novelist can become paradigms of action through the act of reading or other modes of the "reception" of the text.[13] Thus narrativity and morality are more intertwined than might appear to be the case at first approximation.

Now the key to this position is the dialectic of *ipse* and *idem* – the two forms of personal identity at the core of narrative identity. Whereas *idem* is the self viewed in terms of a sameness of substance – one that resembles the permanence in time of the thing – *ipse* is the term for self that captures its motility or lability, its ability to change and develop. *Idem* responds to the question "what am I?" in terms of sameness but the sameness of acquired characteristics – character as the set of lasting dispositions by which a person is recognized. It is the "what" of the "who," but in an internal, not external sense. *Ipse* means a response to the question "Who am I?" with the assertion "Here I am" – wherein the person escapes his or her lasting manner of thinking, feeling, acting and "recognizes himself or herself as the subject of imputation" and thereby stops wandering among the "multitude of models for action and life," that is, responds to the expectation of the other.[14] But neither is simply fixed – their dialectic is an "existential polarity" with an intricate interweaving of sedimentation and innovation.

The promise, for Ricoeur, is a dramatic example of how the *ipse* of self-constancy (*maintenance de soi*) can transcend the *idem* of character – "even when I am by my character resistant to keeping it [my word] I nevertheless do so." Ricoeur even uses here the fine psychological distinction [not retained in the English translation] between perseverance and perseveration: "The perseverance [sic: the French is *persévération*] of character is one thing, the perseverance of faithfulness to a word that has been given is something else again."[15]

While character, then, isn't sameness as such, it represents an overlap of *idem* with *ipse* in the direction of sameness: "the sameness in the mineness." Thus, when character is displayed in narrative literature as *personnage* [here the English must use character], it is driven by the plot in such a way that it initiates the innovations of the plot even as its identity is assimilated into a certain necessity or inevitability. "The person, understood as a character in a story, is not an entity distinct from his or her 'experiences.' Quite the opposite: the person shares the condition of dynamic identity peculiar to the story recounted." The narrative "constructs the identity of the character, what can be called his or her narrative identity, in constructing that of the story told. It is the identity of the story that makes the identity of the character."[16] But fiction, of course, displays a wide range here: characters in folktales are fixed; in classical novels, they are somewhat varied or transformed; in novels of apprenticeship and stream-of consciousness, they become quite variable; and in extreme cases (e.g., Musil's *The Man Without Qualities*) they become "nonidentifiable."[17]

But it is the encounter of our narrative identity with the other that brings out the fuller ethical dimension of the self, viz., "ethical identity." All actions are brought together by rules of practice ("constitutive rules" as in Searle), e.g., in games (higher score wins) or in promising (I oblige myself to do something). But such rules are not ethical until they also involve the other. Promising becomes, then, not just a speech act, but a matter of faithfulness. The question for the narrative imagination: "Who am I?" raised by fiction becomes, Ricoeur says, "Who am I, so inconstant, that *notwithstanding* you count on me? And the answer, then, is "Here I take my stand" not, he adds, in proud Stoic rigidity, but in a "dialectic of ownership and of dispossession, of care and of carefreeness, of self-affirmation and of self-effacement." This is, then, the "stripped self" of Nabert, Marcel and Levinas, but not, Ricoeur says, de-centered to the point of substituting self-hatred for self-esteem, since the "irruption of the other, breaking through the enclosure of the same," must "meet with the complicity of effacement by which the self makes itself available to others."[18] This theme of "*disponibilité*" has also been treated by Ricoeur elsewhere in an essay "Entre éthique et ontologie: la disponibilité," in which he analyzes Marcel's discussion of fidelity.[19]

Even though value seems to be missing in all this discussion, it has not disappeared totally. For example, in the analysis of habit as a sedimentation of character that creates a predominance of *idem* over *ipse* (i.e., the *ipse* announces itself as *idem*), Ricoeur finds the set of acquired identifications by which the other enters into the composition of the same; at the same time, the identification with heroic figures presupposes an "identification with values which make us place a 'cause' above our own survival," as, e.g., in loyalty as it turns character as *idem* toward fidelity and the "self-maintenance" of *ipse*.[20]

Or again, in the notion of self-esteem – the "good life" understood in terms of ends – the notion of "value" surfaces, even if only minimally, in the analysis of the universalism implicit in the ethical aim – especially as self-esteem is tested against the moral norm embodied in self-respect.[21] And in the Ninth Study on practical wisdom – *phronesis* manifested in conviction – value emerges as the underpinning for the claims of human rights: "It is as though universalism and contextualism overlapped imperfectly on a small number of fundamental values, such as those we read of in the universal declaration of the rights of man and of the citizen." Despite complaints of ethnocentrism, one must, he says, "maintain the universal claim attached to a few values where the universal and the historical intersect." In this context, he adds in a footnote, value "corresponds in public discussion to those inchoate universals whose genuine moral tenor will be established only by the subsequent history of the dialogue between cultures." For Ricoeur, value thus features not as a genuine moral concept but a "compromise term" "justified by the cases in which universality and historicity provide mutual comfort to one another, rather than separating off from one another."[22] Since these alleged universals will become authentic values "when they are recognized by all the persons concerned" (Habermas), i.e., in a remote, possible future, one can conclude that values have been situated fully in temporality by way of the narrative context in which they are embedded. In this way of taking time seriously, one can see that values are fully "de-platonized" in Ricoeur's narrativization of ethics. This narrativization is not total, however, since he has affirmed that the ethical self transcends the narrative self.[23] Thus, it is not to be confused with the full-scale narrativizing of ethics in the manner of MacIntyre, e.g., whose "narrative unity of a life" Ricoeur finds too conflative of life and literature and therefore dismissive of the role and variety of the literary work and of the poetic imagination behind it.[24]

Thus, in this attenuated view of value, a key point of Ricoeur's ethics comes through – what I would call his modified post-modernism. More properly, it might be called a hermeneutic pluralism. This is because, while it recognizes the spatial and temporal incommensurability of value systems, both individual and collective, as they figure in a variety of texts and "conflicts of interpretation," it still holds out the possibility – the hope! – of an eventual consensus. And it does this, not merely in contemporary political and social terms, but in the context of the major ethical traditions – Aristotle and Kant, most particularly. Such a hermeneutic pluralism achieves this also with the ordering of the classical ontological paradigms or metacategories – the Same and the Other, the one and the many, potency and act – initiated mainly by Plato but utilized by the whole of western philosophy and, indeed, by non-western traditions as well. That is, it responds to the concerns of diverse groups and traditions without a relativistic levelling or a sheer "heteronomism."

This brief survey cannot do justice to the nuances and compelling cohesiveness of Ricoeur's effort to articulate an ethical theory within the theory of a self and its relation to narrative. In any case, ethical discussion in *Oneself as Another* is not confined to the question of narrative – there are, for example, the practical applications in Study Nine and the discussions of justice in Study Eight. In other writings, there are discussions of the question of evil where narrative plays a central role but only in the form of myth – and then not with the deployment of the theory of narrative developed in his later works. There are also the discussions of ethics in religious contexts, but again, where the narrativity of the Gospels is not focused on.[25]

It is, perhaps, the constant dialogue with Levinas that is most remarkable in this ethics – the constant effort to place the narrative self in relation to the face of the "other" and the resultant responsibility without losing its freedom, its initiative. Levinas's asymmetry is recognized, even accepted and internalized to a degree, but also "domesticated," i.e., rendered compatible with the humanistic core of the western tradition. Put differently, Levinas' unilateralism is countered, not with the egotism of "moral psychology," but with the mediating theme of "*disponibilité*" – which evokes, indeed, the narrativity of life and its authorship by the other.[26]

One might infer that the "poetics of the will" that Ricoeur promised as the culmination of his "philosophy of the will"[27] has essentially been completed, at least in broad outline, with the publication of the works on narrative, and the ethics included in *Oneself as Another* and other writings on ethical themes.[28] But in lieu of a full-scale study with a focus on ethics by Ricoeur himself, and considering the richness and intricacy of his views on ethics and narrative – views that have only been able to be sketched out here – much more work by both commentators and critics would be appropriate.

Notes

1 Paul Ricoeur, *The Symbolism of Evil*, trans. E. Buchanan (New York: Harper & Row, 1967).

2 Paul Ricoeur, *The Rule of Metaphor: Multi-disciplinary Studies of the Creation of Meaning in Language* (Toronto: University of Toronto Press, 1981).

3 Paul Ricoeur, *Time and Narrative*, I–III, trans. K. Blamey and D. Pellauer (Chicago: University of Chicago Press, 1984-88).

4 Paul Ricoeur, *Lectures 2. La contrée des philosophes* (Paris: Seuil, 1992), 195-202.

5 Paul Ricoeur, *Freedom and Nature: The Voluntary and the Involuntary*, trans. E. Kohak (Evanston: Northwestern University Press, 1966), 74-9.

6 Paul Ricoeur, "The Problem of the Foundation of Moral Philosophy," *Philosophy Today* 3 (Fall 1978): 184.

7 Ricoeur, "The Problem of the Foundation of Moral Philosophy," 184-8.

8 Paul Ricoeur, *Soi-même comme un autre* (Paris: Seuil, 1990); *Oneself as Another* (Chicago: University of Chicago Press, 1992).

9 This is a summary of two themes in different studies in *Oneself as Another*: Seventh Study, "The Self and the Ethical Aim," and the Eighth Study, "The Self and the Moral Norm."

10 Ricoeur, *Oneself as Another*, 204.

11 Ricoeur, *Time and Narrative*, I–III.

12 Paul Ricoeur, "De la métaphysique à la morale," *Revue de Métaphysique et de Morale* 4 (1993): 465.

13 Ricoeur, "De la métaphysique à la morale": 476.

14 Ricoeur, *Oneself as Another*, 167.

15 Ricoeur, *Oneself as Another*, 123.

16 Ricoeur, *Oneself as Another*, 147-8.

17 Ricoeur, *Oneself as Another*, 149.

18 Ricoeur, *Oneself as Another*, 168.

19 Ricoeur, *Lectures 2*, 68-78.

20 Ricoeur, *Oneself as Another*, 121.

21 Ricoeur, *Oneself as Another*, 224.

22 Ricoeur, *Oneself as Another*, 289-90.

23 E.g., in "Reply to Peter Kemp," *The Philosophy of Paul Ricoeur*, 398: "To this ethical intention are attached predicates such as good an obligatory, which cannot be derived from the narrative structure of the self but which, in being added to the latter, assure the transition from narrative identity to the moral imputability of the self."

24 Kemp," *The Philosophy of Paul Ricoeur*, 157-60.

25 See Ricoeur, e.g., "Freedom in the Light of Hope," *The Conflict of Interpretations: Essays in Hermeneutics* (Evanston: Northwestern University Press, 1974).

26 Ricoeur, *Oneself as Another*, 189-90.

27 "Les méthodes et tâches de la phénoménologie de la volonté," in Les *Problèmes actuels de la phénoménologie*, ed. H.L. van Breda (Paris: Desclées de Brouwer, 1952), 140. In the "Intellectual Autobiography," in *The Philosophy of Paul Ricoeur*, ed. L. Hahn, Ricoeur adverts (13) to the "abandonment of this grand project."

28 E.g., "Morale, Ethique et Politique," Pouvoirs. *Revue française d'études constitutionnelles et politiques* (Paris: P.U.F., 1993), 5-17, and others listed in the invaluable "Bibliography of Paul Ricoeur," in *The Philosophy of Paul Ricoeur*, 609-815.

Mediation, *Muthos,* and the Hermeneutic Circle in Ricoeur's Narrative Theory

LINDA FISHER

Introduction

A recurring, if overlooked, theme in Paul Ricoeur's thought, particularly in his extensive writings concerning hermeneutics and the theory of interpretation, is the fundamental and exemplary role played by the concept of the hermeneutic circle. The hermeneutic circle describes the fundamentally circular and reflexive nature of understanding, as represented in the classic formulation of the part-whole relation. Dating back to the earliest origins of hermeneutics in the interpretation of classical texts, Biblical exegesis, and early rhetoric, and continuing to the present in various manifestations in contemporary hermeneutic and postmodern theory, the hermeneutic circle figures as a key concept and device throughout the long history of hermeneutics.

Clearly many hermeneutic resonances are to be found in Ricoeur's more recent work on narrative theory, which takes as its task the study of narrative and its role in the unfolding of meaning and understanding, both in forms such as fiction and history, and in the broader description of our lived human and historical world. Given the characteristically dialectical and synthetic tendencies in Ricoeur's thought generally, where his project consists often in realizing a highly complex interaction, if not marriage of diverse themes or discourses,[1] it comes as no surprise that in his work on narrative, Ricoeur focuses on what he identifies as the capacity of narrative to accomplish a "synthesis of the heterogeneous."[2] This capacity, manifested, for example, in the operation of emplotment, serves in a related way both a unifying and a structural function. In unfolding the nature of this unity and structure, we can see how it also displays more fundamentally a mediating, cohering, and circular character. In other words, not only does narrative, and in particular Ricoeur's narrative theory, display many hermeneutic dimensions, but it displays even more profoundly certain crucial aspects and features of the hermeneutic circle.

In this paper, I undertake an examination of the role of the hermeneutic circle in Ricoeur's thought, with particular emphasis on his narrative theory. What becomes clear in such an examination is the extent to which his analysis of time and narrative is informed, if not to say motivated, by themes and ideas derived from the hermeneutic circle. Or to put the point more directly still: the hermeneutic circle, frequently present in Ricoeur's earlier hermeneutic discussions as an important conceptual touchstone, becomes the central structural framework for Ricoeur's discussion of narrative and time in his three-volume study on this topic.[3] As such, the role of the hermeneutic circle evolves from suggestive image or metaphor to an exemplary concept for narrative, leading Ricoeur to claim in a conclusive fashion in *Time and Narrative*, III, that "narrative identity is the poetic resolution of the hermeneutic circle."[4]

While commentators have addressed the hermeneutical issues and aspects in Ricoeur's earlier work – particularly, of course, in terms of his texts dealing specifically with hermeneutics – little attention has been paid to the hermeneutical aspects of his narrative theory. Moreover, there has been virtually no discussion of Ricoeur's employment of the concept of the hermeneutic circle, either in terms of his hermeneutics or narrative theory. Given that, as I will argue, the hermeneutic circle is unfolded as a central influence and motif, if not conceptual paradigm, for Ricoeur's thought, an analysis of his appropriation and development of the hermeneutic circle would appear to be essential.

I begin with a discussion of the general features and structure of the hermeneutic circle, and Ricoeur's incorporation of this concept in earlier texts on hermeneutics. I turn then to an examination of the role of the circle in Ricoeur's narrative theory, in particular its role in structuring the overall framework and parameters of *Time and Narrative.*

Formulations of the Hermeneutic Circle

While the history of hermeneutics bears witness to a number of distinct conceptions and analyses of the hermeneutic circle, there has been, nonetheless, a consistent conceptual structure, constituting the circle as a central thematic continuity throughout hermeneutic theory and history. Without doubt, the two primary formulations, each a watershed in its own right in the history of hermeneutics, are the part/whole relation and the circular and presuppositional character of understanding. Indeed, these are the two formulations that appear most frequently in Ricoeur's writing on hermeneutics.

As stated above, in its classic formulation, the circle represents the well-known principle of whole and parts: the parts can only be understood in relation to the whole, and vice versa. For example, a particular poem can only be understood in the context of the poet's other poems, or larger oeuvre, or even the poetic genre as such. Correspondingly, the whole which is the genre can only be grasped in relation to the individual poems that constitute poetry and the poetic genre. Subsequent formulations of the circle have unfolded any number of variations or applications of this principle. One of the more significant and far-reaching contemporary applications is Heidegger's formulation of the circle. Grounded in his project of fundamental ontology, and motivated by his analysis of understanding as *Vorverständnis*, Heidegger's hermeneutic circle emphasizes the anticipatory structure of understanding, or presuppositional understanding: understanding as projected toward possibilities, where the projecting is guided and mediated by what has come before; inquiry is guided beforehand by what is sought.[5]

It is these two versions of the circle in particular – the whole/part relation and Heidegger's presuppositional formulation – that serve as the prevailing models for Ricoeur's analysis and elaboration of conceptions of circularity and reflexivity in his earlier writings on hermeneutics,[6] in texts such as *Interpretation Theory*,[7] *The Conflict of Interpretations*,[8] and the essays collected in *Hermeneutics and the Human Sciences*.[9] While different aspects and nuances are explored in various contexts, and while these formulations of the circle are refashioned by Ricoeur in significant and original ways in keeping with the overall aims of his project, he is clearly appropriating existing conceptions of the circle. That is to say, Ricoeur is very much entering into a dialogue with, and contributing to the development of the tradition of the hermeneutic circle.

At the same time, while these two formulations each constitute distinct moments in the conceptual history of the circle, they remain fundamentally related. Indeed, what becomes evident is the extent to which the various versions of the hermeneutic circle are in fact so many variations on a theme – more or less complex, more or less developed, more or less ontological formulations of an essential conceptual character of reflexivity, in the sense of mutual implication. The hermeneutic circle is, fundamentally, a dialectical and reflexive principle wherein two terms come into relation with one another, but not merely in an alternating, seesaw reciprocity, but in a progressive, mutually informing activity; the sense of circularity coming from the continual deepening and developing of the relation in what is often described as a spiraling movement. As such, a comparative analysis of diverse formulations of the circle reveals both their common theoretical and conceptual origins and their methodological and generative co-dependence, the elements of one being unfolded from the other.

Ricoeur's various formulations of hermeneutic circularity acknowledge and build on this fundamental continuity in the conceptual structure of the circle, at once identifying the essential character common to all versions, while also laying out a progressive taxonomy of formulations moving from least complex, or most basic, in the statements of straightforward reflexivity, to the more complex, in the appropriations of the Heideggerian ontological/phenomenological model.[10] In "The Task of Hermeneutics," for example, Ricoeur invokes the basic form of the circle, as simple reflexivity, to describe the manner in which the subject and object are mutually implicated in the human sciences:

> The subject itself enters into the knowledge of the object; and in turn, the former is determined, in its most subjective character, by the hold which the object has upon it, even before the subject comes to know the object.[11]

In the context of other discussions, one concerning symbolism, another on Bultmann and religion, Ricoeur formulates this idea in the following way: "You must understand in order to believe, but you must believe in order to understand."[12] What is clear in such formulations is the developed nature of the reflexivity at issue – a much more sophisticated vision of reflexivity than the simple "seesaw" versions often depicted, where *a* is to *b* as *b* is to *a*: too much the legacy of logical models, they never seem to overcome their one-sidedness. The hermeneutic relation of mutual implication, however, must be grasped in its circular and reflexive character; going beyond the simple logical relation, it is constituted as an instance of the hermeneutic circle.

The part/whole relation, as the next level of the circle, has become, as stated earlier, the classic formulation of the hermeneutic circle. One particularly salient application of the part/whole relation takes place in the context of interpretation theory – specifically, the theory of the text and text-reading. Historically, the principle of part/whole undergoes a particularly dialectical transformation and reading with Friedrich Schleiermacher in the nineteenth century, when the latter undertook to delineate a set of principles and general methodology for interpretation, seeking to provide a "general" or universal hermeneutics.[13] Corresponding to Schleiermacher's circular dialectic between the "divinatory" and "grammatical" sides of interpretation, Ricoeur elaborates what he terms "the dialectic of guessing and validation," which constitutes in turn one dimension of the dialectic between comprehension and explanation.[14]

> Why do we need an art of guessing? Why do we have to "construe" the meaning?
> ... a text has to be construed because it is not a mere sequence of sentences, all on an
> equal footing and separately understandable. A text is a whole, a totality.... The re-
> construction of the text as a whole necessarily has a circular character, in the sense
> that the presupposition of a certain kind of whole is implied in the recognition of the
> parts. And reciprocally, it is in construing the details that we construe the whole.[15]

Furthermore, Ricoeur specifies the relation of guess and validation as corresponding to subjective and objective approaches to the text (the subjective/objective dialectic also being found in Schleiermacher). Arguing against the critic E.D. Hirsch, Ricoeur states that this circularity is not a vicious circularity; that would only be the case if we were unable to escape the kind of "self-confirmability" which threatens the relation of guess and validation, according to Hirsch, as a form of question-begging – a criticism often leveled at the hermeneutic circle. Instead, this process involves a methodical procedure of interpretation validation, where interpretations are neither self-validating, nor automatically correct and beyond critique: "To the procedures of validation also belong procedures of invalidation similar to the criteria of falsifiability emphasized by Karl Popper in his *Logic of Scientific Discovery*.[16]

The key features of the first, basic formulation of mutual implication are still present in this version of the circle, but raised to a higher level: the dialectic of reciprocal interaction is reinscribed in a more sophisticated theoretical relationship, according to the terms of an ontological and epistemological status, and in this manner anticipating the final significant formulation of the circle for Ricoeur.

This is, of course, the anticipatory or presuppositional character of understanding, derived from Heidegger's analysis of the *Vorstruktur des Verstehens*.[17] In the Heideggerian hermeneutic phenomenology, where the project is framed as the question of the meaning of Being, Heidegger states that in order properly to formulate and elucidate the question of Being, it is essential to find an exemplary being and to give an explication of it with regard to its Being, and in this manner to gain access to Being. This being is, of course, *Dasein*, the being for whom its own Being is at issue, and for whom the question of Being is precisely a mode of Being. As Heidegger states:

> If we must first define an entity *in its Being*, and if we want to formulate the question
> of Being only on this basis, what is this but going in a circle? In working out our
> question, have we not "presupposed" something which only the answer can bring?[18]

This *is* indeed circular reasoning, but once again, it is not of a question-begging type. Rather, what is at issue is a "'relatedness backward or forward' which what we are asking about (Being) bears to the inquiry itself as a mode of Being of an entity."[19] *Dasein* is a being that asks about Being, and this asking, as a mode of its Being, enables the elucidation of Being. Moreover, what is disclosed in this analysis is the inherently anticipatory and presuppositional component of understanding: in order to formulate the question, we must know something about that which we are questioning. So, Heidegger states, "Inquiry, as a kind of seeking, must be guided beforehand by what is sought. So the meaning of Being must already be available to us in some way."[20] These presuppositional elements are subsequently unfolded in the notion of projective understanding – which, as *Dasein*, is the existential significance of its Being-toward-possibilities – so the full circle, as it were, consists in the modalities of presupposition and projection in the circularity of understanding.

Following this model, Ricoeur states: "The most fundamental condition of the hermeneutical circle lies in the structure of pre-understanding which relates all explication to the understanding which precedes and supports it."[21] This formulation proves particularly fruitful for Ricoeur in his discussions of metaphor, whose key characteristics include a "polarity between sense and reference"[22] – thus playing on the earlier formulations of the circle – but also the capacity to create and project a world of its own. Ricoeur also states that the understanding of metaphor can serve as a guide to the understanding of longer texts, such as a literary work; thus in this context interpretation deals with the "*power of a work* to project a world of its own,"[23] and in terms of the anticipatory dimension, "to set in motion the hermeneutical circle, which encompasses in its spiral both the apprehension of projected worlds and the advance of self-understanding in the presence of these new worlds."[24]

Again, fundamental to this formulation are the resonances of the earlier dialectics of reflexivity and mutual implication. The new dimension, unfolded by the higher sophistication of the Heideggerian model, are the latent elements of mediation and projection. Mediation is implicit in the Heideggerian formulation of the role of *Dasein* in the inquiry into Being, and it is implicit for Ricoeur in an analysis like that of metaphor. Other theorists have identified this mediating capacity in metaphor, but I believe Ricoeur is unique in developing it in the context of a discussion of the hermeneutic circle. At any rate, the foregoing analysis of the various formulations of the circle for Ricoeur serves to ground my earlier claim about the interrelatedness of these formulations. The final, most developed formulation is not so distinct from the earlier ones, but rather is grounded in and unfolded from them, even the most basic form, the different and deepening versions evolving in their own spiral development. And conversely, the later presuppositional version is anticipated in Ricoeur's interpretation of the earlier version: recall his language in the formulation of the part/whole principle, referring to "the presupposition of a certain kind of whole [which] is implied in the recognition of the parts."[25] The circularity of understanding the whole in terms of the parts and the parts in terms of the whole, and back to a more developed whole, and so on, has been deepened by disclosing the presuppositional structure underlying such movement; a structure implicit in the very character of the part/whole relation, but not especially thematized before Heidegger.

Particularly significant for a discussion of narrative is the sense in which various key themes of Ricoeur's narrative theory are themselves anticipated and unfolded through his earlier invokings of the hermeneutic circle. In other words, these earlier hermeneutic discussions help to lay the groundwork for the development of Ricoeur's narrative theory, and to the extent that the concept of the hermeneutic circle figures importantly in the hermeneutic discussions, it points to the significance in turn of the circle for Ricoeur's narrative theory.

The Hermeneutic Circle and Narrative Theory

Indeed, the seminal first part of *Time and Narrative*, I, is entitled "The Circle of Narrative and Temporality."[26] What is this circle? On the very first page, Ricoeur makes his thesis, and his framework of analysis, undeniably clear: narrativity and temporality stand in a fundamentally circular relation to each other. In other words:

> ... what is ultimately at stake in the case of the structural identity of the narrative function as well as in that of the truth claim of every narrative work, is the temporal character of human experience. The world unfolded by every narrative work is always a temporal world. Or, as will often be repeated in the course of this study: time becomes human time to the extent that it is organized after the manner of a narrative; narrative, in turn, is meaningful to the extent that it portrays the features of temporal experience.[27]

Continuing, Ricoeur states that while this thesis is undoubtedly circular, he will endeavor to show that what is at issue is not a vicious, but a healthy circularity – thus following in the footsteps of Heidegger, among others, in acknowledging and answering the traditional objection to formulations of the hermeneutic circle.

In the discussion that follows, several crucial themes of Ricoeur's narrative theory are developed within the dialectical framework of time and narrative; themes that are individually significant for their character of circularity: time, emplotment, and mimesis. Moving from an analysis of time in Augustine's *Confessions* to an analysis of emplotment (*muthos*) in Aristotle's *Poetics*, Ricoeur attempts in the third chapter to bring these elements of time and narrative together, by way of an analysis of mimesis. This analysis will reveal three distinct moments of mimesis – $mimesis_1$, $mimesis_2$, and $mimesis_3$ – which will constitute in turn what Ricoeur calls "the circle of mimesis." As such, Ricoeur states:

> By moving from the initial question of the *mediation* between time and narrative to the new question of connecting the three stages of mimesis, I am basing the whole strategy of my work on the subordination of the second problem to the first one. In constructing the relationship between the three mimetic modes I constitute the mediation between time and narrative.[28]

Given the breadth of Ricoeur's study, it is impossible to elaborate all the relevant aspects of this analysis in a short essay. In order, however, to sketch some of the details of the analysis, and in this manner to highlight the elements of circularity and the hermeneutic circle that are inherent in Ricoeur's thesis, I will focus on a brief examination of his discussion of emplotment. As will become clear, the analysis of emplotment proves particularly salutary for Ricoeur in his elaboration of narrative; indeed he states that the "dynamic" of emplotment is the key to the problem of the relation between time and narrative.[29]

The larger problematic of Ricoeur's discussion of emplotment – a problematic that runs throughout his discussion of narrative – is the question of the relation of narrative to lived experience. In particular, the question consists in asking whether narrative should be distinguished from lived experience or the "real world," and confined to fiction. Working from his discussion of Aristotle's *Poetics*, Ricoeur borrows two concepts: emplotment (*muthos*) and mimetic activity (*mimesis*). Observing that for Aristotle plot is not a static structure but an operation, a *process of integration*, Ricoeur proceeds to characterize emplotment as the "synthesis of heterogeneous elements."[30] And here we see the first clear resonances of the hermeneutic circle, for the synthesis resembles less the kind of synthesis found, for example, in German idealism,[31] but rather the synthetic dynamic of the part/whole of the hermeneutic circle.

Characteristically, we find that the synthetic operations of emplotment are multi-layered. First, it is a synthesis between multiple events or incidents and a story that is unified and complete – the plot makes *one* story out of the multiple incidents. Second, plot organizes components that are "as heterogeneous as unintended circumstances, discoveries, those who perform actions and those who suffer them."[32] Gathering all these factors into a single story makes the plot a totality which is at once concordant and discordant – or, in a formulation resonant of the aspect of the hermeneutic circle dealing with mutual implication, Ricoeur refers to "discordant concordance", or "concordant discordance." Finally, Ricoeur says, emplotment is a synthesis of the heterogeneous in a more profound sense yet as the temporality specific to all narrative compositions: succession and configuration. Composing a story involves, from a temporal point of view, drawing a configuration out of a succession.

As we saw in the previous section, the interaction or process characteristic of the hermeneutic circle may operate on one level as reflexivity – such as the reflexivity of concordant and discordant – but the "to and fro" movement is soon inflected into a Heideggerian "relatedness backward and forward" where the new relation requires a more complex synthesis of disparate elements – the parts coming together in and composing the totality of the plot; the narrative whole giving form to the individual component parts. Once again, there is a mutual co-dependency here of parts and whole, but the key element in both the hermeneutic circle and the concept of plot is the sense of process – a plot is not the static spine of the narrative, but the evolving narrative process which structures, mediates, and coheres.

The notion of temporality is clearly crucial here as one of the kinds of synthesis, and as a thematic motif for all three. Succession is an open series of discrete incidents integrated into a cohesive configuration. A story – and history – bear these temporal structural features. But it is a temporal structure of mediated parts and whole, anticipated futures and retained pasts: the hermeneutic of temporality. Certainly there are Husserlian elements here, traceable to Husserl's analyses of time-consciousness and Ricoeur's ongoing engagement with Husserl. But read through the motif of the hermeneutic circle, temporality is construable as itself hermeneutically grounded. Thus Ricoeur summarizes:

> ... the manifest circularity of every analysis of narrative, an analysis that does not stop interpreting in terms of each other the temporal form inherent in experience and the narrative structure, is not a lifeless tautology. We should see in it instead a "healthy circle" in which the arguments advanced about each side of the problem aid one another.[33]

And in this manner "the hermeneutic circle of narrative and time never stops being reborn from the circle that the stages of mimesis form."[34] As such, Ricoeur posits a doubled, or meta-hermeneutic circularity: there is the circle of narrative, the circle of time, and the circle of narrative *and* time, the latter spiraling more generally from the circle of mimesis.

Finally, Ricoeur underscores the necessary participation in this process of a reader or spectator, as a *living* receiver of the narrated story. This is the intentional moment in the hermeneutic circle of understanding, where the meaning obtained through the synthetic grasp of parts and whole is a meaning *for* someone. Once again, there are Husserlian elements in such a model – but for now the framework is still prevalently hermeneutical (and Heideggerian) as Ricoeur invokes the presuppositional sense of the circle in discussing the particular act of meaning intention at issue here, the act of following a story: "following a story is a very complex operation, guided by our expectations concerning the outcome of the story, expectations that we readjust as the story moves along, until it coincides with the conclusion."[35] This intentional and presuppositional model, which requires the active participation of the reader or listener, Ricoeur will later characterize as the intersection of the world of the text and the world of the reader: the text opens before it a world of possible experience, a lived world, and a world of life. As such:

> To appropriate a work through reading is to unfold the world horizon implicit in it which includes the actions, the characters and the events of the story told. As a result, the reader belongs at once to the work's horizon of experience in imagination and to that of his or her own real action. The horizon of expectation and the horizon of experience continually confront one another and fuse together.[36]

This begins to sound, of course, quite Gadamerian, and indeed Ricoeur immediately gives the nod to Gadamer and his concept of "fusion of horizons." However, what is also significant in this for my present purposes is the fact that Gadamer's "fusion of horizons" is based in Gadamer's own particular version of the hermeneutic circle, heavily influenced, naturally, by Heidegger.

The other important point in the preceding, given Ricoeur's initially stated problematic of the relation of narrative to lived experience, is the development of the ideas of horizon, world, and the role of the reader. It *is* the case that narrative and lived experience are related – not only does life configure narrative, but narrative configures and reconfigures life. And so once again, if fiction is completed in life and if that life can only be understood through the stories we tell about it, then, in a Socratic play, Ricoeur states that an *examined* life is a life *recounted*.[37]

At the end of this first section of *Time and Narrative*, I ("The Circle of Narrative and Temporality"), Ricoeur summarizes and looks ahead to the rest of the study. Outlining the manner in which the discussions that follow will interweave the analysis of time and narrative with history and fiction, he states that it is probable that "the hermeneutic circle of narrativity and temporality will be enlarged well beyond the circle of mimesis,"[38] indicating the key structural and thematic function of the hermeneutic circle, not only for the immediate analysis of the first part, but for the entire study. This is consistent both with his earlier treatments of the circle, and also underscores the hermeneutic continuity between Ricoeur's earlier texts and the work on narrative.

Indeed, an interesting aspect of the foregoing appropriations of the hermeneutic circle is the manner in which they reflect Ricoeur's earlier treatments. If we recall how it was possible to distinguish several inter-related formulations of the circle in Ricoeur's other treatments, formu-lations that moved progressively through several levels of development and complexity, we find parallels with the unfolding of the circle and its role in the beginning of *Time and Narrative*. Here, as we have seen, Ricoeur begins with the basic, preliminary formulation of the circle as principle of reflexivity or mutual implication. He then moves to a more devel-oped characterization of the circle in terms of the mediating movement of the part/whole interaction. Finally, we see the echo of the Heideggerian presuppositional model in the analysis of the role of mean-ing intention and the living receiver of the narrated story who, in fol-lowing the story, contributes to its constitution as a story, helping to mediate the parts into an intelligible whole.

Conclusion

I have attempted in this essay to establish the crucial importance of the hermeneutic circle for Ricoeur's thought, particularly with respect to its formative structural role in *Time and Narrative*. Running throughout the discussions of narrative as *leitmotiv* and model for his framework of analysis, the hermeneutic circle undeniably plays a pivotal role, point-ing in turn to the hermeneutic character, among other elements, of Ricoeur's narrative theory and the continuity of these analyses through-out Ricoeur's work. While I am not suggesting at any point that this is the only key analysis for Ricoeur, given the breadth of his intellectual interests and influences, I am arguing that the significance of the hermeneutic circle in Ricoeur's thought has not been sufficiently recog-nized and analyzed. This is perhaps true even of Ricoeur himself who, while incorporating the hermeneutic circle throughout his work as any-thing from illustrative metaphor at certain junctures to exemplary con-cept in others, never at any point engages in a direct conceptual analysis of the circle, but instead invokes and unfolds it from his discussions as they progress. This too, finally, would be in keeping with the nature of the hermeneutic circle: as Heidegger pointed out, interpretation, inflected by the character of hermeneutical circularity, always involves the work-ing-out of possibilities projected in understanding. Thus any analysis must proceed by interpreting and unfolding that which has already been understood.

Notes

1   As just one example, Ricoeur's project to bring together phenomenology and hermeneutics in a "hermeneutic phenomenology" is seen in essays such as Paul Ricoeur, "Phenomenology and Hermeneutics," in *Hermeneutics and the Human Sciences*, ed. and trans. John B. Thompson (Cambridge: Cambridge University Press, 1981), 101-28. Many of these essays appeared originally in Ricoeur, *Du texte à l'action: Essais d'herméneutique*, II (Paris: Seuil, 1986).

2   Paul Ricoeur, *Time and Narrative*, I, trans. Kathleen McLaughlin and David Pellauer (Chicago: University of Chicago Press, 1984), 66.

3   Indeed, this is consistent with the significant structural and determinative character often attributed to the circle throughout its history.

4   Paul Ricoeur, *Time and Narrative*, III, trans. Kathleen Blamey and David Pellauer (Chicago: University of Chicago Press, 1988), 248.

5   Martin Heidegger, *Being and Time*, trans. John Macquarrie and Edward Robinson (New York: Harper & Row, 1962). For a more extensive discussion of the hermeneutic circle in Heidegger, see my "Heidegger's Hermeneutic Circle," *Eidos*, Special Double Issue on Hermeneutics and Critical Theory, XI (June/December 1993): 1-11.

6   There are references to the hermeneutic circle, for example, in discussions of the text, metaphor, religion, the understanding of symbols, and the work on Freud.

7   Paul Ricoeur, *Interpretation Theory: Discourse and the Surplus of Meaning* (Fort Worth: Texas Christian University Press, 1976).

8   Paul Ricoeur, *The Conflict of Interpretations: Essays in Hermeneutics*, ed. Don Ihde (Evanston: Northwestern University Press, 1974).

9   Paul Ricoeur, *Hermeneutics and the Human Sciences*, ed. and trans. John B. Thompson (Cambridge: Cambridge University Press, 1981).

10 This may not seem so significant a claim, except for the fact that the presuppositional version, usually attributed to Heidegger, is also often credited as Heidegger's unique and original contribution to the history of the concept of the circle. This is Gadamer's position, and it is one which Ricoeur also seems at some points to share. Not to say that Heidegger's formulation is not a significant turning point; but also not to overlook the extent to which his formulation, and his hermeneutics generally, were firmly grounded in the prior hermeneutic history and tradition.

11 Ricoeur, "The Task of Hermeneutics," in *Hermeneutics and the Human Sciences*, 57.

12 Ricoeur, *The Conflict of Interpretations*, 298; 389.

13 F.D.E. Schleiermacher, *Hermeneutik*, ed. and introduced by Heinz Kimmerle (Heidelberg: Carl Winter Universitätsverlag, 1959).

14 Ricoeur, "The Model of the Text," in *Hermeneutics and the Human Sciences*, 211.

15 Ricoeur, "The Model of the Text," 211.

16 Ricoeur, "The Model of the Text," 213.

17 Consisting in the moments of *Vor-habe, Vor-sicht, Vor-griff*: fore-having, fore-sight, and fore-conception.

18 Heidegger, *Being and Time*, 27.

19 Heidegger, *Being and Time*, 28.

20 Heidegger, *Being and Time*, 25.

21 Ricoeur, "Phenomenology and Hermeneutics," in *Hermeneutics and the Human Sciences*, 108.

22 Ricoeur, "Metaphor and the Problem of Hermeneutics," in *Hermeneutics and the Human Sciences*, 171.

23 Ricoeur, "Metaphor and the Problem of Hermeneutics," 171.

24 Ricoeur, "Metaphor and the Problem of Hermeneutics," 171.

25 Ricoeur, "The Model of the Text," in *Hermeneutics and the Human Sciences*, 211.

26 Ricoeur, *Time and Narrative*, I, 3-87.

27 Ricoeur, Time and *Narrative*, I, 3.

28 Ricoeur, *Time and Narrative*, I, 53.

29 Ricoeur, *Time and Narrative*, I, 53.

30 Ricoeur, *Time and Narrative*, I, 66.

31 Not that there aren't resonances of German idealism throughout Ricoeur's discussions of circularity. In many ways, he plays the notions of mediation and synthesis derived from the hermeneutic circle against parallel notions in German idealism. His overall thematic framework, however, still appears to be primarily modeled on the hermeneutic circle, more than on a Hegelian circle. Nevertheless, comparing these two models of circularity, both in terms of each other and in terms of Ricoeur's appropriation of them, suggests itself as the further stage in this analysis.

32 Paul Ricoeur, "Life in Quest of Narrative," in *On Paul Ricoeur: Narrative and Interpretation*, ed. David Wood (London and New York: Routledge, 1991), 21.

33 Ricoeur, *Time and Narrative*, I, 76.

34 Ricoeur, *Time and Narrative*, I, 76.

35 Ricoeur, "Life in Quest of Narrative, 21-2.

36 Ricoeur, "Life in Quest of Narrative," 26.

37 Ricoeur, "Life in Quest of Narrative," 31.

38 Ricoeur, *Time and Narrative*, I, 84.

Notes on Contributors

Pamela Anderson is Senior Lecturer in Philosophy at the University of Sunderland, England. Anderson received a DPhil from the University of Oxford in 1989 and has since published *Ricoeur and Kant* (Atlanta, GA: Scholars Press, 1993), as well as other articles on Ricoeur. Her current project is a book for Basis Blackwell, *The Rationality and Myths of Religious Belief: A Feminist Critique of Philosophy of Religion.*

David D. Brown completed his PhD in Sociology at the University of Alberta in 1990. His thesis was entitled "Ricoeur's Narrative Methodology and the Interpretation of Life History Texts." Brown, an Associate Professor of Sociology at the University of Lethbridge, teaches in the areas of contemporary theory and research methodology. His recent publications include "Discursive Moments of Identification," *Current Perspectives in Social Theory* 14 (1994): 269-92, and (with R.A. Morrow) *Critical Theory and Methodology: Interpretive Structuralism as a Research Program* (Sage, 1994). He organized an Internet electronic discussion group called "Narrative-L," which provided an international forum for scholars concerned with narrative in everyday life.

Helen M. Buss is Associate Professor of English at the University of Calgary and has published articles, books and monographs on Canadian literature and women's life writing. Her most recent book is *Mapping Our Selves: Canadian Women's Autobiography in English* (McGill-Queen's UP, 1993). She is currently at work on a study of women's uses of the memoir form in English.

Bernard P. Dauenhauer is University Professor of Philosophy at the University of Georgia. In his work, he has paid particular attention to existential and hermeneutic phenomenology. His writings have regularly dealt with issues in political philosophy and with the topic of the self. His published work includes: *The Politics of Hope* (Routledge & Kegan Paul, 1986), *At the Nexus of Philosophy and History* (University of Georgia Press, 1987), and *Textual Fidelity and Textual Disregard* (P.D. Lang, 1990).

Jocelyn Dunphy Blomfield completed her doctorate in philosophy in Paris under the supervision of Paul Ricoeur. She teaches philosophy at Deakin University, Geelong, Victoria (Australia) and has developed her thought around Ricoeur's work. She participated in celebrations in Ricoeur's honor at the Sorbonne in 1983 and at Cerisy-la-Salle in 1988.

Lori Egger received her doctorate in psychology from the University of Calgary in 1994. Since then, she has worked as a clinical psychologist in private practice. She is interested in postmodern approaches to the study of gender issues in psychology, in general, and therapy, in particular.

Linda Fisher received her BA from Wilfrid Laurier University; MA from the University of Ottawa, and PhD from Pennsylvania State University. She is Assistant Professor of Philosophy at the University of Windsor and has taught previously at McGill University and the University of Ottawa. She is currently President of the Canadian Society for Hermeneutics and Postmodern Thought. Her area of specialization and research is contemporary European philosophy, in particular phenomenology, hermeneutics and feminism. She has published articles on hermeneutics, phenomenology, postmodernism, and feminist theory. She is currently writing a book on Husserl's critique of naturalism in the context of phenomenological analyses of science and scientism.

Jim Fodor is author of *Christian Hermeneutics: Paul Ricoeur and the Refiguring of Theology* (Oxford University Press, 1995); he currently teaches in the Department of Religion, Washington and Lee University, Lexington, Virginia. He holds a PhD in theology from Cambridge University and has just completed three years of post-doctoral studies at Duke University exploring the theological interrelationships between practical rationality, character formation, and self-identity with a view to the work of Paul Ricoeur, Charles Taylor, and Stanley Hauerwas.

Hermina Joldersma received her PhD in Germanic Languages and Literatures from Princeton University in 1983. She has taught at Calvin College (Michigan) and at the University of Manitoba and is currently Associate Professor of German, and Associate Dean of Humanities, at the University of Calgary. While she works in German and Dutch women's literature, and late-medieval/early-modern literature, the focus of her research is popular song, including vernacular religious song.

Morny Joy is Associate Professor in the Department of Religious Studies at the University of Calgary. She is interested in hermeneutics, narrative, and the integration of the work of Paul Ricoeur with aspects of current feminist theory. Her publications include: "Derrida and Ricoeur: A Case of Mistaken Identity and Difference," *Journal of Religion* 68(4) (1988), "Divine Reservations," *Derrida and Negative Theology* (SUNY, 1992), and "Feminism and the Self," *Theory & Psychology* 3(3) (1993).

Graham Livesey is currently an Assistant Professor in the Architecture program at the University of Calgary. Educated at McGill University, he worked for a number of years in architectural practice in Montreal and London prior to becoming a university teacher. At present, he is responsible for teaching a survey course in the history of Western architecture, design studio and a seminar on urban design. For a number of years, he has maintained a research interest in the interrelationship between narrative, architecture and cities.

David Pellauer is Professor of Philosophy at DePaul University, Chicago, Illinois, and editor of *Philosophy Today*. He is the translator or co-translator of many of Ricoeur's works.

Dominique Perron received her PhD from Université Laval (Québec), writing a thesis on Marcel Proust. She is Assistant Professor of Québec Literature at the University of Calgary. Perron has published several papers on Québec Popular Literature (Yves Beauchemin, Denise Bombardier) and Marie-Claire Blais. Her main interests are sociocriticism, particularly Bourdieu. She is currently preparing a book on Colette.

C. Bryn Pinchin, Hons. BA (Toronto), BEd, MA (Calgary), is a PhD student in the Department of English, University of Calgary. Her areas of interest include literary theory and contemporary Canadian literature. Her thesis research focuses on metaphor as a locus of power in language. Mrs. Pinchin is an instructor in the Humanities Department of the Alberta College of Art. She is also a textile artist. Her work is included in the Alberta Art Foundation collection as well as in numerous private collections.

Jamie S. Scott received his doctorate in Religion and Literature from the Divinity School of the University of Chicago. He is Coordinator of the Religious Studies program and Associate Professor in the division of Humanities at York University, Toronto, Canada. His book, *Christians and Tyrants: The Prison Testimonies of Boethius, Thomas More and Dietrich Bonhoeffer*, is in press, and he has co-edited *Sacred Places and Profane Spaces: Essays in the Geographics of Judaism, Christianity and Islam* (Greenwood Press, 1991). Dr. Scott has published articles in several scholarly journals on topics in the interdisciplinary study of religion, literature and geography.

Henderikus J. Stam is a Professor in the Department of Psychology at the University of Calgary. His recent publications focus on social constructionist and discursive approaches to psychology and the history of psychological practices. He is the editor of the journal *Theory & Psychology*, and, with Lorraine Radtke, editor of *Power/Gender: Social Relations in Theory and Practice* (Sage, 1993).

Robert Sweeney, Professor of Philosophy at John Carroll University, Cleveland, received his PhD from Fordham University in 1962. His dissertation topic was Max Scheler's philosophy of value. He has published numerous articles in phenomenology and hermeneutics, including "A Survey of Recent Ricoeur Literature (By and About): 1975-1984," *Philosophy Today*, 1985. Sweeney has also translated several articles by Paul Ricoeur, including: "Structure, Word, Event," "Freedom in the Light of Hope," "The Myth of Punishment," "Fatherhood: From Phantasm to Symbol" (all of which appear in *The Conflict of Interpretations*) and "Narrated Time," *Philosophy Today*, 1986.

Terrence W. Tilley (PhD, Graduate Theological Union, Berkeley) has taught at Georgetown University, St. Michael's College (Vermont), and the Florida State University. He is currently Chair and Director of Graduate Studies in the Department of Religious Studies at the University of Dayton. He is the author of five books, most recently *Postmodern Theologies* (Orbis, 1995, with seven chapters co-authored with his graduate students) and *The Wisdom of Religious Commitment* (Georgetown University Press, 1995).

Index